LOOK WOT THEY DUN!

The Ultimate Guide to UK Glam Rock on TV in The '70s

Peter Checksfield

Copyright © 2019 Peter Checksfield

All rights reserved.

The editorial arrangement, analysis, and professional commentary are subject to this copyright notice. No portion of this book may be copied, retransmitted, reposted, duplicated, or otherwise used without the express written approval of the author, except by reviewers who may quote brief excerpts in connection with a review.

FOR HEATHER

ALSO SHERRY AND MATTHEW

Peter Checksfield

ACKNOWLEDGEMENTS

This book wouldn't have been possible without the help of a great many archivists and music historians over the years. These include, but are not limited to, Ray Langstone, Robert Reinstein, Wolfgang Guhl, Philip Brown, Ritchie Finney, James Ross, Gordon Irwin, Jock Barnson, Bobby Baity, Keith Badman, Kev Mulrenan, Gary Quinn, William McGregor, Jean François Bouquin, Kev Hunter, Terry Fendley, S-M-S, Gareth and Alex Radov. Special thanks to Dee Dee Wilde for her wonderful foreword and photos!

FOREWORD by DEE DEE WILDE

It's great to be asked to contribute to this book.

Pan's People, the dance group I was part and also a founder member of was a fantastic period of my life. Dancing was the only career I ever wanted and hey, what a dance experience I had! I think I met every pop star of the era, which included, Stevie Wonder, The Jackson Five with a very young Michael at the helm, Jimi Hendrix, The Beatles and many others.

In fact, when I'm asked who have I worked with or encountered on my long dance career, I always say, I regret never having met Frank Sinatra or Elvis as I've met most of the other iconic stars of my generation.

Dancing in Pan's with the other girls was a delight and we all became life-long friends. Sadly some of them are not with us now. My, the memories go on forever.

I have been dancing for 69 years and am STILL dancing, teaching around the West Country. Myself and my group, Pan's Fans, all ladies of a certain age, entertain the crowds at festivals, demonstrations, etc, and recently we were seen on TV on 'The Greatest Dancer'.

All the best with the book and to its readers, enjoy!

Dee Dee Wilde

Peter Checksfield

CONTENTS

	Introduction	1
1	T. Rex	5
2	David Bowie	17
3	The Kinks	26
4	The Move	31
5	Elton John	34
6	The Sweet	44
7	The Rolling Stones	54
8	Slade	63
9	Middle Of The Road	77
10	The Faces	84
11	Rod Stewart	88
12	Chicory Tip	97
13	Gary Glitter	99
14	The Electric Light Orchestra	107
15	Mott The Hoople	114
16	10cc	118

17	Blackfoot Sue	124
18	Roxy Music	125
19	Lieutenant Pigeon	131
20	Geordie	133
21	Wizzard	136
22	Mud	141
23	Suzi Quatro	149
24	Barry Blue	156
25	David Essex	158
26	Alvin Stardust	165
27	Cozy Powell	170
28	Leo Sayer	171
29	The Bay City Rollers	179
30	Paper Lace	190
31	Mick Ronson	193
32	Queen	194
33	The Glitter Band	202
34	Sparks	205

35	The Rubettes	210
36	Paul Da Vinci	215
37	Steve Harley and Cockney Rebel	216
38	Showaddywaddy	219
39	The Arrows	228
40	The Heavy Metal Kids	232
41	Pilot	233
42	Hello	235
43	Kenny	237
44	Fox	239
45	The Sensational Alex Harvey Band	242
46	Chris Spedding	245
47	Sailor	246
48	Be-Bop Deluxe	250
49	Bilbo Baggins	252
50	Slik	254
	Pan's People	256
	Bibliography & Websites	276

Look Wot They Dun!

INTRODUCTION

It was over 30 years ago when I first started researching the TV and movie appearances of musicians from the '50s, '60s and '70s, and by 2012 I decided it was time to do something with all the information I'd amassed. Six more years and much additional research later resulted in 2018's 'CHANNELLING THE BEAT – The Ultimate Guide to UK '60s Pop on TV', followed in 2019 by this book, 'LOOK WOT THEY DUN – The Ultimate Guide to UK Glam Rock on TV in The '70s.

All performances listed in this book **in bold** are known to still survive, either in TV vaults or private collections. Dates, unless specified otherwise, refer to broadcast dates; taping dates for pre-recorded shows have been added only when known. Occasionally, shows were broadcast on more than one date, in different regions of the UK; in these cases I've listed the earliest known date only. For concert footage, I've usually listed the date of the actual concerts, only adding broadcast dates where known.

Although this book is primarily about the artists' TV and movie appearances, I've often included additional info, such as chart positions, outfits and context, commenting on many key TV shows and songs. I hope this book proves to be both enjoyable and informative. If you've any serious comments or additional info, contact me via either my website or the email address at the back of the book.

GLAM ROCK

As with so many music genres, everyone has a different idea of what and who represents "Glam Rock". For this book, it encompasses a wide variety of acts. All of the expected are here, T. Rex, David Bowie, Slade, The Sweet, Mud, Roxy Music, Mott The Hoople, et al, as well as the poppier "Class of '74" acts, such as The Bay City Rollers, The Rubettes, Paper Lace, Pilot and Kenny.

Others are perhaps a little more controversial: The Rolling Stones, The Kinks, The Faces/Rod Stewart, Elton John, The Electric Light Orchestra, David Essex, 10cc… acts whom few would truly regard as "Glam", but who directly influenced the genre, and/or dabbled in the music, and/or the imagery. I've generally avoided USA acts such as Alice Cooper, Lou Reed, Iggy and The Stooges, Kiss, The New York Dolls and The Osmonds (whose 'Crazy Horses' outclassed anything The New York Dolls ever did). I've also included Gary Glitter. This book is about the music, the TV, the chart positions and the outfits, and I'd feel that I was cheating both myself and those who want a true representation of the '70s Glam Rock era if I didn't include him.

Any book on UK Glam Rock would be unthinkable without the Queen of Glam herself, Ms Suzi Quatro; she based herself in the UK, used British musicians, and recorded songs written by UK Glam's most prolific hitmakers, Nicky Chinn and Mike Chapman. Other US acts that based themselves in the UK with British musicians, and are therefore also included, are Sparks and The Arrows.

Despite the androgyny of the acts and the presence of Suzi, Glam Rock was a very male-dominated genre. To balance things out a little bit, I've included both Middle Of The Road and Fox; it is debatable how much "Glam" both of these are, but, with their memorable front-women Sally Carr and Noosha Fox, respectively, they deserve wider recognition.

There is also a bonus chapter, on dance troupe Pan's People's appearances on 'Top Of The Pops'. While not strictly a musical act in their own right (despite issueing a couple of singles and even being featured on their own BBC 'In Concert' episode), they were household names in the '70s, with individual members being more famous than many of the other acts mentioned in this book.

1970 – 1979?

With every artist, I've used a last date "cut-off" point of 31st December 1979. The Glam Rock scene was long over by then, but this gives a good indication of what they all did next. I did, briefly, consider bringing the listings right up to date, but as well as making for an unwieldy and often boring book, this would involve many far inferior spin-off acts; groups like Les Gray's Mud, Brian Connolly's/Andy Scott's/Steve Priest's Sweet, Tin Machine, Slade II, Queen + Paul Rodgers/Adam Lambert, etc.

I've generally started chapters at no earlier than 1970, though, despite the title of the book, I have made a few exceptions. NOTE: For full '60s listings on The Kinks, The Move, The Rolling Stones, The Small Faces and Alvin Stardust (in his Shane Fenton days), see my earlier book, 'CHANNELLING THE BEAT – The Ultimate Guide to UK '60s Pop on TV'!

WHAT IS AND ISN'T INCLUDED IN THESE BOOKS

Generally speaking, I've only listed complete or near-complete musical performances – whether that is on TV shows, in movies, as live concert footage, or promotional videos. NOT usually mentioned are documentaries (unless the include full-length, exclusive, performances), interviews, news footage, appearances in quiz shows, and amateur footage filmed from the audience. Nor have I mentioned non-musical appearances in movies, such as David Essex in 'That'll Be The Day' and David Bowie in 'The Man Who Fell To Earth', essential viewing though those particular films are.

"LOST" TV SHOWS

Although the situation is better than with earlier TV shows from the '50s and '60s, there is still a large amount of Glam-era UK shows lost forever. Pre-1976 surviving 'Top Of The Pops' appearances are far more miss than hit, and only a small percentage of shows like 'Lift Off' (later 'Lift Off With Ayshea') and '45' (later 'Rock On With 45') are still around. Mike Mansfield's 'Supersonic' shows largely survive intact (occasionally complete with outtakes), though as the show didn't really get going until late 1975, it missed the peak Glam years of 1971-1974. Fortunately, many acts also appeared on overseas TV shows like 'Musikladen', 'Top Pop', 'Hits A Go Go' and 'The Midnight Special', shows whose survival rate is generally far higher than those in the UK.

AT THE MOVIES

Another source for quality footage is the movies. Many of these are available on officially-released DVDs, and almost all of the rest circulate among collectors. Essential movies from this era include 'Born To Boogie' (T. Rex), 'Ziggy Stardust and The Spiders From Mars' (David Bowie), 'Stardust' (David Essex), 'Slade In Flame' (Slade), 'Remember Me This Way' (Gary Glitter), 'Tommy' (Elton John) and 'Never Too Young To Rock' (an admittedly awful movie, saved by Mud, The Rubettes, The Glitter Band and Slik).

PETER CHECKSFIELD

www.peterchecksfield.com

T. REX

12-11-65 – 'Ready, Steady, Go!' (UK): The Wizard *(Taped on 09-12-65, this was Marc Bolan's debut TV appearance, and, like all other pre-Tyrannosaurus Rex performances, it is almost certainly lost forever)* – **MARC BOLAN**

23-11-65 – 'Five O' Clock Fun Fair' (UK): The Wizard – **MARC BOLAN**

MARC BOLAN was scheduled to appear on 'Thank Your Lucky Stars' on 18-12-65, but this appearance was postponed.

19-02-66 – 'Thank Your Lucky Stars' (UK): The Wizard – **MARC BOLAN**

16-12-66 – 'Ready, Steady, Go!' (UK): Hippy Gumbo *(This was taped on 13-12-66)* – **MARC BOLAN**

00-06-67 – Promo Video (UK): Desdemona – **JOHN'S CHILDREN**

23-09-67 – **Middle Earth, London (UK): Sara Crazy Child** *(Although rather poorly lit in black and white and with thin sound, this is essential viewing as it's the earliest surviving footage of a Tyrannosaurus Rex performance)* – **TYRANNOSAURUS REX**

10-08-68 – **'18th National Jazz, Blues & Pop Festival', Sunbury-On Thames (UK): Deborah / Mustang Ford** *(In full colour, this includes the duo's first hit 'Deborah', which got to No. 34 in the UK charts a few months earlier. Other late '60s UK hits were 'One Inch Rock' at No. 28 and 'King Of The Rumbling Spires' at No. 44)* – **TYRANNOSAURUS REX**

23-08-68 – Unknown TV show (Belgium) *(This is the taping date; all other details are unknown)* – **TYRANNOSAURUS REX**

Spring 1969 – 'John Peel's In Concert' (UK) *(This pilot for a proposed TV series was taped in March or April 1969; it was never broadcast, and all other details are unknown)* – **TYRANNOSAURUS REX**

27-06-69 – **'Tous En Scene' (France): Stacey Grove / Salamanda Palaganda** *(Taped in late 1968, 'Stacey Grove' is performed on the back of a flatbed truck, while 'Salamanda Palaganda' is on a concert stage, introduced by French hosts who try and fail several times to say the word 'Tyrannosaurus') **TYRANNOSAURUS REX**

10-09-69 – **'Hy Lit Show' (USA): Warlord Of The Royal Crocodiles / The Seal Of Seasons** *(Marc's debut US TV appearance, these performances feature suitably way-out quasi-psychedelic backdrops)* **TYRANNOSAURUS REX**

28-06-70 – **'Kralingen Festival', Rotterdam (Holland): By The Light Of A Magical Moon** *(This footage captures a transitional period where the duo's name has yet to be shortened, but Marc is standing up playing an electric guitar and Steve Peregrin Took has been replaced by Mickey Finn. Huge chart success wouldn't be too far off now)* – **TYRANNOSAURUS REX**

Summer 1970 – **'London Rock' (UK): Suneye / The Children Of Rarn** *(Although this is still part of the Tyrannosaurus Rex era, this is technically a Marc Bolan solo appearance. It features him playing songs alone in his flat, interspersed with snippets of interviews)* – **TYRANNOSAURUS REX**

12-11-70 – 'Top Of The Pops' (UK): Ride A White Swan *(This was taped on 11-11-70)*

26-11-70 – 'Top Of The Pops' (UK): Ride A White Swan

10-12-70 – 'Top Of The Pops' (UK): Ride A White Swan *(This is a repeat of an earlier performance)*

30-01-71 – **'Point Chaud' (France): Ride A White Swan** *(Taped on 22-12-70, this is the earliest known surviving footage of the newly christened T. Rex. Filmed in a small underground club that's reminiscent of Liverpool's The Cavern, it features Mickey Finn pretending to play bass. This footage is sometimes, wrongly, identified as 'Pop Match' due to the large lettering on the screen, but this simply refers to a contest between T. Rex and the group 'Rotation'. 'Ride A White Swan' reached No. 2 in the UK charts)*

20-02-71 – **'Pop Deux' (France): Jewel / Ride A White Swan / Elemental Child / Summertime Blues** *(Taped at the Tavern D'Olympia in Paris on 28-01-71, this exciting concert footage features the band expanded to a trio with Steve Currie on bass)*

27-02-71 – **'Beat Club' (Germany): Ride A White Swan / Jewel** *(Another superb live performance by the T. Rex trio of Marc, Mickey and Steve, this time featuring OTT colour video effects that aren't to everyone's taste)*

11-03-71 – **'Top Of The Pops' (UK): Hot Love** (Taped on 10-03-71, this is where the Glam really starts! Although Marc wears a sombre black suit, he now has glitter on his cheeks, while Steve looks cool on bass and Mickey Finn "plays" drums. With the addition of the magical 6-piece line-up of Pan's People dancing behind them, this remains one of the defining early moments of Glam Rock. The performance was also broadcast on 'Disco', German TV, on 05-06-71. 'Hot Love' was the group's first UK No. 1, also reaching the top spot in Ireland)

18-03-71 – **'Top Of The Pops' (UK): Hot Love** (This is probably a repeat of the 11-03-71 performance)

25-03-71 – **'Top Of The Pops' (UK): Hot Love** (Again featuring Pan's People, this 2nd performance of 'Hot Love' features Marc in a silver suit. This was probably taped on 24-03-71, though some sources date this appearance as being broadcast on 18-03-71)

01-04-71 – **'Top Of The Pops' (UK): Hot Love** (This is a repeat of an earlier performance)

08-04-71 – **'Top Of The Pops' (UK): Hot Love** (This is a repeat of an earlier performance)

15-04-71 – **'Top Of The Pops' (UK): Hot Love** (This is a repeat of an earlier performance)

27-06-71 – **'Hits A Go Go' (Switzerland): Hot Love** (Miming in a TV studio, this performance now features the full classic early T. Rex line-up of Marc Bolan with Steve Currie on bass, Mickey Finn on percussion and Bill Legend on drums. This performance also features publicist BP Fallon as a 2nd percussionist)

08-07-71 – **'Top Of The Pops' (UK): Get It On** (Taped on 07-07-71, this survives in incomplete form only, thanks to a partial broadcast on 'Disco', German TV, on 09-10-71. Probably the most famous T. Rex song, it reached No. 1 in the UK, No. 12 in Canada and No. 10 in the US, where the song was renamed 'Bang A Gong (Get It On)'. As well as the usual band, this performance includes the addition of King Crimson saxophonist Ian MacDonald)

22-07-71 – **'Top Of The Pops' (UK): Get It On** (This is a repeat of the 08-07-71 performance)

29-07-71 – **'Top Of The Pops' (UK): Get It On** (This is a repeat of the 08-07-71 performance)

05-08-71 – 'Top Of The Pops' (UK): Get It On *(This was taped on 04-08-71)*

12-08-71 – 'Top Of The Pops' (UK): Get It On *(This is a repeat of an earlier performance)*

30-09-71 – **'Starparade' (Germany): Hot Love / Get It On** *(Mimed performances, these are notable for the background special effects, in particular, a leather hot-pants-clad woman on a motorbike during 'Get It On')*

01-10-71 – **'Beat Club' (Germany): Jeepster / Life's A Gas / Baby Strange** *(Again featuring the garish special effects that seemed almost de rigueur on German TV at the time, these are impressive performances throughout, with even 'Life's A Gas' performed on electric guitar and with a full band. 'Baby Strange' is an outtake that was not originally broadcast)*

00-11-71 – **Promo Video (UK): Jeepster** *(Compiled from live concert footage, this video was broadcast on 'Top Of The Pops' on 18-11-71. 'Jeepster' reached No. 2 in both the UK and Ireland)*

25-12-71 – 'Top Of The Pops' (UK): Hot Love *(This was taped on 20-12-71)*

26-12-71 – **'Top Of The Pops' (UK): Get It On** *(Taped on 20-12-71, this performance is notable for featuring Elton John on piano. Although Elton had at this point only had one major UK hit single, he was already starting to have huge success worldwide)*

04-01-72 – **'Disco' (Germany): Jeepster** *(A mimed performance on this important German TV show)*

14-01-72 – **'Hits A Go Go' (Switzerland): Jeepster / Mambo Sun** *(Taped on 03-01-72, Marc put more effort into posing and showmanship than he did miming to the songs)*

20-01-72 – **'Top Of The Pops' (UK): Telegram Sam** *(Taped on 19-01-72, this performance includes 'Dr Who'-like special effects that were often used for TOTP Glam Rock performances during the early 70s. It was also broadcast on 'Disco', German TV, on 29-04-72. 'Telegram Sam' became T. Rex's 3rd UK and Ireland No. 1 in the opening weeks on 1972, though stalled at No. 67 in the US, where it was the band's final chart entry)*

27-01-72 – **'Top Of The Pops' (UK): Telegram Sam** *(This is a repeat of the 20-01-72 performance)*

03-02-72 – **'Top Of The Pops' (UK): Telegram Sam** *(This is a repeat of the 20-01-72* performance)

12-02-72 – **'Rock En Stock' (France): Jeepster / Hot Love / Cadilac / Telegram Sam** *(Taped in black and white, live in a French studio on 03-02-72, this is one of T. Rex's best performances)*

18-03-72 – **Empire Pool, Wembley – Show 1: Cadilac / Jeepster / Baby Strange / Spaceball Ricochet / Girl / Cosmic Dancer / Telegram Sam / Hot Love / Get It On / Summertime Blues** *(One of two concerts filmed especially for the 'Born To Boogie' movie, these feature T. Rex mania at full pelt)*

18-03-72 – **Empire Pool, Wembley – Show 2: Cadilac / Jeepster / Baby Strange / Spaceball Ricochet / Girl / Cosmic Dancer / Telegram Sam / Hot Love / Get It On / Summertime Blues** *(This 2nd performance ended up being the only one used for 'Born To Boogie', albeit with overdubs. When the movie was issued on DVD in 2005, both concerts were included un-dubbed and uncut. As for the actual movie, it rivals David Bowie's 'Ziggy Stardust and The Spiders From Mars' as one of the most vital artefacts of the era)*

00-03-72 – **Apple Studios, London (UK): Tutti Frutti / Children Of The Revolution** [both songs feature Elton John and Ringo Starr] *(These are hot, playful, inspired performances, filmed at the very peak of Marc's commercial and critical success. They were featured in the Ringo Starr-directed 'Born To Boogie' movie)*

28-03-72 – **'Whatever Happened To Tin Pan Alley?' (UK): Jeepster** *(This incomplete but exciting live performance was taped at The Starlight Rooms in Boston, UK, on 15-01-72)*

Spring 1972 – **John Lennon's Estate, Ascot (UK): Medley: Jeepster – Hot Love – Get It On – The Slider** *(Performed acoustically, outdoors, and with a string quartet, this became one of the most memorable sequences of 'Born To Boogie')*

23-04-72 – **'Music In The Round' (UK): Jeepster / Cadilac / Spaceball Ricochet / Telegram Sam** *(Taped over 4 months earlier on 08-12-71, all songs are performed with live vocals over a pre-recorded backing with the exception of the fully live, acoustic, 'Spaceball Ricochet')*

11-05-72 – 'Top Of The Pops' (UK): Metal Guru *(This was taped on 10-05-72)*

18-05-72 – 'Top Of The Pops' (UK): Metal Guru *(This is a repeat of the 11-05-72 performance)*

25-05-72 – **'Top Of The Pops' (UK): Metal Guru** *(Wearing a blue jacket with black trousers, this mimed performance was taped on 24-05-72, though some sources claim that this surviving performance is instead from the 11-05-72 show. Whatever, it was also broadcast on 'Disco', German TV, on 24-06-72. 'Metal Guru' reached No. 1 in both the UK and Ireland)*

31-05-72 – **'The Dave Cash Radio Programme' (UK): Get It On** or **Jeepster** *(Often mistaken as promo videos, these performances, filmed in a darkened TV studio, were actually taped especially for this TV series. It is probable that only one song was broadcast on this date, with the other song broadcast on 12-07-72; however, it is uncertain which song was shown on which episode. 'The Dave Cash Radio Programme' is often wrongly identified as 'Music Unlimited', owing to the fact that highlights from the shows were issued on VHS tapes under this name in the early '80s. Throughout this book, the original, correct, programme title is used)*

01-06-72 – 'Top Of The Pops' (UK): Metal Guru *(This is a repeat of an earlier performance)*

08-06-72 – 'Top Of The Pops' (UK): Metal Guru *(This is a repeat of an earlier performance)*

10-06-72 – **Capitol Theatre, Cardiff (UK): Cadillac** *(Superb close-up live footage, unfortunately, this is the only song from this show that is known to survive)*

12-07-72 – **'The Dave Cash Radio Programme' (UK): Get It On** or **Jeepster** *(See 31-05-72!)*

00-09-72 – **Promo Video (UK): Children Of The Revolution** *(A straight, mimed studio performance, by this point, Marc's OTT performances were starting to veer into self-parody. One of T. Rex's most memorable songs, 'Children Of The Revolution' got to No. 2 in the UK charts, though again reached No. 1 in Ireland)*

00-09-72 – **Promo Video (UK): Buick Mackane** *(Another mimed performance, from the same studio session as the 'Children Of The Revolution' video, and another powerful song)*

14-09-72 – **'Top Of The Pops' (UK): Children Of The Revolution** *(Another mimed TOTP performance, this was taped on 30-08-72. It was also broadcast on 'Disco', German TV, on 11-11-72)*

28-09-72 – **'Top Of The Pops' (UK): Children Of The Revolution** *(This is a repeat of the 14-09-72 performance)*

07-12-72 – **'Top Of The Pops' (UK): Solid Gold Easy Action** *(Taped on 22-11-72, this performance features a female vocal trio, including Joe Brown's wife Vicki. This was also broadcast on 'Disco', German TV, on 03-02-73. 'Solid Gold Easy Action' got to No. 2 in the UK and No. 4 in Ireland)*

14-12-72 – **'Top Of The Pops' (UK): Solid Gold Easy Action** *(This is a repeat of the 07-12-72 performance)*

25-12-72 – 'Top Of The Pops' (UK): Telegram Sam *(This was taped on 21-12-72)*

28-12-72 – **'Top Of The Pops' (UK): Metal Guru** *(Taped on 21-12-72, this is easy to tell apart from the May '72 performance by Marc's black jacket and silver trousers)*

04-01-73 – **'Top Of The Pops' (UK): Solid Gold Easy Action** *(This is a repeat of the 07-12-72 performance)*

27-01-73 – **'Cilla!' (UK): Mad Donna / Life's A Gas** [with Cilla Black] *(On paper, Marc and Cilla are a very unlikely combination, but this duet is surprisingly listenable. 'Mad Donna' is from the 'Tanx' album, and is the only time it was performed on TV)*

21-02-73 – **'Musikladen' (Germany): 20th Century Boy / Buick Mackane** *(Taped on 19-02-73, these are loud 'n' heavy versions of two of T. Rex's most hard-rockin' songs. 'Buick Mackane' is an outtake that was not originally broadcast)*

01-03-73 – **'Top Of The Pops' (UK): 20th Century Boy** *(A straight run-through of the current hit, this was taped on 28-02-73, and also broadcast on 'Disco', German TV, on 26-05-73. '20th Century Boy' reached No. 3 in the UK and No. 11 in Ireland. Incidentally, a "promo video" exists for this song, but as it was compiled long after the '70s it isn't listed here)*

08-03-73 – **'Top Of The Pops' (UK): 20th Century Boy** *(This is a repeat of the 01-03-73 performance)*

10-03-73 – **'Devine Qui Est Derrier La Porte' (France): 20th Century Boy / Children Of The Revolution** *(Mimed performances in colour, '20th Century Boy' features Marc at the top of a long glittering staircase, while 'Children Of The Revolution' includes garish background effects similar to some of the band's earlier German TV appearances)*

24-03-73 – **'T. Rex In Brussels' (Belgium): 20th Century Boy** *(As well as interview and airport arrival footage, this TV appearance includes a solo acoustic performance of T. Rex's current big hit)*

01-05-73 – **'In Concert' (USA): The Groover / Jeepster** *(Taped in the UK for US TV broadcast, this live performance features the classic early '70s 4-piece T. Rex, though now with the addition of backing singers that include Marc's girlfriend Gloria Jones)*

30-05-73 – 'Top Of The Pops' (UK): The Groover

00-06-73 – **Promo Video (UK): The Groover** *(This video mixes live footage with film of a solo Marc at a studio photoshoot. 'The Groover' got to No. 4 in the UK, as well as No. 11 in Ireland, but it was to be his last top 10 hit)*

15-06-73 – 'Top Of The Pops' (UK): The Groover *(This is a repeat of the 30-05-72 performance)*

29-09-73 – **'The Midnight Special' (USA): Hot Love / Get It On** *(Taped on 12-08-73, this live performance would be one of the last TV appearances to feature all of the classic early '70s T. Rex line-up, albeit augmented by guitarist Jack Green and backing singers. The performances are OK, but Marc is looking a little overweight and those backing singers are a bit overpowering at times)*

19-12-73 – 'Lift Off With Ayshea' (UK): Truck On (Tyke) *(The only TV promotion for this single, this is one of many long lost gems of the Glam Rock era that were featured on Ayshea Brough's TV show. Very much "T. Rex-by-numbers", 'Truck On (Tyke)' stalled at No. 12 in the UK charts, the lowest chart placing since the pre-'Ride A White Swan' Tyrannosaurus Rex days)*

00-02-74 – **Scorpio Studios, London (UK): Get It On** *(Interesting footage of Marc Bolan rehearsing the band, he is the only one seen on camera, but the band by now almost certainly includes new drummer Paul Fenton as Bill Legend quit around November 1973)*

07-02-74 – **'Top Of The Pops' (UK): Teenage Dream** *(Taped on 05-02-74, this dramatic ballad is performed solo without the rest of T. Rex. Credited on record to 'Marc Bolan and T. Rex', 'Teenage Dream' was a No. 13 UK hit)*

14-04-74 – **'Disco' (Germany): Teenage Dream** *(Taped on 03-04-74, this is the only other TV performance of 'Teenage Dream')*

00-07-74 – **Promo Video (UK): Light Of Love** *(Taped in Paris on 07-05-74, this straight studio performance includes some interesting visual special effects. By now the band line-up was Marc, Steve, Mickey, another new drummer in Davey Lutton and Gloria Jones on keyboards and backing vocals. While not a bad song, 'Light Of Love' got to just No. 22 in the UK charts)*

08-10-74 – **'Don Kirshner's Rock Concert' (USA): Jeepster / Zip Gun Boogie / Token Of My Love / Get It On** *(By now looking very bloated, this patchy performance features the same band as on the 'Light Of Love' video, though with additional 2nd keyboardist Dino Dines. 'Zip Gun Boogie' was issued as a single in the UK, where it reached a disastrous No. 41)*

00-06-75 – **Promo Video (UK): New York City** *(Another simple studio promo, though sadly without Mickey Finn who had left the band by now, this video was broadcast on 'Shang-A-Lang' on 11-08-75. 'New York City' was T. Rex's biggest hit in nearly 18 months, reaching No. 15 in the UK charts)*

03-07-75 – **'Top Of The Pops' (UK): New York City** *(Taped on 02-07-75, this was T. Rex's first 'Top Of The Pops' appearance in almost 18 months)*

17-07-75 – 'Top Of The Pops' (UK): New York City *(This was taped on 16-07-75)*

24-07-75 – 'Rock On With 45' (UK): New York City

31-07-75 – **'Top Of The Pops' (UK): New York City** *(This is a repeat of the 03-07-75 broadcast)*

00-09-75 – **Promo Video (UK): Dreamy Lady** *(In a video featuring Marc Bolan alone and wearing a pink glittering suit, 'Dreamy Lady' got to No. 30 in the UK charts)*

11-10-75 – **'Supersonic' (UK): Dreamy Lady** *(Taped on 30-09-75, this is the first of two performances of 'Dreamy Lady' on this essential late era Glam TV show. This one features Marc alone wearing a white suit and getting covered in fake snow)

23-10-75 – 'Top Of The Pops' (UK): Dreamy Lady *(This was taped on 22-10-75)*

25-10-75 – **'Supersonic' (UK): Dreamy Lady** *(For this 2nd 'Supersonic' performance to promote the latest single, Marc is wearing a blue cat-suit, and with hair and make-up that was clearly the inspiration for punk singer Siouxsie Sioux's early look)*

21-02-76 – **'Supersonic' (UK): Telegram Sam / London Boys** *(Both songs are unconvincingly mimed by Marc alone, with 'Telegram Sam' being a weak remake of the classic 1972 single. 'London Boys' was another small hit, reaching No. 40 in the UK charts)*

11-03-76 – 'Top Of The Pops' (UK): London Boys *(This was taped on 10-03-76)*

17-06-76 – **'Top Of The Pops' (UK): I Love To Boogie** *(Taped on 16-06-76, by now Marc had slimmed down and cut his hair shorter, and the band had also been revamped, with Gloria Jones leaving to concentrate on motherhood and Miller Anderson joining on guitar. 'I Love To Boogie' was T. Rex's biggest hit in quite a while, getting to No. 13 in the UK charts)*

01-07-76 – 'Top Of The Pops' (UK): I Love To Boogie *(This was taped on 30-06-76)*

28-08-76 – **'Rollin' Bolan' (UK): I Love To Boogie / Funky London Childhood / The Soul Of My Suit / New York City / Laser Love** *(Taped on 13-07-76, this fine live performance includes two future singles in 'The Soul Of My Suit' and 'Laser Love', both sounding far more powerful here than on their studio counterparts. This would be the final TV performance to feature original bassist Steve Currie)*

07-10-76 – **'Top Of The Pops' (UK): Laser Love** *(Taped on 06-10-76, even an appearance on the nation's most important music TV show couldn't prevent 'Laser Love' stalling at No. 41 in the UK charts. This performance is notable for featuring the TV debut of a revamped T. Rex featuring Miller Anderson on guitar, Dino Dines on keyboards, Herbie Flowers on bass and Tony Newman on drums)*

16-10-76 – **'Supersonic' (UK): Ride A White Swan / Laser Love** *(Taped on 05-10-76, this is more promotion for the new single plus a tepid version of T. Rex's first hit)*

02-11-76 – **'The Arrows' (UK): Laser Love** *(Yet more 'Laser Love' promotion, as with*

'Supersonic', this features Marc alone without the rest of the band)

25-12-76 – **'Supersonic' (UK): I Love To Boogie / The Soul Of My Suit / New York City / We Wish You A Merry Christmas** [Finale, with Gary Glitter, Guys and Dolls, Russell Harty and Joanna Lumley] *(Taped at The Theatre Royal in Drury Lane, London, on 19-12-76, this is an exciting but slightly under-rehearsed performance)*

21-01-77 – **'Hit Kwiss' (Germany): Laser Love / Get It On** *(T. Rex's only post-1974 TV appearance outside the UK, this mimed performance features a one-off appearance by ex-The Pretty Things Jon Povey on drums, with Miller Anderson playing bass)*

12-02-77 – **'Supersonic' (UK): To Know Him Is To Love Him** [with Gloria Jones] *(Released in the UK as a flop single, this performance features enough dry ice to almost completely engulf Marc and Gloria)*

12-03-77 – **'Supersonic' (UK): Crimson Moon** *(A weak song from the 'Dandy In The Underworld' album, this features a solo Marc miming while sitting upon a glittering crescent "moon" prop)*

00-03-77 – **Promo Video (UK): The Soul Of My Suit** *(With a video that was taped in a hall of mirrors at The Belle Vue in Manchester on 12-03-77, 'The Soul Of My Suit' reached just No. 42 in the UK charts. It was destined to be the final hit of Marc's lifetime)*

24-03-77 – **'Top Of The Pops' (UK): The Soul Of My Suit** *(Looking good in a yellow suit, this TOTP performance, taped on 23-03-77, was Marc's last)*

02-04-77 – **'Supersonic' (UK): Soul Of My Suit / Sweet Little Rock 'n' Roller** [Finale, with Dave Edmunds, Dave Davies, Alvin Stardust, Elkie Brooks, Gloria Jones and John Lodge] *(Taped on 29-03-77, this final edition of 'Supersonic' includes the best known live version of 'The Soul Of My Suit' plus a fun but messy finale with other artists from the show)*

27-04-77 – **'Get It Together' (UK): The Soul Of My Suit** *(Taped on 20-04-77, this features another rather good live performance of the latest single)*

29-06-77 – **'Get It Together' (UK): Dandy In The Underworld** *(Taped on 26-06-77, Marc hadn't looked as good or released such a fine single in years, though none of this helped as the song failed to chart)*

24-08-77 – **'Marc' (UK): Sing Me A Song / I Love To Boogie / Celebrate Summer /**

Jeepster *(A trim and fit-looking Marc Bolan finally got his own TV series in August 1977, though unfortunately, the actual performances were far from ideal. Much of the newer material, including the latest, flop, single, 'Celebrate Summer', was weak, and when older classics were performed they were often insipid updates. Part of this was down to the band, which no longer included Miller Anderson, though with such stellar musicians as Herbie Flowers and Tony Newman at least part of the blame must lie with the studio engineers. Whatever, these were T. Rex's final TV appearances. This first edition's guests are The Jam, Stephanie De Sykes, The Radio Stars and Showaddywaddy)*

31-08-77 – **'Marc' (UK): Celebrate Summer / New York City / Ride A White Swan / Endless Sleep** *(Today's guests are Alfalfa, The Bay City Rollers, Mud and 10cc)*

07-09-77 – **'Marc' (UK): Sing Me A Song / Groove A Little / Let's Dance / Hot Love** *(Today's guests are The Boomtown Rats, Jamie Wild, Alan David and Hawkwind)*

14-09-77 – **'Marc' (UK): Endless Sleep / Dandy In The Underworld** *(Today's Denis Conly, The Steve Gibbons Band, Robin Askwith and Roger Taylor)*

21-09-77 – **'Marc' (UK): Celebrate Summer / Get It On** *(The first of two editions to be broadcast posthumously, today's guests are Rosetta Stone, Blue, The Radio Stars and Thin Lizzy)*

28-09-77 – **'Marc' (UK): Deborah / Standing Next To You** [with David Bowie] *(Today's guests are Generation X, Lip Service, Eddie and The Hot Rods and David Bowie)*

Glam Rock's first major casualty, Marc Bolan died in a car crash on 15th September 1977, just two weeks short of his 30th birthday. Original percussionist Steve Peregrin Took died in 1980, with bassist Steve Currie following him in 1981, percussionist Mickey Finn in 2003 and keyboardist Dino Dines in 2004. Of the classic 1971 to 1973 era, drummer Bill Legend alone survives.

Look Wot They Dun!

DAVID BOWIE

21-06-64 – 'Ready Steady Go!' (UK): Liza Jane *(Taped on 19-06-64, as with all pre-1969 David Bowie TV performances, it no longer exists)* – **DAVIE JONES and THE KING BEES**

27-07-64 – 'The Beat Room' (UK): Liza Jane – **DAVIE JONES and THE KING BEES**

08-03-65 – 'Gadzooks! It's All Happening' (UK): I Pity The Fool – **THE MANISH BOYS**

04-03-66 – 'Ready Steady Go!' (UK): Can't Help Thinking About Me – **DAVID BOWIE and THE BUZZ**

10-11-67 – 'Fenkleur' (Holland): Love You Till Tuesday *(This was taped on 08-11-67)*

16-03-68 – '4-3-2-1, Musik Fur Junge Leute' (Germany): Love You Till Tuesday / Did You Ever Have A Dream / Please Mr Gravedigger *(This was taped on 27-02-68)*

20-09-68 – '4-3-2-1, Musik Fur Junge Leute' (Germany)

11-11-68 – 'Fur Jeden Etwas Musik' (Germany)

00-02-69 – **'Love You Till Tuesday' (UK): Love You Till Tuesday / Sell Me A Coat / When I'm Five / Rubber Band / The Mask** (a mime) / **Let Me Sleep Beside You / Ching-A-Ling / Space Oddity / When I Live My Dream** *(Taped from 26-01-69 to 07-02-69, this is the earliest surviving David Bowie performance footage. Mainly consisting of Anthony Newley inspired whimsy and mime routines, this is largely more of a visual than audio treat, though it's one saving grace is a new song that David had just written… 'Space Oddity'. When issued as a single later in the year the song would get to No. 5 in the UK charts, as well as No. 13 in Ireland and No. 4 in Holland)*

14-06-69 – 'Colour Me Pop' (UK) [with The Strawbs] *(Taped on 10-05-69, Bowie did a mime routine during The Strawbs' song 'Poor Jimmy Wilson')*

30-08-69 – 'Doebidoe' (Holland): Space Oddity *(This was taped on 25-08-69, and was repeated on 31-12-69)*

09-10-69 – 'Top Of The Pops' (UK): Space Oddity *(This was taped on 02-10-69)*

16-10-69 – 'Top Of The Pops' (UK): Space Oddity *(This is a repeat of the 09-10-69*

performance)

12-11-69 – **'Hits A Go Go' (Switzerland): Space Oddity** *(This is a black and white performance, featuring a perm-haired Bowie miming on a long staircase in dry ice)*

22-11-69 – '4-3-2-1, Musik Fur Junge Leute' (Germany): Space Oddity *(This was taped on 29-10-69)*

05-12-69 – 'Like Now' (Republic of Ireland): Space Oddity

22-02-70 – **The Roundhouse, London (UK): Waiting For The Man** *(Backed by 'The Hype', short multi-angle clips of this performance circulate)*

27-02-70 – 'Cairngorm Ski Night' (UK): London Bye Ta-Ta *(This was taped on 29-01-70)*

10-05-70 – **'The Ivor Novello Awards' (UK): Space Oddity** *(Backed by an orchestra while playing an acoustic 12-string guitar, David Bowie is seen with long hair, a flowery shirt and huge flared trousers)*

00-06-70 – Six-O-One (UK): Memory Of A Free Festival *(As with the preceding 'The Prettiest Star' single, this was not a hit)*

15-08-70 – 'Eddy Ready Go' (Holland): Memory Of A Free Festival

20-01-71 – 'Newsday' (UK): Holy Holy *(Taped on 18-01-71, this performance failed to generate any major interest, and the single did not chart)*

10-06-71 – 'Top Of The Pops' (UK): Oh! You Pretty Things [Performed by Peter Noone, with David Bowie on keyboards] *(This was taped on 09-06-71)*

08-02-72 – **'The Old Grey Whistle Test' (UK): Oh! You Pretty Things / Queen Bitch / Five Years** *(Taped on 07-02-72 and backed by the legendary trio of Mick Ronson, Trevor Bolder and Mick 'Woody' Woodmansey, this superb live performance was really the TV debut of the David Bowie that would very soon become the most influential rock star of the '70s. Alternate versions of both 'Oh! You Pretty Things' and 'Queen Bitch' are available. Around this time the single 'Changes' would become a minor hit)*

01-04-72 – **'Pop 2' (France): Suffragette City** *(This live performance of the 'Ziggy Stardust' classic was taped at The Imperial College, London, on 12-02-72)*

21-06-72 – **'Lift Off With Ayshea' (UK): Starman** *(Taped on 15-06-72, as this book was* going to press, it was announced that this long-lost footage had been found on an old off-air tape)

21-06-72 – **Civic Hall, Dunstable (UK): Ziggy Stardust** *(With a soundtrack taped in Santa Monica four months later on 20-10-72, this footage successfully captures all of the excitement of an early 'Ziggy Stardust' gig)*

06-07-72 – **'Top Of The Pops' (UK): Starman** *(Taped the previous day on 05-07-72, this memorable performance was THE defining moment in Glam Rock. The single got to No. 10 in the UK charts, and was a small hit in several other countries including the USA and Australia)*

20-07-72 – **'Top Of The Pops' (UK): Starman** *(This is a repeat of the 06-07-72 performance)*

00-09-72 – **Promo Video (UK): John, I'm Only Dancing** *(Taped at The Rainbow Theatre, London, in August 1972, this moodily-lit video features mostly a straight mime, though there are some cool shots of Bowie smoking. Outtakes of this video shoot are also available. As for the single, it was a No. 12 UK hit, also reaching No. 19 in Ireland)*

00-11-72 – **Promo Video (USA): The Jean Genie** *(Mostly taped at The Winterland, San Francisco, in late October 1972, this also includes a few outdoors shots. The single became Bowie's biggest UK hit yet, reaching No. 2 in the UK, No. 3 in Ireland and No. 4 in Holland, though he was still struggling chart-wise in the USA and Australia)*

00-12-72 – **Promo Video (USA): Space Oddity** *(A simple mimed performance that was taped at RCA Studios, New York, on 13-12-72, this video was made primarily to promote the US reissue of the song. It worked too, as the single reached No. 15 in the US, as well as No. 9 in Australia. When the single was reissued in the UK in 1975 it became a No. 1 hit)*

04-01-73 – **'Top Of The Pops' (UK): The Jean Genie** *(Taped on 03-01-73, this brilliant live performance was thought to be long lost until being rediscovered in 2011)*

20-01-73 – **'Russell Harty Plus' (UK): Drive-In Saturday / My Death** *(Taped on 17-01-73, this is yet another superb live performance. 'Drive-In Saturday' was a No. 3 UK hit and a No. 4 in Ireland)*

05-06-73 – **'Nationwide' (UK): Watch That Man / Hang On To Yourself** *(Generally, this book doesn't feature documentaries or news items, however, this, and the later 'Cracked Actor', just HAVE to get a mention. Taped at The Winter Gardens in Bournemouth on 25-05-73, it includes incomplete clips of the two songs listed, as well as a backstage interview and chats with fans. Essential viewing)*

00-06-73 – **Promo Video (UK): Life On Mars** *(Taped at Blandford West Ten Studio, London, on 13-06-73, this is another simple mimed studio performance, albeit with excellent 'bleached' effects. Around 13 minutes of outtakes from the taping circulate among collectors. The song was a No. 3 UK hit, also reaching No. 4 in Ireland, but struggled in most other countries)*

03-07-73 – **Hammersmith Odeon, London (UK): Hang On To Yourself / Ziggy Stardust / Watch That Man / Wild Eyed Boy From Freecloud / All the Young Dudes / Oh! You Pretty Things / Moonage Daydream / Changes / Space Oddity / My Death / Cracked Actor / Time / The Width Of A Circle / Let's Spend The Night Together / Suffragette City / White Light/White Heat / Medley: The Jean Genie - Love Me Do** [with Jeff Beck] **/ Around and Around** [with Jeff Beck] **/ Rock 'N' Roll Suicide** *(This legendary performance is, along with 'Born To Boogie', the most essential concert movie of the '70s. As well as saying "goodbye" to Ziggy Stardust, Bowie also said farewell to his band; this was Woody Woodmansey's final show, and by the end of the year both Mick Ronson and Trevor Bolder would be gone too, though pianist Mike Garson would be retained for a while longer. The songs featuring Jeff Beck aren't included on the official DVD of the show, and both 'Changes' and 'Rock 'N' Roll Suicide' – with further edits – have been used for latter-day promo videos. 'Rock 'N' Roll Suicide' was issued as a UK single, where it got to No. 22, while in Holland 'Let's Spend The Night Together' was a single, reaching No. 19 in the charts)*

16-11-73 – **'The 1980 Floor Show' (USA): Medley: 1984 - Dodo / Sorrow / Everything's Alright / Space Oddity / Medley: 1984 - I Can't Explain / Time / The Jean Genie / I Got You Babe** [with Marianne Faithfull] **/ Medley: 1984 - Dodo** *(This was taped at The Marquee, London, from 18-10-73 to 20-10-73, for US TV broadcast. Featuring guests Marianne Faithfull, The Troggs and Carmen, the show includes excellent versions of several songs from the 'Pin Ups' album, though the undoubted highlight is the bizarre* duet with Marianne. Multiple alternate takes and rehearsals of every song circulate unofficially. 'Sorrow' was released as a single, and was a No. 3 UK hit, also getting to No. 1 in Australia, No. 2 in Ireland and No. 29 in Holland)

04-03-74 – **'Top Pop' (Holland): Rebel Rebel** (Looking resplendent in red dungarees, black platform boots, an eye patch and an orange mullet, this is one of Bowie's most visually appealing TV appearances. Taped on 13-02-74, according to some sources it was broadcast just two days later but 04-03-74 is a much more likely date. A worldwide hit, 'Rebel Rebel' got to No. 5 in the UK, No. 2 in Ireland, No. 8 in Holland, No. 33 in Germany, No. 28 in Australia and No. 64 in the USA. Also released as a 1974 single was 'Diamond Dogs', which got to No. 21 in the UK, No. 27 in Ireland and No. 66 in Australia)

00-10-74 – **Promo Video (UK): Knock On Wood** (Before official promo videos became commonplace, the usual practice on 'Top Of The Pops' would be to either feature Pan's People dancing to the record, or to compile a specially-made video, as seen here. This video was broadcast just once, on the 04-10-74 edition of the show. 'Knock On Wood' was a UK No. 10 hit, also getting to No. 4 in Ireland and No. 49 in Australia)

04-12-74 – **'The Dick Cavett Show' (USA): 1984 / Young Americans / Footstompin'** (By now deeply into his "soul" period, Bowie looked very different to how he did on 'Top Pop' earlier in the year, not least because he'd become so painfully gaunt-looking, and was clearly intoxicated during the lengthy interview also featured on the show. Taped on 02-11-74, 'Footstompin'' was later reworked as 'Fame', while 'Young Americans' was a No. 18 UK hit when issued as a single, also getting to No. 13 in Ireland, No. 27 in Australia and No. 28 in the USA)

26-01-75 – **'Cracked Actor' (UK) : Cracked Actor / Sweet Thing /Candidate / Moonage Daydream / Aladdin Sane / Time / Diamond Dogs / John, I'm Only Dancing (Again)** + more (Again breaking my "no documentaries" rule for this book, as with the 1973 'Nationwide' profile, this is essential viewing. This was filmed during the 1974 US 'Diamond Dogs' tour, and includes some fascinating live excerpts from a show at The Universal Amphitheatre in Los Angeles on 02-09-74)

04-11-75 – **'Soul Train' (USA): Golden Years / Fame** (Although Elton John beat him to it six months earlier, it was still extremely unusual for a white rock act to appear on this influential US TV show. At last reaching the kind of US success that Elton had, 'Fame' was a No. 1 hit in the country when issued as a single, also reaching No. 17 in the UK and No. 6 in Holland, while the follow-up 'Golden Years' was a US No. 10 hit, as well as No. 8 in the UK, No. 6 in Holland, No. 9 in Germany and No. 34 in Australia)

23-11-75 – **'Cher' (USA): Fame / Can You Hear Me** [with Cher] / **Young Americans Medley** [with Cher] *(A live vocal performance, Cher is a bit of an unlikely duet partner, though 'Can You Hear Me' works surprisingly well. 'Young Americans Medley' though is far less essential, featuring as it does a lengthy medley of many other songs, all performed in a cringe-worthy "showbiz" manner)*

03-01-76 – **'The Dinah Shore Show' (USA): Stay / Five Years** *(David Bowie's 3rd US TV performance in two months, this features a fine live version of his latest single 'Stay', though the new arrangement of 'Five Years' isn't a patch on the original. 'Stay' unfortunately sold poorly)*

02-02-76 – **'Station To Station' Tour Rehearsals, PNE Coliseum, Vancouver (Canada): Station To Station / Suffragette City / Waiting For The Man / Word On A Wing / Stay / TVC 15 / Sister Midnight / Life On Mars / Five Years / Panic In Detroit / Fame / Changes / The Jean Genie / Queen Bitch / Rebel Rebel** *(Live Bowie footage from the mid '70s is very thin on the ground, but this full dress rehearsal gives us a good idea of what the shows were like in early '76. When issued as a single, 'TVC 15' was a UK No. 15 and US No. 64 hit. Far more successful was the more commercial follow-up 'Sound and Vision', which got to No. 3 in the UK, No. 2 in Holland, No. 6 in Germany and No. 69 in the US)*

15-04-77 – **'The Dinah Shore Show' (USA): Funtime / Sister Midnight** [Both songs are sung by Iggy Pop, with Bowie on Keyboards] *(Touring as a back-up musician for his friend Iggy Pop, both the performances and Iggy's lengthy interview are a lot of fun)*

00-06-77 – **Promo Video (UK): Be My Wife** *(Although there's nothing wrong with the video featuring a heavily made-up Bowie playing a red guitar, 'Be My Wife' rivals 'Holy Holy' as his worst single of the '70s, and failed to chart in any major territories. Alternate edits of the video are also available)*

00-09-77 – **Promo Video (UK): Heroes** *(A simple but effective performance in a darkened studio, outtakes from this video circulate unofficially, along with incomplete performances of 'Blackout' and 'Sense Of Doubt'. Snippets of the latter two songs were used in a TV commercial for the 'Heroes' album. Remarkably, failing to chart in the US, 'Heroes' reached No. 24 in the UK, No. 8 in Ireland, No. 9 in Holland and No. 11 in Australia)

28-09-77 – **'Marc' (UK): Heroes / Sleeping Next To You** [with Marc Bolan] *(Taped on 09-09-77, 'Heroes' is a fine live performance, though the duet is little more than an incomplete jam. It was Marc's final TV appearance)*

01-10-77 – **'Odeon' (Italy): Sense Of Doubt / Heroes** *(Miming in a studio with a red backdrop while wearing a leather jacket, Bowie never looked cooler than here, though it is curious to see him playing keyboards during the instrumental first song)*

20-10-77 – **'Top Of The Pops' (UK): Heroes** *(With an official video and no less than five TV performances, no single before or since received as much promotion as 'Heroes'. Taped on 19-10-77 and featuring a terrific live vocal, this sees Bowie return to the 'Top Of The Pops' studio for the first time in almost five years)*

03-11-77 – **'Top Of The Pops' (UK): Heroes** *(This is a repeat of the 20-10-77 performance)*

06-11-77 – **'Top Pop' (Holland): Heroes** *(Another return to a show for the first time in years, and another fine live vocal performance)*

24-12-77 – **'The Bing Crosby Christmas Show' (UK): Medley: Peace On Earth - Little Drummer Boy** [with Bing Crosby] / **Heroes** *(taped on 11-09-77, 'Heroes' features Bowie superimposed on himself, so that he is both singing and doing a mime, while the Bing 'n' Bowie duet is something else altogether! When released as a UK single in 1982, the latter got to No. 3 in the charts)*

10-04-78 – **'David Bowie On Stage', Dallas (USA): What In The World / Blackout / Sense Of Doubt / Speed Of Life / Hang On To Yourself / Ziggy Stardust** *(Some excellent live footage from his 1978 world tour)*

08-07-78 – **'The London Weekend Show' (UK): Star / Heroes / Hang On To Yourself** *(A feature on Bowie's 1978 tour, this includes incomplete excerpts of the three listed songs, taped at Earl's Court, London, on 30-06-78)*

04-08-78 – **'Musikladen Extra' (Germany): Sense Of Doubt / Beauty And The Beast /**

Heroes / Stay / The Jean Genie / TVC 15 / Alabama Song / Rebel Rebel / What In The World *(Taped on 30-05-78, this is a relaxed live-in-the-studio performance that was broadcast a couple of months later, though 'What In The World' is an outtake that was only featured on later broadcasts. Released as singles, 'Beauty and The Beast' got to No. 39 in the UK charts, while 'Breaking Glass' stalled at No. 54)*

12-12-78 – **NHK Hall, Tokyo (Japan): Warszawa / Heroes / Fame / Beauty And The Beast / Five Years / Soul Love / Star / Hang On To Yourself / Ziggy Stardust / Suffragette City / Station To Station / TVC 15** *(More live footage, this captures Bowie on the final date of his 1978 tour)*

00-04-79 – **Promo Video (UK): Boys Keep Swinging** *(Although largely a simple mimed studio performance, Bowie amusingly dresses as up as three women at the end of the clip. His biggest UK hit in 3 years, it got to No. 7 in the charts, as well as No. 19 in Ireland and No. 16 in Holland)*

23-04-79 – **'The Kenny Everett Video Show' (UK): Boys Keep Swinging** *(At first glance this performance is very similar to the official promo video, but this time Bowie is dressed entirely in black rather than the white shirt with tie that he wears in the video, and instead of the three "women" he is seen playing the violin on a roof at the end)*

00-06-79 – **Promo Video (UK): DJ** *(Up until now, Bowie had rarely used his visual flair in promo videos, largely being satisfied with in-the-studio mimed performances. Things changed with this video, which features him both playing a DJ in a club and about town in night-time London. Not the greatest thing he ever recorded, 'DJ' was a UK No. 29 hit, though did worse elsewhere)*

00-08-79 – **Promo Video (UK): Look Back In Anger** *(Another imaginative video, this sees Bowie as a painter in an attic, whose face gradually gets weirder. Not that it helped the single, as 'Look Back In Anger' did even worse than 'DJ', not charting at all. More successful in 1979 was the single 'John, I'm Only Dancing (Again)', which got to No. 12 in the UK and No. 29 in Ireland)*

31-12-79 – **'Will Kenny Everett Make It To 1980?' (UK): Space Oddity** *(Miming to a stripped-down new version, this video sees Bowie largely in a padded cell, though also with some location shots. Liking this performance/video so much, Bowie repeated some *of the ideas for 1980's 'Ashes To Ashes' promo video)*

31-12-79 – **'Souvenirs of the Seventies' (USA): Space Oddity** *(Again miming to the new version, though this time in an on-stage setting)*

05-01-80 – **'Saturday Night Live' (USA): The Man Who Sold The World / TVC 15 / Boys Keep Swinging** *(Performing live, this is one of Bowie's most memorably weird TV appearances. 'The Man Who Sold The World' sees him in an oversized tuxedo and bow-tie, for 'TVC 15' he is wearing a skirt, and 'Boys Keep Swinging' features him like a puppet with a huge head. Although not broadcast until 1980, this bizarre performance was taped on 15-12-79, so it is a valid, vital, inclusion for this book)*

Releasing one more universally acclaimed album with 1980's 'Scary Monsters (and Super Creeps)', David Bowie went on to less acclaim but far greater success for the next decade. Largely reclaiming his mojo throughout the '90s and the new millennium, he shocked the world by dying on the 10th January 2016, just two days after his 69th birthday and the release of his final album 'Blackstar'.

Peter Checksfield

THE KINKS

18-04-70 – 'Point Chaud' (France) (on film)

18-06-70 – **'Top Of The Pops' (UK): Lola** (Taped on 21-05-70, the band started the '70s not only with a great record but with one of their biggest ever worldwide smashes. It got to No. 2 in the UK, also reaching the top 10 almost everywhere else, including the US and Australia. In 1970 the band featured Ray Davies (vocals, guitar), Dave Davies (vocals, lead guitar), John Dalton (bass), John Gosling (keyboards) and Mick Avory (drums))

09-07-70 – **'Top Of The Pops' (UK): Lola** (This is a repeat of the 18-06-70 performance)

17-07-70 – 'The David Frost Show' (USA): Lola (This was taped on 22-06-70)

30-07-70 – **'Top Of The Pops' (UK): Lola** (This is a repeat of the 18-06-70 performance)

31-07-70 – 'The Kenny Everett Explosion' (UK): Lola

08-08-70 – '4-3-2-1, Hot and Sweet' (Germany): Lola

21-08-70 – **'Jazz Bilzen Festival' (Belgium): Sunny Afternoon** + probably other songs

15-10-70 – **'Play For Today – The Long Distance Piano Player' (UK): Long Distance Piano Player / Got To Be Free / Marathon** (Taped from 21-03-70 to 23-03-70, these are Ray solo performances) – **RAY DAVIES**

00-11-70 – **Promo Video (UK): Apeman** (Performed here in an amusing video filmed outdoors, 'Apeman' did almost as well as the previous single in the UK at No. 5, also doing well elsewhere with the notable exception of the US)

03-12-70 – **'Top Of The Pops' (UK): Apeman** (This was taped on 04-11-70)

26-12-70 – 'Top Of The Pops' (UK): Lola (This was taped on 15-12-70)

07-01-71 – 'Top Of The Pops' (UK): Apeman (This was taped on 06-01-71)

21-01-71 – 'Top Of The Pops' (UK): Apeman (This is a repeat of an earlier performance)

11-02-71 – 'Top Of The Pops' (UK): Powerman / Got To Be Free (This was taped on 10-02-71)

04-01-72 – **'The Old Grey Whistle Test' (UK): Have A Cuppa Tea / Acute Schizophrenia Paranoia Blues** *(An excellent live studio performance)*

07-05-72 – **'Beat Club' (Germany): Muswell Hillbilly / You're Looking Fine / Alcohol / Holiday / Lola / Medley: You Really Got Me - All Day And All Of The Night** *(Taped on 12-04-72, this is another fine live performance. Only 'Muswell Hillbilly' was originally broadcast, the other songs are outtakes that were shown at later dates)*

00-05-72 – **Promo Video (UK): Supersonic Rocket Ship** *(An amusing location video, this was filmed outside Ray's London home. 'Supersonic Rocket Ship' was a No. 16 UK hit, also getting to No. 25 in Holland, but sadly it was The Kinks' final UK hit of the decade)*

01-06-72 – 'Top Of The Pops' (UK): Supersonic Rocket Ship

15-06-72 – 'Top Of The Pops' (UK): Supersonic Rocket Ship

21-07-72 – **'The Kinks At The Rainbow' (UK): Till The End Of The Day / Waterloo Sunset / Top Of The Pops / The Moneygoround / Sunny Afternoon / She's Bought A Hat Like Princess Marina / Alcohol / Acute Schizophrenia Paranoia Blues / Medley: You Really Got Me - All Day And All Of The Night** *(Featuring the five-piece The Kinks, occasionally augmented by a horn section, this was taped on 31-01-72, with the exception of 'The Moneygoround', which was taped without an audience on 30-01-72)*

15-03-73 – **'In Concert', London (UK): Victoria / Acute Schizophrenia Paranoia Blues / Dedicated Follower Of Fashion / Lola / Holiday / Good Golly Miss Molly / Medley: You Really Got Me - All Day And All Of The Night / Waterloo Sunset / The Village Green Preservation Society / Village Green Overture** *(Taped in London on 24-01-73, this superb performance is a strong candidate for the best The Kinks footage ever filmed)*

00-06-73 – **Promo Video (UK): Sitting In The Midday Sun** *(With a video notable for featuring close-ups of a camp-looking Ray brushing his long hair, the song was not a hit)*

22-09-73 – **'It's Lulu' (UK): Lola** *(This was taped on 08-09-73)*

07-06-74 – **'The Midnight Special' (USA): You Really Got Me / Money Talks / Here Comes Yet Another Day / Celluloid Heroes / Medley: Skin and Bone – Dry Bones** *(Taped on 07-05-74, incredibly, this was The Kinks first US TV appearance since 'Piccadilly Palace' way back in 1967. With a flamboyantly dressed Ray, the band now features female backing singers, as well as the horn section)

16-08-74 – **'ABC In Concert' (UK): Here Comes Yet Another Day / Here Comes Flash / Skin And Bone / Celluloid Heroes** *(This was taped in London for US TV broadcast on 04-06-74. Again, it sometimes features far too many musicians and singers on stage)*

04-09-74 – **'Starmaker' (UK): Everybody's A Star (Starmaker) / Ordinary People / Rush Hour Blues / Nine To Five / Have Another Drink / You Make It All Worthwhile / A Face In The Crowd / You Can't Stop The Music** *(Taped on 25-07-74, this is a stage musical, complete with dramatic scenes)*

14-11-74 – '45' (UK): Holiday Romance

00-05-75 – **The Beacon Theatre, New York (USA): Alcohol / Slum Kids / Ordinary People / Sunny Afternoon / Everybody's A Star (Starmaker) / Rush Hour Blues / Nine To Five / When Work Is Over / Have Another Drink / Underneath The Neon Sign** *(Taped on either the 7th, 8th or 9th of May 1975, this ambitious stage show, complete with dialogue, dramatic scenes and backdrops, was critically mauled at the time, but is fascinating in retrospect. Unfortunately, the surviving poorly lit black and white footage doesn't really do the show any justice)*

03-01-76 – **'Supersonic' (UK): No More Looking Back / Medley: You Really Got Me – All Day And All Of The Night** *(Taped on 29-12-75, this was one of the last TV appearances to feature the horn section)*

24-01-76 – Unknown TV show (UK) *(Reportedly, the band taped 2 songs on this date for a proposed TV special, but this was later scrapped, and the songs were never broadcast)*

06-03-76 – **'Supersonic' (UK): No More Looking Back** *(This is a repeat of the 03-01-76 performance)*

26-02-77 – **'Saturday Night Live' (USA): Medley: You Really Got Me – All Day And All Of The Night – A Well Respected Man – Lola / Sleepwalker** *(Heavily promoting their back-to-basics new single 'Sleepwalker', by now John Dalton had left the band to be replaced by bassist Andy Pyle)*

00-03-77 – **Promo Video (UK): Sleepwalker** *(With their popularity on the rise again in the USA, 'Sleepwalker' was a No. 48 US hit, also getting to No. 54 in Canada)*

08-03-77 – **'The Mike Douglas Show' (USA): Sleepwalker / Celluloid Heroes** *(This was taped on 22-02-77)*

02-04-77 – **'Supersonic' (UK): Sleepwalker / Sweet Little Rock 'n' Roller** [Finale, with Dave Davies, Dave Edmunds, Alvin Stardust, Elkie Brooks, Gloria Jones and John Lodge] *(This was taped on 29-03-77)*

26-04-77 – **'The Old Grey Whistle Test' (UK): You Really Got Me / Sleepwalker / Life Goes On / Stormy Sky / Celluloid Heroes / Muswell Hillbilly / Full Moon / Life On The Road / Juke Box Music** *(Taped 28-03-77, this live in the studio performance features the line up of Ray, Dave, Mick, John Gosling and Andy Pyle, as well as a couple of female backing singers)*

06-05-77 – **'The Midnight Special' (USA): Sleepwalker / Juke Box Music / Lola** *(This was taped on 23-04-77)*

00-11-77 – **Promo Video (UK): Father Christmas** *(An excellent video featuring the band in Santa outfits, the actual song is nothing special, and failed to chart)*

24-12-77 – **'The Old Grey Whistle Test: Kinks Christmas Concert' (UK): Juke Box Music / Sleepwalker / Life On The Road / Medley: A Well Respected Man - Death Of A Clown - Sunny Afternoon / Waterloo Sunset / All Day And All Of The Night / Slum Kids / Celluloid Heroes / Get Back In Line / The Hard Way / Lola / Alcohol / Medley: Skin And Bone - Dry Bones / Father Christmas / You Really Got Me** *(Broadcast live, from The Rainbow Theatre in London, this was the final The Kinks performance to feature John Gosling and Andy Pyle, as well as the last to include the backing singers)*

13-05-78 – 'What's On' (UK): Out Of The Wardrobe – ***RAY DAVIES***

06-07-78 – **'On Site' (UK): Life On The Road / Misfits / Live Life / Celluloid Heroes / Waterloo Sunset** *(Taped on 04-07-78, The Kinks' line-up was now Ray, Dave and Mick, with new members Gordon Edwards on keyboards and Jim Rodford on bass. Around this time, the single 'Rock 'N' Roll Fantasy' got to No. 30 in both the US and Canada)*

The band was scheduled to tape a performance for 'The Leo Sayer Show' on 26-10-78, but this was cancelled.

18-11-78 – **'Plattenkueche' (Germany): Father Christmas** *(This features the new line-up* *of the band miming to a year old single)*

23-09-79 – 'One For The Road', Rhode Island (USA): All Day And All Of The Night / Lola / Low Budget / (Wish I Could Fly Like) Superman / Attitude / Celluloid Heroes / The Hard Way / Where Have All The Good Times Gone / You Really Got Me / Pressure / Catch Me Now I'm Falling / Victoria *(Now featuring a line-up of Ray, Dave, Mick, Jim and another new keyboardist in Ian Gibbons, this inspired performance was issued as both a live album and an official VHS tape, as well as, later, an official DVD. Released as a single, '(Wish I Could Fly Like) Superman' got to No. 41 in the US and No. 43 in Canada)*

23-09-79 – 'One For The Road', Rhode Island (USA): Live Life *(This is an outtake that was not included on the official VHS and DVD releases. Other outtakes, not currently available, are 'Sleepwalker', 'Life On The Road', 'Misfits', 'A Gallon Of Gas' and 'Twist And Shout')*

The Kinks early '80's singles generally sold better than they had for much of the '70s, in particular, 1982's 'Come Dancing' (No. 12 in the UK and No. 6 in the USA). The band split in 1996, with both Ray and Dave pursuing solo careers, and several other ex-members forming The Kast-Off Kinks. 1978 keyboardist Gordon John Edwards died in 2003, original bassist Peter Quaife died in 2010, and latter-day bassist Jim Rodford died in 2018, the same year it was announced that Ray, Dave and Mick are recording again.

THE MOVE

28-03-70 – 'Disco 2' (UK): Brontosaurus

09-04-70 – 'Top Of The Pops' (UK): Brontosaurus

18-04-70 – **'Beat Club' (Germany): Brontosaurus** *(For the '70s, 'Beat Club' moved on from the black and white, often mimed, in front of an audience, performances of old. Instead, bands performed live in the studio, in colour, and without an audience. This format suited The Move perfectly, particularly now that future ELO-leader Jeff Lynne was in the band, and they were pursuing a more heavy/progressive direction. 'Brontosaurus' got to No. 7 in the UK charts)*

30-04-70 – 'Top Of The Pops' (UK): Brontosaurus *(This is a repeat of the 09-04-70 performance)*

14-05-70 – 'Top Of The Pops' (UK): Brontosaurus *(This is a repeat of the 09-04-70 performance)*

26-06-70 – 'Pop Scotch' (UK)

31-10-70 – 'Disco 2' (UK): When Alice Comes Back To The Farm

12-11-70 – 'Top Of The Pops' (UK): When Alice Comes Back To The Farm

25-11-70 – 'Lift Off' (UK): When Alice Comes Back To The Farm

31-12-70 – **'Beat Club' (Germany): When Alice Comes Back To The Farm** *(Another live and heavy performance, this song is from the 'Looking On' album)*

29-05-71 – **'Whittaker's World Of Music' (UK): Tonight** *(Back to more lightweight pop, and featured here with a live vocal, 'Tonight' got to No. 11)*

24-06-71 – 'Top Of The Pops' (UK): Tonight

03-07-71 – **'Disco' (Germany): Tonight** *(A mimed German TV performance of their latest single)*

08-07-71 – 'Top Of The Pops' (UK): Tonight

24-08-71 – 'Lift Off' (UK): Tonight

14-10-71 – 'Top Of The Pops' (UK): Chinatown *(This was a No. 23 hit)*

04-11-71 – 'Top Of The Pops' (UK): Chinatown

11-11-71 – 'Top Of The Pops' (UK): Chinatown *(This is a repeat of an earlier performance)*

24-11-71 – 'Lift Off' (UK): Chinatown

27-11-71 – **'Beat Club' (Germany): Down On The Bay** *(Performed live, this up-tempo '50s styled song is also available without the special effects that were used on the broadcast version)*

00-11-71 – **'Beat Club' Outtakes (Germany): The Words Of Aaron / Ella James** (Take 1) / **Ella James** (Take 2) *(Although taped at the same time as 'Down On The Bay', these songs weren't broadcast at the time)*

30-11-71 – **'The Old Grey Whistle Test' (UK): Ella James / The Words Of Aaron** *(Another fine live performance. Some sources list 'Ella James' as an un-broadcast outtake)*

12-04-72 – 'Lift Off With Ayshea' (UK): California Man *(This show also featured a Roy Wood solo performance of 'When Grandma Plays The Banjo')*

04-05-72 – 'Top Of The Pops' (UK): California Man

25-05-72 – 'Top Of The Pops' (UK): California Man

08-06-72 – 'Top Of The Pops' (UK): California Man *(This is a repeat of an earlier performance)*

22-06-72 – **'Top Of The Pops' (UK): California Man** *(A rock 'n' roll song similar to what both ELO and Wizzard would have success with in the future, 'California Man' was The Move's final hit at No. 7)*

08-07-72 – **'2 G's and The Pop People' (UK): California Man** *(Performed here with a live vocal, this show also features The Electric Light Orchestra performing '10538 Overture', though oddly, Roy Wood isn't featured on the latter song)*

25-12-72 – 'Top Of The Pops' (UK): California Man *(This is a repeat of an earlier performance)*

When The Move split in 1972, Roy Wood and Rick Price formed Wizzard, and Jeff Lynne, Bev Bevan (and, initially, Roy Wood) formed The Electric Light Orchestra, with both bands achieving huge success. There were occasional one-off partial reunions from 1981 onwards, though Bev Bevan put together a more permanent line-up from 2004 to 2014, with Trevor Burton joining him from 2007 to 2014. Carl Wayne became the lead singer of The Hollies in 2000, staying with them until his death in 2004.

ELTON JOHN

19-03-69 – 'The Discotheque' (UK) *(Elton's 1st known TV appearance, the song performed was probably his 2nd single 'Lady Samantha')*

10-01-70 – **'Disco 2' (UK)** *(Elton John and his band back Lou Christie on 'She Sold Me Magic', but unfortunately they do NOT perform by themselves)*

02-04-70 – 'Top Of The Pops' (UK): Border Song

13-06-70 – '4-3-2-1, Musik Fur Junge Leute' (Germany)

17-06-70 – **'Hits A Go Go' (Switzerland): Border Song** *(The earliest known surviving Elton John performance proper, this features him with a full head of hair and dressed soberly in a smart grey jacket and black shirt. A chart failure in the UK, 'Border Song' got to No. 25 in Holland, No. 34 in Canada and No. 92 in the US)*

23-10-70 – **'In Concert' (UK): Your Song / Border Song / Sixty Years On / Take Me To The Pilot / The Greatest Discovery / I Need You To Turn To / Burn Down The Mission** *(Taped on 22-05-70, 'In Concert' is musically superb though-out, even though at this point in his career Elton didn't incorporate much showmanship into his act. What's more, he is wearing a horrible outfit of faded blue jeans, a long-sleeved orange T-shirt and a sleeveless striped cardigan, clothing that in the near future he wouldn't be seen dead in. Outtakes from this show survive in the BBC archives)*

03-12-70 – 'The David Frost Show' (USA)

19-12-70 – 'Disco 2' (UK)

31-12-70 – **'Top Of The Pops: Into '71' (UK): Your Song** / People Can I Put You On *(Elton's 1st UK hit single, 'Your Song' got to No. 7 in the UK, No. 8 in the US, No. 3 in Canada, No. 10 in Holland and No. 11 in Australia. Wearing a red shirt with a white rhinestone jacket, Elton is at last beginning to look more interesting visually. Unfortunately only 'Your Song' from this 'Top Of The Pops' appearance survives, with 'People Can I Put You On' being long lost)*

14-01-71 – **'Top Of The Pops' (UK): Your Song** *(This is a repeat of the 31-12-70*

performance)

16-01-71 – **'The Andy Williams Show' (USA): Your Song / Heaven Help Us All** [with Ray Charles, Cass Elliott and Andy Williams] *(Elton's earliest known surviving US TV appearance, this performance was also broadcast in the UK on 11-03-71, and repeated on 14-09-71)*

23-01-71 – 'It's Cliff Richard!' (UK)

24-01-71 – **'Cannes A L'heure Du Midem' (France): Your Song**

04-02-71 – 'Top Of The Pops' (UK): Your Song / Ballad Of A Well Known Gun / Where To Now St. Peter

17-02-71 – 'Eddy Ready Go' (Holland): Your Song

22-02-71 – 'Bobbie Gentry' (UK)

02-03-71 – **'Top Pop' (Holland): Your Song** (on film) *(Filmed outdoors in the countryside while he mimes into a microphone, Elton John here looks more like a regional news reporter than a rock star. An alternate version of this film exists, much the same except that he is surrounded by photographers)*

18-03-71 – **'GTK' (Australia): Take Me To The Pilot** *(This is a specially made promo film)*

30-03-71 – 'The Dick Cavett Show' (USA)

03-04-71 – **'Aquarius: Elton John – Mr Superfunk' (UK): Your Song / Country Comfort / Border Song / Tiny Dancer / Sixty Years Old / Talking Old Soldiers** *(Although mostly performing slower songs, Elton is, at last, upping the showmanship stakes, eventually jumping around like a loony while dressed from head to toe in red. This broadcast was repeated on 24-07-71 and 02-09-72)*

09-06-71 – 'The Dick Cavett Show' (USA)

00-10-71 – **Japan Tour (Japan): Sixty Years On / It's Me That You Need** *(These songs were taped in either Tokyo or Osaka, exact date unknown)*

07-12-71 – **'The Old Grey Whistle Test' (UK): Tiny Dancer / All The Nasties** *(Although standard singer-songwriter stuff performed alone at a piano, Elton John is at least wearing a multi-coloured shiny jacket. Released as a single, 'Tiny Dancer' got to just No.*

70 in the UK, but reached No. 41 in the US and No. 19 in Canada)

29-01-72 – 'It's Cliff Richard!' (UK)

19-02-72 – **'Aquarius: Elton John and The Royal Philharmonic Orchestra' (UK): Rocket Man / Honky Cat / Mona Lisas and Mad Hatters / Your Song / Take Me To The Pilot / Sixty Years On / Tiny Dancer / The King Must Die / Indian Sunset / Border Song / Madman Across The Water / Burn Down The Mission / Goodbye** *(This was taped at The Royal Festival Hall, London, on 05-02-72. For the first three songs Elton John is "casually" dressed in a purple glitter jacket, then after that, he leaves the stage before returning in white top hat and tails, to be backed by The Royal Philharmonic Orchestra. The opening two songs would be released as his next two singles, and never sounded better than at this concert)*

00-04-72 – Promo Video (UK): Rocket Man

27-04-72 – **'Top Of The Pops' (UK): Rocket Man** *(Seen here in rare footage that only recently surfaced, 'Rocket Man' got to No. 2 in the UK, No. 6 in the USA, No. 8 in Canada and No. 18 in Germany. One person who was less than pleased with the record's success was David Bowie, who, allegedly, considered the song a rip-off of 'Space Oddity')*

29-04-72 – **'Sounds For Saturday' (UK): Tiny Dancer / Rotten Peaches / Razor Face / Holiday Inn / Indian Sunset / Levon / Madman Across The Water / Goodbye** *(Backed by his superb band, this inspired performance is one of his best. It was taped nearly 5 months earlier on 08-12-71, hence no 'Rocket Man')*

11-05-72 – **'Top Of The Pops' (UK): Rocket Man** *(This is a repeat of the 27-04-72 performance)*

25-05-72 – 'Top Of The Pops' (UK): Rocket Man

02-05-72 – 'Top Pop' (Holland): Rocket Man

31-08-72 – **'Top Of The Pops' (UK): Honky Cat** *(Not quite as successful as the last single, 'Honky Cat' stalled at No. 31 in the UK, though did scrape into the top 10 in both the US and Canada)*

05-11-72 – **'The Royal Variety Performance' (UK): I Think I'm Going To Kill Myself / Crocodile Rock** *(Taped on 30-10-72, this is classic Glam-era Elton. Wearing a red, white* and blue shiny suit with white framed glasses, 'Crocodile Rock' is a particularly strong version of his, at the time, latest single. A huge hit worldwide, it reached No. 5 in the UK, No. 1 in both the US and Canada, No. 2 in Australia and No. 3 in Germany. The performance was also broadcast on 'Top Pop', Holland, on 15-01-73)

09-11-72 – **'Top Of The Pops' (UK): Crocodile Rock (Video)** *(Filmed in the USA, this video was specially compiled for 'Top Of The Pops'. The same footage was later dubbed with 'Goodbye Yellow Brick Road')*

07-12-72 – 'Top Of The Pops' (UK): Crocodile Rock

25-12-72 – **'Top Of The Pops' (UK): Rocket Man** *(Notable for Elton wearing yellow glasses that spell out the word "zoom", unfortunately only a short segment of this performance survives)*

11-01-73 – **'Top Of The Pops' (UK): Daniel** *(The 1st of two surviving 'Top Of The Pops' performances of this excellent song, for this one Elton wears a blue and silver jacket. This performance was also broadcast on 'Top Pop', Dutch TV, on 05-03-73, and on 'Disco', German TV, on 28-04-73. 'Daniel' got to No. 4 in the UK, No. 4 in Ireland, No. 2 in the US, No. 1 in Canada and No. 7 in Australia)*

25-01-73 – **'Top Of The Pops' (UK): Daniel** *(A 2nd 'Top Of The Pops' performance, this time featuring Elton wearing a brown fur jacket)*

27-01-73 – **'Russell Harty Plus' (UK): Daniel** *(Wearing an orange teddy boy's jacket, this is another fine surviving performance of 'Daniel'. It was repeated on 'Russell Harty Plus Pop' on 19-01-74)*

17-03-73 – **'Hai Visto Mai' (Italy): Crocodile Rock** *(A live vocal performance over a pre-recorded backing track)*

29-06-73 – 'Top Of The Pops' (UK): Saturday Night's Alright For Fighting *('Saturday Night's Alright For Fighting' got to No. 7 in the UK, No. 12 in both the US and Canada and No. 31 in Australia)*

13-07-73 – 'Top Of The Pops' (UK): Saturday Night's Alright For Fighting *(This is a repeat of the 29-06-73 performance)*

01-11-73 – **'Top Of The Pops' (UK): Goodbye Yellow Brick Road** *(Wearing a blue satin* jacket and white glasses with orange lenses, this is yet more classic Elton. Another giant hit, 'Goodbye Yellow Brick Road' got to No. 6 in the UK, No. 2 in the US, No. 1 in Canada and No. 4 in Australia)

00-11-73 – **Promo Video (UK): Step Into Christmas** *(A simple mimed studio video, the song was released as a UK single, where it just missed the top 10 at No. 11)*

22-12-73 – **'Gilbert O'Sullivan: Welcome To My Show' (UK): Step Into Christmas / Get Down** [with Gilbert O'Sullivan] *(The only TV performance to promote the 'Step Into Christmas' single, also included is a fun duet with fellow piano-playing singer-songwriter Gilbert O'Sullivan)*

14-03-74 – **Randwick Racecourse, Sydney (Australia): Crocodile Rock / Goodbye Yellow Brick Road** *(This superb colour footage was broadcast, in black and white, on 'GTK')*

21-03-74 – 'Top Of The Pops' (UK): Candle In The Wind

30-03-74 – **'Russell Harty Plus' (UK): Candle In The Wind** *(Another classic single and another great live performance, the non-US single 'Candle In The Wind' got to No. 11 in the UK and No. 8 in Ireland)*

05-05-74 – **Watford Stadium (UK): Daniel / Country Comfort** [with Rod Stewart] *('Country Comfort' is an Elton John composition that Rod Stewart recorded for his 1970 'Gasoline Alley' album, so it was the perfect choice for a live duet. Unfortunately, this footage is marred by the fact that Rod's voice is almost inaudible throughout)*

09-07-74 – **'The Old Grey Whistle Test' (UK): Ticking / Grimsby** *(Dressed a little more soberly than of late, this is singer-songwriter fare performed without a band, similar to some of his TV appearances a couple of years previously)*

29-07-74 – **'Top Pop' (Holland): Don't Let The Sun Go Down On Me** *(Surprisingly, 'Don't Let The Sun Go Down On Me' only got to No. 16 in the UK, though it did get to No. 2 in the US, No. 1 in Canada and No. 13 in Australia)*

05-09-74 – **'Top Of The Pops' (UK): The Bitch Is Back** *(Singing live while surrounded by a close-up audience, this is another fine performance. Again only a moderate UK hit at No. 15, 'The Bitch Is Back' reached No. 1 in both the US and Canada, though failed to reach the top 50 in Australia)*

05-09-74 – **'Top Of The Pops' (UK): The Bitch Is Back** *(This is a repeat of the 05-09-74 performance)*

12-12-74 – **'Top Of The Pops' (UK): Lucy In The Sky With Diamonds** *(A classic song by The Beatles of course, Elton John's version features backing vocals and guitar by none other than John Lennon himself. Performed here while wearing enormous multi-framed glasses, 'Lucy In The Sky With Diamonds' got to No. 10 in the UK, No. 1 in both the US and Canada and No. 3 in Australia)*

24-12-74 – **'The Old Grey Whistle Test' Christmas Eve Concert (UK): Grimsby / Rocket Man / Goodbye Yellow Brick Road / Daniel / Grey Seal / Bennie and The Jets / Lucy In The Sky With Diamonds / I Saw Her Standing There / Don't Let The Sun Go Down On Me / Honky Cat / Saturday Night's Alright For Fighting / Crocodile Rock / The Bitch Is Back / Your Song / White Christmas** [with Rod Stewart and Gary Glitter] *(This is it, Elton John at the very peak of his formidable mid '70s powers. Taped at The Hammersmith Odeon, London, the first 4 songs weren't included on the original TV broadcast, which started part way through 'Grey Seal', but all songs are available unofficially. The show was repeated on 27-12-75)*

12-02-75 – **'Cher' (USA): Lucy In The Sky With Diamonds / Bennie and The Jets** [with Cher] **/ Medley: Mockingbird - Proud Mary - Ain't No Mountain High Enough - Never Can Say Goodbye** [with Cher and Bette Midler] *(Dressed in a particularly OTT silver outfit during The Beatles classic, for the duet with Cher on 'Bennie and The Jets' he is dressed far more sensibly. Once again, the song reached No. 1 in both the US and Canada, and No. 5 in Australia, but only a disastrous No. 37 in the UK)*

Early 1975 – **'Tommy' movie (UK): Pinball Wizard** [with The Who] *(With due respects to Tina Turner and Paul Nicholas, it was Elton John's cameo in 'Tommy' that was the most memorable. Not released as a single in the US or Canada, 'Pinball Wizard' was a No. 7 UK hit, as well No. 13 in Ireland)*

17-05-75 – **'Soul Train' (USA): Philadelphia Freedom / Bennie And The Jets** *(Wearing a hat over his ever-thinning hair, Elton John broke new ground by being the first major white rock act to appear on this famous soul music show, almost 6 months prior to David Bowie doing the same thing. 'Philadelphia Freedom' was a No. 12 UK hit, but, yet again, reached the top spot in both the US and Canada, as well as No. 4 in Australia)*

19-12-75 – **'Russell Harty' (UK): Your Song / Bennie and The Jets / Goodbye Yellow Brick Road / The Bitch Is Back / Pinball Wizard** *(Interspersed with interviews, these songs were taped live at Dodger Stadium, Los Angeles, USA, on 26-10-75. The broadcast was repeated on 29-08-76)*

07-02-76 – **'Parkinson' (UK): We All Fall In Love Sometimes**

12-05-76 – **Earl's Court, London (UK): Grow Some Funk Of Your Own / Goodbye Yellow Brick Road / Island Girl / Rocket Man / Hercules / Bennie and The Jets / Funeral For A Friend / Love Lies Bleeding** *(While not a bad performance by any means, Elton seems a little subdued compared to most 1972 – 1975 shows. Released as singles, 'Island Girl' got to No. 14 in the UK, No. 4 in both the US and Canada, and No. 12 in Australia, while 'Grow Some Funk Of Your Own' failed to chart at all in the UK, despite reaching No. 14 in the US and No. 8 in Canada)*

00-07-76 – **Promo Video (UK): Don't Go Breaking My Heart** [with Kiki Dee] *(Seen in a cheap-looking but fun video, this classic duet was, perhaps surprisingly, Elton's only UK No. 1 during the '70s. It also got to No. 1 in the US, Canada and Australia, and hit the top 5 pretty much everywhere else)*

17-09-76 – **Edinburgh Playhouse (UK): Skyline Pigeon / I Need You To Turn To / Sixty Years On / Border Song / Daniel / Love Song / The Greatest Discovery / Candle In The Wind / Bennie and The Jets / Rocket Man / Tonight / Think I'm Going To Kill Myself / Don't Let The Sun Go Down On Me / Better Off Dead / Sorry Seems To Be The Hardest Word / Someone Saved My Life Tonight / Sweet Painted Lady / Your Song / Island Girl / Don't Go Breaking My Heart / Saturday Nights Alright For Fighting** *(Bravely performing alone without a band, this superb performance shows just what a brilliant pianist Elton was, and still is. The show was broadcast on BBC Scotland in 2 parts: Live on 17-09-76, and the remainder a week later on 24-09-76. The single release, 'Someone Saved My Life Tonight' reached just No. 22 in the UK and No. 54 in Australia, though got to No. 4 in the US and No. 2 in Canada)*

00-10-76 – **Promo Video (UK): Sorry Seems To Be The Hardest Word** *(Mimed to in a plain white studio, this video is notable for featuring Elton without glasses for the first time on TV. With one of his most impressive vocal performances, 'Sorry Seems To Be The Hardest Word' reached No. 11 in the UK, No. 6 in the US, No. 3 in Canada and No. 19 in*

Australia, but after this Elton would struggle chart-wise in the US and Canada. Some claim this is because Elton had announced he was gay, but probably at least as much blame must be the undoubted downturn in quality of the singles. The UK follow-up was 'Crazy Water', which got to No. 27)

25-11-76 – **'Top Of The Pops' (UK): Sorry Seems To Be The Hardest Word** (Looking sharp in a grey suit, shirt and tie, this is a live performance without a band)

25-12-76 – **'The Morecambe and Wise Christmas Show' (UK): Sorry Seems To Be The Hardest Word** (Also featuring the inevitable comedy sketch, this is another live performance of Elton's current hit. The show was repeated on 02-04-77)

25-12-76 – **'The Parkinson Music Show' (UK): We All Fall In Love Sometimes** (This is a repeat of the 'Parkinson' performance from 07-02-76)

08-01-77 – **'Disco' (Germany): Sorry Seems To Be The Hardest Word** (A live vocal performance while wearing a red and yellow suit, this is notable for being probably Elton John's final "bald" performance, as during the early months of 1977 he decided to do something about his ever-decreasing hair, opting for a hair transplant)

29-05-77 – 'The Royal Windsor Big Top Show' (UK): Don't Let the Sun Go Down On Me

03-11-77 – **Wembley Arena, London (UK): Better Off Dead / Daniel / Roy Rogers / The Goaldigger's Song / Where To Now St. Peter? / Shine On Through / Tonight / I Heard It Through The Grapevine / Island Girl / Candle In The Wind / One Horse Town / Bennie and The Jets / Sorry Seems To Be The Hardest Word / Philadelphia Freedom / Medley: Funeral For A Friend - Love Lies Bleeding / Rocket Man / (Gotta Get A) Meal Ticket / Your Song / Don't Go Breaking My Heart** [with Kiki Dee] / **Bite Your Lip (Get Up and Dance)** [with Stevie Wonder] (A somewhat patchy performance featuring Elton with longer hair and a beret, a 45 minute edit of this show was broadcast in the UK on 07-11-77. 'Bite Your Lip (Get Up and Dance)' was a minor hit single, getting to No. 28 in both the UK and US, No. 51 in Canada and No. 72 in Australia)

18-12-77 – 'The Big Match' (UK): The Goaldigger's Song

25-12-77 – **'The Morecambe and Wise Christmas Show' (UK): Shine On Through** (Following another comedy sketch, Elton performs this song solo without a band)

08-01-78 – **'The Muppet Show' (USA): Crocodile Rock / Bennie and The Jets / Goodbye Yellow Brick Road / Don't Go Breaking My Heart** [with Miss Piggy] *('The Muppet Show' was incredibly popular during the late '70s and early '80s, with many a superstar eager to appear on it. This was broadcast in the USA on 04-02-78, and repeated in the UK on 04-06-78)*

00-03-78 – **Promo Video (UK): Ego** *(A forgettable song, it really was alarming just how below par many of Elton's singles were post '76. Only a mediocre hit, 'Ego' got to No. 15 in the UK but failed to crack the top 20 in the US, Canada and Australia)*

29-04-78 – 'Our Show' (UK)

00-10-78 – **Promo Video (UK): Part Time Love** *(One of Elton John's better late '70s singles, the video features a performance on a set that's made to look like a '60s TV show, complete with Cathy McGowan of 'Ready Steady Go!' fame sitting nearby. 'Part Time Love' got to No. 15 in the UK, No. 22 in the US, No. 13 in Canada and No. 14 in Australia)*

14-10-78 – **'Bruce's Big Night' (UK): Your Song** [with Bruce Forsyth] *(A duet that's even weirder than the one Elton did with Miss Piggy!)*

00-11-78 – **Promo Video (UK): Song For Guy** *(Although a No. 4 hit in the UK, No. 13 in Canada and No. 14 in Australia, the touching semi-instrumental 'Song For Guy' failed to reach the top 100 in the US. This would've been unthinkable a couple of years earlier)*

08-11-78 – **'Rock-Pop' (Germany): Return To Paradise / Part Time Love** *('Return To Paradise' was a Dutch hit at No. 49)*

31-10-78 – **'The Old Grey Whistle Test' (UK): Shooting Star / Song For Guy**

02-12-78 – **'Parkinson' (UK): Every Mother Wants A Son Like Elton** [with Dame Edna Everage]

14-12-78 – **'Top Of The Pops' (UK): Song For Guy** *(A live version performed without a band)*

31-12-78 – **'Disco Dance' (France): Part Time Love** *(A mimed performance on an expensive looking set)*

04-01-79 – **'Top Of The Pops' (UK): Song For Guy** *(This is a repeat of the 14-12-78*

performance)

Elton John was scheduled to appear on 'David Frost Presents The Gift Of Song' (UK) on 13-01-79, but cancelled due to illness.

00-04-79 – **Promo Video (UK): Are You Ready For Love** *(With a video largely filmed in a recording studio, the disco-flavoured 'Are You Ready For Love' got to No. 42 in the UK and didn't do much better elsewhere. The follow-ups 'Mama Can't Buy You Love' and 'Victim Of Love' also did poorly in most countries they were released in)*

00-05-79 – **'From Russia With Elton' (USSR): Your Song / Daniel / Medley: Funeral For A Friend – Tonight / Part Time Love / Bennie and The Jets / Sixty Years On / Candle In The Wind / Better Off Dead / Rocket Man / I Think I'm Gonna Kill Myself / Medley: Saturday Night's Alright For Fighting – Pinball Wizard** *(A fascinating documentary on Elton John's ground-breaking visit to Russia in 1979, he is accompanied by percussionist Ray Cooper, with no other additional musicians present. The performance was taped at The Great October Hall, Leningrad, in late May 1979)*

02-12-79 – **'Countdown' (Australia): Johnny B. Goode** *(One of Elton John's most bizarre singles, this performance of his disco-flavoured version of Chuck Berry's 'Johnny B. Goode' was taped in London, for Australian TV broadcast. The final single of the '70s, it was probably also his poorest selling, failing to chart anywhere)*

As well as many more hits, Elton John's subsequent decades have included celebrity duets (including Luciano Pavarotti, Leon Russell, George Michael and Cliff Richard), a knighthood, marriages to both a woman and a man, royal weddings and funerals, Disney soundtracks, drugs, wigs and tantrums... all of which have made it all too easy to forget the remarkable run of records he released from 1970 to 1976.

THE SWEET

31-10-66 – 'Herd At The Scene' (UK) *(One of Andy Scott's early bands, no footage of The Silverstone Set are known to survive)* – **THE SILVERSTONE SET**

12-11-66 – 'Opportunity Knocks' (UK) – **THE SILVERSTONE SET**

19-11-66 – 'Opportunity Knocks' (UK) – **THE SILVERSTONE SET**

26-11-66 – 'Opportunity Knocks' (UK) – **THE SILVERSTONE SET**

03-12-66 – 'Opportunity Knocks' (UK) – **THE SILVERSTONE SET**

10-12-66 – 'Opportunity Knocks' (UK) – **THE SILVERSTONE SET**

17-12-66 – 'Opportunity Knocks' (UK) – **THE SILVERSTONE SET**

21-06-68 – **'Mr. Rose: The Unlucky Dip' (UK): Do Unto Others** *(Another band featuring Andy Scott, and this time footage does still exist. With a line-up that includes a flute, the music sounds at times closer to Jethro Tull than it does The Sweet)* – **THE ELASTIC BAND**

26-04-69 – 'Colour Me Pop' (UK) – **THE ELASTIC BAND**

26-09-69 – **'The Contenders' (UK)** – **THE ELASTIC BAND**

30-12-70 – 'Lift Off' (UK): Funny Funny *(The Sweet's 5th single, 'Funny Funny' was the breakthrough they'd been waiting for, reaching No. 13 in the UK and the top 10 in most of Europe. They debuted the song on this show)*

30-03-71 – 'Top Pop' (Holland): Funny Funny

01-04-71 – 'Top Of The Pops' (UK): Funny Funny

08-04-71 – 'Top Of The Pops' (UK): Funny Funny

17-06-71 – **'Top Of The Pops' (UK): Co-Co** *('Co-Co' was The Sweet's first giant hit, getting to No. 13 in the UK and the top 3 in much of Europe. This 'Top Of The Pops' performance is the earliest known surviving footage of the band who, apart from Brian in his yellow top and red trousers, are all looking a little dowdy)*

01-07-71 – **'Top Of The Pops' (UK): Co-Co** *(This is a repeat of the 17-06-71 performance)*

07-07-71 – 'Eddy Ready Go' (Holland): Co-Co

10-08-71 – 'Lift Off' (UK): Co-Co

07-09-71 – 'Lift Off' (UK): Co-Co

11-09-71 – **'Disco' (Germany): Co-Co** *(While Brian wears the same clothes as on the earlier 'Top Of The Pops', the other three are all dressed in white)*

07-10-71 – 'Top Of The Pops' (UK): Alexander Graham Bell *(A blip in their world domination plans, 'Alexander Graham Bell' reached just No. 33 in the UK, with only Germany doing better at No. 24)*

28-10-71 – 'Lift Off' (UK): Alexander Graham Bell

06-11-71 – **'Die Aktuelle Schaubude' (Germany): Co-Co** *(Filmed in what looks like a small club, this mimed performance features the band in matching outfits consisting of green trousers with orange and green jackets, a combination that looks as bad as it sounds)*

22-12-71 – 'Lift Off' (UK): Funny Funny / Alexander Graham Bell / Co-Co

07-02-72 – 'Top Pop' (Holland): Poppa Joe

13-02-72 – 'The Golden Shot' (UK): Poppa Joe

17-02-72 – **'Top Of The Pops' (UK): Poppa Joe** *(Also broadcast on 'Disco', German TV, on 11-03-72, this sees all the band starting to look a little more colourful, though it's still Brian in his black and yellow trousers and yellow jacket that is the most eye-catching. 'Poppa Joe' just missed the top 10 at No. 11 in the UK, and did well in much of Europe)*

24-02-72 – 'Top Of The Pops' (UK): Poppa Joe

17-03-72 – **'Hits A Go Go' (Switzerland): Poppa Joe** *(This features some interesting special effects that see each band member repeated many times)*

04-04-72 – **'Tienerklanken' (Belgium): Poppa Joe** *(This fun video sees The Sweet miming outdoors in a Belgian street, and clearly having a lot of fun in the process)*

17-05-72 – **'The Dave Cash Radio Programme' (UK): Alexander Graham Bell** *(As with videos of other artists who appeared on this show, such as T. Rex, Slade and Middle Of*

The Road, performances from 'The Dave Cash Radio Programme' are often mistaken as general promo videos rather than those made specifically for a TV show. This video features the band miming on a studio set with a backdrop featuring outdoor night-time scenery)

07-06-72 – 'Lift Off With Ayshea' (UK): Little Willy

08-06-72 – **'Top Of The Pops' (UK): Little Willy** (Also broadcast on 'Disco', German TV, on 22-07-72, this is the first of many TV appearances where bassist Steve Priest steals the show, this time by wearing tight hot pants and boots. A tougher record than their previous hits, 'Little Willy' finally broke the band across the Atlantic, reaching No. 3 in the US and No. 1 in Canada, as well as getting to No. 4 in the UK and No. 1 in Germany)

15-06-72 – 'Top Of The Pops' (UK): Little Willy

21-06-72 – **'The Dave Cash Radio Programme' (UK): Poppa Joe / Jeanie** (Miming on a beach while wearing colourful – but not quite Glam – clothing, 'Poppa Joe' also includes a steel drum player and an exotic-looking black female dancer)

22-06-72 – 'Top Of The Pops' (UK): Little Willy

06-07-72 – 'Top Of The Pops' (UK): Little Willy

14-09-72 – 'Top Of The Pops' (UK): Wig Wam Bam

18-09-72 – 'Top Pop' (Holland): Wig Wam Bam

21-09-72 – 'Top Of The Pops' (UK): Wig Wam Bam

05-10-72 – **'Top Of The Pops' (UK): Wig Wam Bam** (Again, also broadcast on 'Disco', German TV, on 11-11-72, 'Wig Wam Bam' sees Steve memorably wearing a full-length red Indian feathered head-dress. 'Wig Wam Bam' got to No. 4 in the UK, No. 1 in Germany and No. 15 in Australia, but failed to chart in the US and Canada)

16-11-72 – **'The Dave Cash Radio Programme' (UK): Co-Co** (Featuring the band miming outdoors, intercut with studio footage of the same exotic dancer as seen in the 'Poppa Joe' video, this performance was taped some months earlier)

24-12-72 – 'Christmas Lift Off' (UK)

11-01-73 – 'Top Of The Pops' (UK): Blockbuster

14-01-73 – 'The Golden Shot' (UK): Blockbuster

15-01-73 – **'Top Pop' (Holland): Blockbuster** *(By now rivalling Slade and Bowie as the most flamboyant looking act on TV, this excellent TV performance features individual close-ups of each band member in all their made-up glory. 'Blockbuster' was a UK No. 1, one place ahead of David Bowie's similarly-riffed 'The Jean Genie', as well as No. 1 in Germany and Holland, No. 29 in Australia, No. 30 in Canada and No. 73 in the US. It was the band's sole UK No. 1, though they did have five No. 2's)*

18-01-73 – 'Top Of The Pops' (UK): Blockbuster

25-01-73 – **'Top Of The Pops' (UK): Blockbuster** *(The first of three surviving 'Top Of The Pops' performances of this song, this one is distinguished by Brian wearing a silver and black outfit. It was also broadcast on 'Disco', German TV, on 03-03-73)*

01-02-73 – **'Top Of The Pops' (UK): Blockbuster** *(Only surviving in black and white, this time all band members are in dark clothing)*

02-02-73 – 'Crackerjack' (UK): Blockbuster

08-02-73 – 'Top Of The Pops' (UK): Blockbuster *(This is a repeat of an earlier performance)*

15-02-73 – 'Top Of The Pops' (UK): Blockbuster *(This is a repeat of an earlier performance)*

22-02-73 – 'Top Of The Pops' (UK): Blockbuster *(This is a repeat of an earlier performance)*

00-04-73 – Promo Video (UK): Hellraiser *(This was broadcast on 'Top Pop' on 21-05-73, among other shows)*

27-04-73 – 'Top Of The Pops' (UK): Hellraiser

28-04-73 – **The Floral Hall, Southport (UK): Rock 'N' Roll Disgrace / Wig Wam Bam / I'm A Boy / Little Willy** *(This stunning albeit it black and white footage captures the band at their outrageous live best, despite the guitar being a little low in the mix. As well as the hits, a highlight is their version of The Who's 'I'm A Boy', with Steve Priest singing the Pete Townshend parts, and Andy Scott doing some incredibly high harmonies)*

04-05-73 – 'Top Of The Pops' (UK): Hellraiser

18-05-73 – 'Top Of The Pops' (UK): Hellraiser

25-05-73 – 'Top Of The Pops' (UK): Hellraiser *(This is a repeat of an earlier performance)*

23-06-73 – **'Disco' (Germany): Blockbuster / Hellraiser** *(Featuring Steve in a purple high-collared cape, this performance includes their latest, hard-rocking, single, 'Hellraiser'. The song got to No. 2 in the UK, No. 1 in Germany and No. 49 in Australia, but the title was far too controversial to get much airplay state-side. 'Hellraiser' was repeated on 06-07-74)*

00-09-73 – **Promo Video (UK): Ballroom Blitz** *(Seen here miming on a concert stage, 'Ballroom Blitz' is perhaps the definitive single by The Sweet. It got to No. 2 in the UK, No. 1 in Australia, Germany, Holland and Canada, and No. 5 in the USA)*

13-09-73 – 'Top Of The Pops' (UK): Ballroom Blitz

20-09-73 – **'Top Of The Pops' (UK): Ballroom Blitz** *(Apart from the promo video, this is the only known surviving footage to feature a contemporary performance of this song)*

04-10-73 – 'Top Of The Pops' (UK): Ballroom Blitz

21-12-73 – **The Rainbow Theatre, London (UK): Hellraiser / You're Not Wrong For Loving Me** *(Although the whole show is available officially on audio, only these two songs are known to survive on video – and that's only because they were featured in a BBC documentary on The Sweet entitled 'All That Glitters', broadcast on 28-02-74)*

25-12-73 – **'Top Of The Pops' (UK): Blockbuster** *(Featuring Steve Priest in his infamous "gay Hitler" German army outfit, rehearsal footage for this performance also exists, again courtesy of 'All that Glitters')*

00-01-74 – **Promo Video #1 (UK): Teenage Rampage** *(Filmed in a recording studio, 'Teenage Rampage' reached No. 2 in the UK, No. 1 in Germany and Ireland, and No. 10 in Australia, though oddly failed to chart in the US and Canada, where their career was very much hit and miss)*

00-01-74 – **Promo Video #2 (UK): Teenage Rampage** *(Featured in the 'All That Glitters' documentary on 28-02-74, this features concert and off-stage footage intercut with the recording studio video)*

10-01-74 – **'Top Of The Pops' (UK): Teenage Rampage** *(The first of two surviving 'Top Of The Pops' performances of this song, this one features an introduction by DJ Johnnie Walker and shows Brian dressed in blue)*

18-01-74 – **'Crackerjack' (UK): Teenage Rampage** *(A fully live performance, this must've left the young audience's ears ringing for hours afterwards)*

24-01-74 – **'Top Of The Pops' (UK): Teenage Rampage** *(This time the band are introduced by Jimmy Savile and Brian wears silver)*

The band was due to appear on 'Cilla!' on 02-02-74, but the show was cancelled due to technicians strike.

20-02-74 – **'Musikladen' (Germany): Teenage Rampage / Sweet F.A.** *(Only 'Teenage Rampage' was originally broadcast, with the hard-rocking 'Sweet F.A.' first being shown at a later date)*

00-07-74 – **Promo Video (UK): The Six Teens** *(In early 1974, Brian Connolly was badly beaten while out drinking, resulting in damaged vocal cords. Although he did recover, his voice was a little deeper and rougher afterwards, though this song was probably a little easier to sing than most of their hits. A welcome change of pace, 'The Six Teens' was a slightly lesser hit at No. 9 in the UK and No. 1 in Germany. The video was filmed on a concert stage, intercut with old photos of band members)*

15-07-74 – **'Lift Off With Ayshea' (UK): The Six Teens** *(During the summer of '74 no 'Top Of The Pops' shows were broadcast for seven weeks in a row, resulting in relatively few opportunities for established acts to plug their latest releases. 'Lift Off With Ayshea' was the next best thing, and, unusually for the show, this particular clip still survives. As well as Brian's voice changing, the band were now moving away from the over-the-top costumes of late, opting instead for leather and T-shirts)*

00-11-74 – **Promo Video (UK): Turn It Down** *(Seen here in a filmed-on-stage video, 'Turn It Down' was banned by the BBC, and consequently stalled at No. 41 in the UK, though it did get to No. 4 in Germany. Uniquely, Australia had 'Peppermint Twist' as a single, where it got to No. 1)*

13-11-74 – **'Musikladen' (Germany): Burn On The Flame / No You Don't / Turn It Down / Breakdown / Solid Gold Brass / Sweet F.A. / Andy Scott Guitar Solo / Man With The**

Golden Arm / The Six Teens *(Taped on 11-11-74, only 'Turn It Down' was originally broadcast, but all songs from this superb live performance have been seen since. Essential viewing)*

23-11-74 – **'Disco' (Germany): Turn It Down** *(An enthusiastically mimed performance of their No. 4 German hit)*

28-11-74 – **'45' (UK): The Six Teens / You're Not Wrong For Loving Me / Lady Starlight** *(Although an odd choice considering it had dropped out of the charts months earlier, this is still a superb live version of 'The Six Teens', followed by acoustic harmony-led versions of two slower songs, including a number later released by Andy Scott as a solo single)*

30-11-74 – **'The Geordie Scene' (UK): Breakdown / Solid Gold Brass / Turn It Down** *(Taped ten days earlier on 20-11-74, this is another excellent fully live performance)*

31-12-74 – **'Sylvester-Tanzparty' (Germany): The Ballroom Blitz / The Six Teens / Blockbuster** *(A mimed performance for an end-of-year German TV show. The Sweet would appear on the show again a year later)*

00-03-75 – **Promo Video (UK): Fox On The Run** *(Up until now, all of The Sweet's singles had been composed by Nicki Chinn and Mike Chapman, songwriters who also supplied many of the hits for Mud and Suzi Quatro. By now though, particularly following a couple of relative chart flops, The Sweet wanted to write their own songs, starting with this one. Seen in a simple studio video, 'Fox On The Run' was broadcast on 'Top Pop' on 28-03-75 and 'Disco' on 26-04-75, among other shows. The song was a worldwide hit, getting to No. 2 in the UK and Canada, No. 1 in Germany and Australia, and No. 5 in the USA)*

13-03-75 – **'Top Of The Pops' (UK): Fox On The Run** *(The first of two surviving 'Top Of The Pops' performances of this song, this is introduced by Noel Edmonds and sees the whole band dressed in black and white)*

27-03-75 – 'Top Of The Pops' (UK): Fox On The Run

03-04-75 – 'Top Of The Pops' (UK): Fox On The Run

10-04-75 – **'Top Of The Pops' (UK): Fox On The Run** *(Introduced by Emperor Rosko, Andy, Steve and Mick are again all in black and white, but Brian opts for a pale blue* *outfit)*

00-07-75 – **Promo Video (UK): Action** *(A mimed performance filmed on a concert stage featuring the band dressed in black leather and T-shirts, 'Action' got to No. 15 in the UK, No. 2 in Germany, No. 4 in Australia, No. 5 in Canada and No. 20 in Australia)*

10-07-75 – **'Top Of The Pops' (UK): Action** *(Dressed similarly to the promo video, with Mick in a dark waistcoat, this is the first of two 'Top Of The Pops' performances)*

24-07-75 – 'Top Of The Pops' (UK): Action *(This time Mick wears a white T-shirt with the word 'Bravo' on it)*

14-08-75 – 'Rock On With 45' (UK): Action

16-10-75 – **'Supersonic' (UK): Action / Burn On The Flame** *(With Brian looking great in a white suit, these are exciting performances. 'Fox On The Run', 'Action' and other recent recordings were sometimes criticized for sounding like Queen with their multi-part harmonies, but in truth, The Sweet were doing it first)*

00-12-75 – **Promo Video (UK): Lady Starlight** *(Although there were many great groups that emerged during the Glam era, only two could boast that every member was a great singer, one of those being 10cc, and the other The Sweet. A one-off solo single, Andy Scott's 'Lady Starlight' wasn't a hit)* – **ANDY SCOTT**

11-12-75 – **'Supersonic' (UK): Lady Starlight** *(The only solo TV performance to plug 'Lady Starlight')* – **ANDY SCOTT**

20-12-75 – 'Saturday Scene' (UK): Action *(This is probably a repeat of an earlier performance)*

23-12-75 – **'Top Of The Pops' (UK): Fox On The Run** *(This is a repeat of the 10-04-75 performance)*

25-12-75 – **'The Supersonic Christmas Show' (UK): Action** *(This is a repeat of the 16-10-75 performance)*

31-12-75 – **'Sylvester-Tanzparty' (Germany): Fox On The Run / Action** *(Another performance for this end-of-year German TV show)*

00-01-76 – **Promo Video (UK): The Lies In Your Eyes** *(With another simple mimed on-*

stage video, 'The Lies In Your Eyes' got to No. 35 in the UK, No. 5 in Germany and No. 14 in Australia)

17-01-76 – **'Supersonic' (UK): The Lies In Your Eyes** (With their homeland popularity waning, British TV appearances were becoming rarer. It would be two years before they appeared on a UK TV show again)

07-02-76 – **'Supersonic' (UK): The Lies In Your Eyes** (This is a repeat of the 17-01-76 performance)

00-10-76 – **Promo Video (UK): Lost Angels** (Good though the music is, most of The Sweet's later promo videos were a little boring, this one included. By now struggling in most countries, this did get to No. 13 in Germany)

11-12-76 – **'Musikladen' (Germany): Lost Angels** (The first of two major German TV show performances for 'Lost Angels', it's Andy Scott who looks the sharpest here in his white suit and scarf)

08-01-77 – **'Disco' (Germany): Lost Angels** (Repeated on 23-07-77, it's now Brian's turn to wear the white suit)

00-02-77 – **Promo Video (UK): Fever Of Love** (Another fine song with a mediocre video, this was a No. 9 hit in Germany. The follow-up, 'Stairway To The Stars', was a German No. 15)

20-08-77 – **'Disco' (Germany): Live For Today** (An exciting song from The Sweet's 'Off The Record' album, this again features Brian in white)

00-01-78 – **Promo Video (UK): Love Is Like Oxygen** (After a couple of years in the semi-wilderness, 'Love Is Like Oxygen' finally gave The Sweet another big worldwide hit, getting to No. 9 in the UK and Australia, No. 8 in the US and Canada, and No. 10 in Germany)

00-01-78 – **Promo Video (UK): California Nights** ('California Nights' was sung by Steve, with Andy harmonizing)

00-01-78 – **Promo Video (UK): Fountain** (Andy sings lead on 'Fountain')

00-01-78 – **Promo Video (UK): Lettres D'Amour** ('Lettres D'Amour' does feature Brian on lead vocals, though this time as a duet with female guest vocalist Stevie Lange)

19-01-78 – **'Top Of The Pops' (UK): Love Is Like Oxygen** *(In an expanded line-up featuring Gary Moberly on keyboards and Nico Ramsden on guitar, this is a welcome return to UK TV screens)*

02-02-78 – **'Top Of The Pops' (UK): Love Is Like Oxygen** *(This is a repeat of the 19-01-78 performance)*

16-02-78 – **'Top Of The Pops' (UK): Love Is Like Oxygen** *(This is a repeat of the 19-01-78 performance)*

17-02-78 – **'Szene '78' (Germany): California Nights / Love Is Like Oxygen** *(The first of several German TV appearances in two months, with both Brian and Mick having their hair cut shorter than usual, and all of them wearing white with the exception of Steve who's mostly in black. 'California Nights' was a No. 23 German hit, as well as a minor chart entry in both the US and Canada. Alternate, rehearsal, footage from this show circulates)*

11-03-78 – **'Hit Kwiss' (Germany): Love Is Like Oxygen** *(This time everyone is dressed in white)*

20-03-78 – **'Disco' (Germany): Love Is Like Oxygen** *(For this performance Brian wears a black outfit while the others wear lighter colours)*

22-04-78 – **'Hit Kwiss' (Germany): California Nights** *(Another performance of the Steve-sung German hit)*

22-03-79 – **'Musikladen' (Germany): Call Me** *(Due to his increasing alcoholism and unreliability, Brian Connolly was fired from the band in late 1978, with the other three continuing without him. Mick looks very youthful here with his shorter hair, and Andy looks like Andy, but Steve has chosen to have a perm, along with a Jason King style moustache, resulting in him looking far more of a prat than he ever did the Glam years. Sung by Steve, 'Call Me' isn't actually a bad song, but few people were really interested in the post-Brian band, despite the ever-loyal Germans getting this to No. 29)*

Early 1979 – **'Pop '79' (Germany): Call Me** *(Another German TV promotion for 'Call Me', though by this time Steve had wisely shaven off his moustache)*

Andy, Steve and Mick continued as a trio before disbanding in 1981. Brian formed The New Sweet, later renamed Brian Connolly's Sweet, in 1984. Andy and Mick reformed The Sweet with new additional members in 1985, a band that would be renamed Andy Scott's Sweet following Mick's departure in 1991. Sadly, Brian Connolly died in 1997, and Mick Tucker died in 2002, but both Andy Scott and Steve Priest currently tour with their own, separate, versions of the band.

THE ROLLING STONES

00-08-70 – **'Performance' Movie (UK): Come On In My Kitchen / Me and The Devil Blues / Memo From Turner** (*Although filmed from 01-09-68 to 11-11-68, this movie was not released until 1970. The first 2 songs are brief performances only. Mick Jagger's look in this, as 'Turner', inspired a host of future stars*) – **MICK JAGGER**

00-10-70 – **'Ned Kelly' Movie (Australia): Wild Colonial Boy** (*Taped in September 1969, this movie was released in 1970. This time, Jagger's look didn't inspire anyone, least of all movie-watchers. 'Ned Kelly' was a critical disaster*) – **MICK JAGGER**

26-03-71 – **The Marquee, London – Rehearsal (UK): Bitch / Brown Sugar**

26-03-71 – **The Marquee, London – Rehearsal (UK): Live With Me / Dead Flowers / I Got The Blues** [Take 1] / **I Got The Blues** [Take 2] / **Let It Rock / Midnight Rambler / (I Can't Get No) Satisfaction / Bitch** [Take 1] / **Brown Sugar / Bitch** [Take 2] (*Not only did The Rolling Stones largely inspire the glam rock stars of the '70s, but they also continued to incorporate the look. Although Keith looks a mess here and the others just look plain dowdy, Mick is wearing an open gold glittering jacket. As for the performance, this is a fine showcase for their-then new album 'Sticky Fingers'*)

15-04-71 – **'Top Of The Pops' (UK): Brown Sugar** (*Taped on 11-03-71, this is a superb live-vocal version of The Rolling Stones' current single, with Mick resplendent in a satin pink suit, multi-coloured cap and studded collar. 'Brown Sugar' got to No. 2 in the UK and France, No. 1 in the US and Holland, No. 4 in Germany and No. 5 in Australia*)

22-04-71 – **'Top Of The Pops' (UK): Brown Sugar** / Bitch / Wild Horses (*'Brown Sugar' is a repeat of the 15-04-71 performance, and all songs were taped on 11-03-71 with the latter two lost. 'Wild Horses' was released as a single in the US, where it got to No. 28*)

06-05-71 – **'Top Of The Pops' (UK): Brown Sugar** (*This is a repeat of the 15-04-71 performance*)

18-05-72 – **Rialto Theatre, Montreux (Switzerland): Shake Your Hips / Instrumental Jam / Tumbling Dice** [Take 1] / **Tumbling Dice** [Take 2] / **Loving Cup** (*'Shake Your Hips' and 'Tumbling Dice' [Take 1] was broadcast on 'Beat Club' on 27-05-72, while

'Instrumental Jam' and *'Loving Cup'* was broadcast on *'Beat Club'* on 24-06-72. When issued as a single, *'Tumbling Dice'* got to No. 5 in the UK and Holland, No. 7 in the US, No. 17 in Germany and No. 22 in Australia. Unfortunately, there was no promo video or TV performances for the song, so the best we have are these slightly hesitant run-throughs)

24-06-72 – **Tarrant County Convention Center, Fort Worth – 1st Show (USA): Gimme Shelter / Dead Flowers / Happy / Sweet Virginia / Rip This Joint** *(These songs were included as part of the 'Ladies and Gentleman, The Rolling Stones' movie, first premiered in 1974, as were the listed songs for the next three shows. Also worth checking out is the notorious, officially-unreleased 'Cocksucker Blues' documentary movie from this tour, though there's not much actual music included. Released as a US single, 'Happy' was a No. 22 hit)*

24-06-72 – **Tarrant County Convention Center, Fort Worth – 2nd Show (USA): Bitch** *(This song was included as part of the 'Ladies and Gentleman, The Rolling Stones' movie, first premiered in 1974)*

25-06-72 – **Hofheinz Pavilion, Houston – 1st Show (USA): Tumbling Dice / Love In Vain / You Can't Always Get What You Want / Bye Bye Johnny / Jumping Jack Flash** *(These songs were included as part of the 'Ladies and Gentleman, The Rolling Stones' movie, first premiered in 1974)*

25-06-72 – **Hofheinz Pavilion, Houston – 2nd Show (USA): Brown Sugar / All Down The Line / Midnight Rambler / Street Fighting Man** *(These songs were included as part of the 'Ladies and Gentleman, The Rolling Stones' movie, first premiered in 1974)*

25-07-72 – **Madison Square Garden, New York – 1st Show (USA): Brown Sugar / Street Fighting Man** *(These songs were broadcast on 'The Dick Cavett Show', on 11-08-72, along with backstage interviews)*

17-02-73 – **Kooyong Tennis Courts, Melbourne – 1st Show (Australia): Brown Sugar / Bitch** *(These songs were broadcast on 'GTK', on 05-03-73. Both songs featured the studio recordings as the soundtrack instead of the original live audio)*

00-08-73 – **Promo Video #1 (UK): Angie** *(Taped on 30-06-73 along with all other 'Goat's Head Soup' promo videos. 'Angie' got to No. 5 in the UK, No. 1 in the US, Holland, France* and Australia and No. 2 in Germany. The follow-up in the US was 'Doo Doo Doo Doo Doo (Heartbreaker)', where it got to No. 15, while France had a No. 2 hit with 'Star Star'. For this 1st video, Mick Taylor plays the piano while Mick Jagger stands up to sing while wearing gold trousers and waistcoat with a wide-brimmed hat)

00-08-73 – **Promo Video #2 (UK): Angie** (Featuring a live vocal, this time Mick Jagger sits down to sing while wearing a blue polka-dot shirt and a white suit, and Mick Taylor joins Keith on acoustic guitars)

00-09-73 – **Promo Video (UK): Silver Train** (For this song Mick wears a blue flared jump-suit with a silver belt, and heavy blue eye make-up. Despite his protestations at the time, Jagger looked as "glam" as anybody in 1973)

00-09-73 – **Promo Video (UK): Dancing With Mr D** (Again with heavy make-up, this time Mick wears shiny gold trousers and matching waistcoat. The song was released as the flip-side to the US 'Doo Doo Doo Doo Doo (Heartbreaker)' single)

30-09-73 – **Festhalle, Frankfurt – 2nd Show (Germany): Street Fighting Man** (This was broadcast on 'The Old Grey Whistle Test' on 23-10-73)

00-05-74 – **Promo Video #1 (UK): Monkey Grip Glue** (Increasingly frustrated in his role as 'only' the bass player for The Rolling Stones, Bill Wyman was the first band member to release a solo album, with 1974's 'Monkey Grip'. Five promo films were made, all simple studio mimed performances, though sometimes accompanied by scantily-clad dancers. For this one, Bill plays the piano while wearing a white suit with a straw boater hat) – **BILL WYMAN**

00-05-74 – **Promo Video #2 (UK): Monkey Grip Glue** (Similar to the 1st promo video, though this time Bill wears a casual jacket and no hat, while surrounded by even more dancers) – **BILL WYMAN**

00-05-74 – **Promo Video (UK): I Wanna Get Me A Gun** – **BILL WYMAN**

00-05-74 – **Promo Video (UK): What A Blow** – **BILL WYMAN**

00-05-74 – **Promo Video (UK): White Lightnin'** – **BILL WYMAN**

00-07-74 – **Promo Video (UK): It's Only Rock 'N Roll** (Mick Jagger has often insisted that 'It's Only Rock 'N Roll' was the band's only concession to glam rock. He's wrong of course, but there's no doubt that of all their recordings it is this one that would sound most at home on any glam rock compilation CD. Taped on 01-06-74 along with videos for two other songs, this features the band dressed as sailors who slowly get covered in foam in a marquee. 'It's Only Rock 'N Roll' got to No. 10 in the UK, No. 16 in the USA, No. 36 in Germany, No. 17 in Holland and Australia, and No. 3 in France)

14-07-74 – **Kilburn Gaumont State Theatre, London (UK): Intro [instrumental]** / **Am I Grooving You** / **Cancel Everything** / **If You Gotta Make A Fool Of Somebody** [with Rod Stewart] / **Mystifies Me** [with Rod Stewart] / **Take A Look At The Guy** [with Rod Stewart] / **Act Together** / **Shirley** / **Forever** / **Sure The One You Need** / **I Can't Stand The Rain** / **Crotch Music** / **I Can Feel The Fire** *(Promoting his first solo album 'I've Got My Own Album To Do', Ronnie was joined for this one-off concert by both his current Faces colleague Rod Stewart and his future Rolling Stones colleague Keith Richards. It was obvious even here that Ronnie's look and personality were far more suited to The Rolling Stones than the shyer Mick Taylor, despite the latter's impeccable playing)* – **RONNIE WOOD and KEITH RICHARDS**

00-10-74 – **Promo Video (UK): Till The Next Goodbye** *(An under-rated acoustic ballad, for this live vocal video they all dress casually)*

00-10-74 – **Promo Video (UK): Ain't Too Proud To Beg** *(An excellent live vocal version of the old Motown classic, for this video Mick Jagger really goes to town in the wardrobe department, wearing a pink and green jacket, white trousers, pink and white boots, white shirt, and white and green tie, all in shiny satin. What's more surprising is that Charlie Watts wears a similar outfit, with the other three also looking a little more colourful than usual. Released as a single in some countries, 'Ain't Too Proud To Beg' reached No. 17 in the US and No. 11 in France)*

01-05-75 – **5th Avenue, New York City (USA): Brown Sugar** *(This was performed on a flatbed truck as a publicity stunt to announce The Rolling Stones' forthcoming US tour – the first to feature Ronnie Wood instead of Mick Taylor)*

11-07-75 – **Forum, Los Angeles (USA): Honky Tonk Women** / **All Down The Line** / **Medley: If You Can't Rock Me-Get Off Of My Cloud** / **Star Star** / **Gimme Shelter** / **Ain't Too Proud To Beg** / **You Gotta Move** / **You Can't Always Get What You Want** / **Happy** / **Tumbling Dice** / **It's Only Rock 'N Roll** / **Doo Doo Doo Doo Doo** / **Fingerprint File** / **Angie**

/ **Wild Horses** / **That's Life** [performed by Billy Preston] / **Outa Space** [performed by Billy Preston] / **Brown Sugar** / **Midnight Rambler** / **Rip This Joint** / **Street Fighting Man** / **Jumping Jack Flash** / **Sympathy For The Devil** (Although there's no doubting the energy of this concert, Mick Jagger tends to bark and growl his way through it rather than sing)

00-05-76 – **Promo Video (UK): Fool To Cry** (Taped on 01-05-76, along with three other 'Black and Blue' promo videos, Mick still dresses colourfully and flamboyantly throughout, though now he is rivalled by Ronnie Wood. For this video, Mick wears a pink shirt and a black leather jacket. 'Fool To Cry' got to No. 6 in the UK, No. 10 in the US, No. 8 in Holland and No. 2 in France)

00-05-76 – **Promo Video (UK): Hot Stuff** (Proving glam isn't dead yet, Mick wears a silver jacket, green trousers and a long pink scarf. Released as a US single, 'Hot Stuff' got to No. 49)

00-05-76 – **Promo Video (UK): Hey Negrita** (At a time when Bowie, The Sweet and even Slade were dressing down a bit, Mick here wears an open green frilly top with silver and green trousers)

00-05-76 – **Promo Video (UK): Crazy Mama** (Mick is in silver trousers and a leather jacket this time)

04-06-76 – **Les Abattoirs, Paris (France): Angie** (This song was included as part of 'Aux Abattoirs', a 2-part French TV broadcast that featured 16 songs in total. A shorter, 13-song, version, was broadcast in the UK. Generally, these Paris '76 shows are far superior musically to the 1975 L.A. Forum concert)

06-06-76 – **Les Abattoirs, Paris (France): Honky Tonk Women** / **Medley: If You Can't Rock Me-Get Off Of My Cloud** / **Hand Of Fate** / **Hey Negrita** / **Ain't Too Proud To Beg** / **Fool To Cry** / **Hot Stuff** / **Star Star** / **Angie** / **You Gotta Move** / **You Can't Always Get What You Want** / **Happy** / **Tumbling Dice** / **Nothing From Nothing** [performed by Billy Preston] / **Outa Space** [performed by Billy Preston] / **Midnight Rambler** / **It's Only Rock 'N Roll** / **Brown Sugar** / **Jumping Jack Flash** / **Street Fighting Man** (The following songs were included as part of 'Aux Abattoirs', a 2-part French TV broadcast that featured 16 songs in total: Honky Tonk Women / Hand Of Fate / Star / You Gotta Move / You Can't Always Get What You Want / Happy / It's Only Rock 'n Roll / Brown Sugar / Jumping Jack

Flash / Street Fighting Man. *The entire uncut show from this date circulates unofficially)*

07-06-76 – **Les Abattoirs, Paris (France): Fool To Cry / Hot Stuff / Outa Space** [performed by Billy Preston] / **Tumbling Dice / Midnight Rambler** *(These songs were included as part of 'Aux Abattoirs', a 2-part French TV broadcast that featured 16 songs in total)*

21-08-76 – **'Knebworth Fair', Knebworth Park (UK): Around and Around / Little Red Rooster / Stray Cat Blues** (incomplete) / **Hot Stuff / Fool To Cry** (incomplete) / **Star Star / Let's Spend The Night Together** (incomplete) / **Dead Flowers** (incomplete) / **You Gotta Move / Midnight Rambler / Route 66 / Wild Horses / Honky Tonk Women / Tumbling Dice / Midnight Rambler / Jumping Jack Flash / Street Fighting Man** *(Rumoured at the time to be their farewell concert, judging by the above songs that circulate unofficially it was one of the sloppiest shows of their career)*

00-06-78 – **Promo Video (USA): Miss You** *(Taped in New York on 02-05-78 along with two other 'Some Girls' promo videos, Mick has now gone all new wave, with a skinny tie, smart jacket and tight trousers. 'Miss You' was a No. 3 UK hit, also getting to No. 1 in France and the US, No. 2 in Holland and No. 8 in Australia)*

00-06-78 – **Promo Video (USA): Far Away Eyes** *(Released as the B-side to 'Miss You', Mick sings live on this in-studio video)*

00-06-78 – **Promo Video (USA): Respectable** *(Seen here in a suitably energetic mimed-in-the-studio video, 'Respectable' was only released as a single in a few countries, getting to No. 23 in the UK and No. 18 in Holland)*

18-07-78 – **Will Rogers Memorial Center, Fort Worth (USA): Let It Rock / All Down The Line / Honky Tonk Women / Star Star / When The Whip Comes Down / Beast Of Burden / Miss You/ Just My Imagination / Shattered / Respectable / Far Away Eyes / Love In Vain / Tumbling Dice / Happy / Sweet Little Sixteen / Brown Sugar / Jumping Jack Flash** *(Both looking and sounding new wave influenced, the 1978 concerts tended to concentrate on short 'n' sharp songs, ignoring older epics like 'Midnight Rambler' and 'You Can't Always Get What You Want')*

06-10-78 – **'Saturday Night Live' [Rehearsals] (USA): Beast Of Burden / Respectable / Shattered** *(Several takes of each song circulate unofficially, as well as a snippet of*

'Summer Romance', a song that wasn't released until the 1980 'Emotional Rescue' album)

07-10-78 – **'Saturday Night Live' (USA): Beast Of Burden / Respectable / Shattered** (An energetic performance marred by Mick's hoarse vocals. Released as a US-only single, 'Beat Of Burden' got to No. 23)

00-10-78 – **Promo Video (UK): (You Gotta Walk) Don't Look Back** (Signed to Rolling Stones Records, Mick both sings on and guests in the video for Peter Tosh's revival of a song originally recorded by The Temptations. He would reprise the role on 'Saturday Night Live' a few weeks later) – **MICK JAGGER with PETER TOSH**

16-12-78 – **'Saturday Night Live' (USA): (You Gotta Walk) Don't Look Back** – **MICK JAGGER with PETER TOSH**

00-04-79 – **Promo Video (UK): Buried Alive** (One of two promo videos to promote Ronnie's 'Gimme Some Neck' album, this one is notable for featuring Ringo Starr guesting on drums. The video was taped in Los Angeles in April 1979) – **RONNIE WOOD**

00-04-79 – **Promo Video (UK): Seven Days** – **RONNIE WOOD** (This was taped in Los Angeles in April 1979)

05-05-79 – **Capital Center Arena, Largo (USA): Sweet Little Rock 'n' Roller / Buried Alive / F.U.C. Her / Mystifies Me / Infekshun / Rock Me Baby / Sure The One You Need / Lost and Lonely / Love In Vain / Breathe On Me / Let's Go Steady Again / Apartment Number Nine / Honky Tonk Women / Worried Life Blues / I Can Feel The Fire/ Come To Realise / Am I Grooving You / Seven Days / Before They Make Me Run / Jumping Jack Flash** (To promote his new album, as well as to have some fun outside of The Rolling Stones, Ronnie persuaded Keith to help form a temporary band, The New Barbarians. They mainly concentrated on the USA, though they did also support Led Zeppelin at 'Knebworth Fair') – **THE NEW BARBARIANS**

22-05-79 – **Sports Arena, San Diego (USA): Breathe On Me** (incomplete) **/ Love In Vain / Am I Grooving You / Seven Days / Before They Make Me Run / Jumping Jack Flash** – **THE NEW BARBARIANS**

11-08-79 – **'Knebworth Fair', Knebworth Park (UK): Sweet Little Rock 'n' Roller/ F.U.C. Her / Breathe On Me / I Can Feel The Fire / Let's Go Steady Again / Worried Life Blues /**

Honky Tonk Women / Come To Realise / Am I Grooving You / Seven Days / Before They Make Me Run / Jumping Jack Flash – *THE NEW BARBARIANS*

The Rolling Stones have a longevity that all others can only dream of, though they haven't had a UK top 10 hit since 'Start Me Up' in 1981. Bill Wyman left the band in 1993 to pursue other projects, including a prolific post-Stones music career, while all other members have released solo albums to varying degrees of success. Both Bill Wyman and Mick Taylor were featured guests on Rolling Stones concerts in 2012, with Mick Taylor performing on additional dates in 2013 and 2014.

SLADE

00-05-69 – **Promo Video (UK): Genesis** [Ambrose Slade] *(Released as a single, the instrumental 'Genesis' did not chart. This colour video features the group messing around in London's Euston Station)*

00-10-69 – **Promo Video (UK): Wild Winds Are Blowing** *(Now re-inventing themselves as a skin-head group, Slade – or 'The Slade' in this case – are seen in a colour video filmed in a recording studio. 'Wild Winds Are Blowing' was not a hit)*

04-11-69 – **'Monster Music Mash' (UK): Martha My Dear / Wild Winds Are Blowing** *(Playing live, the shaven-headed group perform a wonderful fiddle-led version of The Beatles' classic, as well as plug their latest single)*

21-03-70 – 'Disco 2' (UK): Shape Of Things To Come *(Another single, 'Shape Of Things To Come' was also another non-hit)*

02-04-70 – 'Top Of The Pops' (UK): Shape Of Things To Come *(Slade's first 'Top Of The Pops' appearance, this is unfortunately lost)*

25-04-70 – 'Disco 2' (UK) *(The most likely song here is another performance of 'Shape Of Things To Come')*

31-10-70 – 'Disco 2' (UK): Know Who You Are / Sweet Box *(Slade's 4th single if you include Ambrose Slade's 'Genesis', 'Know Who You Are' is a vocal rewrite of that very song, though again it didn't chart. Both this song and 'Sweet Box' are from the album 'Play It Loud')*

00-05-71 – **Promo Video (UK): Get Down and Get With It** *(Slade didn't entirely give up on the skin-head image straight away, adapting it by keeping their hair short on top but long on the sides, and retaining the boots and braces. This video features the band filmed outdoors, probably in London. At last, hitting the charts, 'Get Down and Get With It' got to No. 16 in the UK, No. 4 in Holland, No. 34 in Germany and No. 78 in Australia)*

22-05-71 – **'Whittaker's World Of Music' (UK): Get Down and Get With It** *(A fine live version of Slade's current hit)*

27-06-71 – **'Hits A Go Go' (Switzerland): Get Down and Get With It** *(Miming, this is the band's first known TV performance outside the UK)*

01-07-71 – 'Campus' (Holland): Raven / Gospel According To Rasputin / One Way Hotel / Sweet Box / Know Who You Are / Born To Be Wild / Get Down and Get With It *(Taped in Wieringerwerf, Holland, this performance featured several songs from the 'Play It Loud' album)*

15-07-71 – 'Top Of The Pops' (UK): Get Down and Get With It

21-10-71 – 'Top Of The Pops' (UK): Coz I Luv You

04-11-71 – 'Top Of The Pops' (UK): Coz I Luv You

11-11-71 – 'Top Of The Pops' (UK): Coz I Luv You

13-11-71 – 'A La Maniere' (France): Coz I Luv You

18-11-71 – **'Top Of The Pops' (UK): Coz I Luv You** *(This is a repeat of an earlier performance, date unknown, and can be distinguished from the later surviving 'Top Of The Pops' performance by Noddy's cap and acoustic guitar. From this single onwards, Slade would have an incredible twelve top 4 UK hits in three years, with six of them getting to No. 1. 'Coz I Luv You' was the first of these No. 1's, also getting to No. 1 in Ireland, No. 2 in Holland, No. 7 in Australia and No. 9 in Germany)*

24-11-71 – 'Eddy Ready Go' (Holland): Coz I Luv You *(This was repeated on 06-06-73)*

25-11-71 – 'Top Of The Pops' (UK): Coz I Luv You *(This is a repeat of an earlier performance)*

27-11-71 – **'Beat Club' (Germany): Coz I Luv You / Hear Me Calling / Get Down and Get With It** *(A truly stunning live performance, though only 'Coz I Luv You' was originally broadcast, with 'Hear Me Calling' and 'Get Down and Get With It' being outtakes that were not originally broadcast. Noddy wears a flat cap, striped shirt, white flares and braces, but Dave upstages him in his orange boiler suit)*

02-12-71 – **'Top Of The Pops' (UK): Coz I Luv You** *(This is a repeat of an earlier performance, the same performance that was repeated on 18-11-71)*

11-12-71 – **'Disco' (Germany): Coz I Luv You** *(A mimed performance on this popular*

German TV show)

13-12-71 – 'Top Pop' (Holland): Coz I Luv You

20-12-71 – 'Top Pop' (Holland): Coz I Luv You *(This is a repeat of the 13-12-71 performance)*

27-12-71 – **'Top Of The Pops' (UK): Coz I Luv You** *(For this performance Noddy dispenses with the cap and plays an electric guitar)*

03-02-72 – 'Top Of The Pops' (UK): Look Wot You Dun

05-02-72 – 'Pop Deux' (France)

17-02-72 – 'Top Of The Pops' (UK): Look Wot You Dun

17-02-72 – **'Hits A Go Go' (Switzerland): Look Wot You Dun** *(Performed here on Swiss TV, 'Look Wot You Dun' was a UK No. 4 hit, as well as No. 2 in Holland, No. 6 in Ireland, No. 14 in Germany and No. 43 in Australia. By now, Noddy was wearing checked "Rupert the bear" trousers with his flat cap, and Dave was wearing a long silver coat and glitter in his hair)*

28-02-72 – 'Top Pop' (Holland): Look Wot You Dun

Spring 1972 – **'The Dave Cash Radio Programme' (UK): Get Down and Get With It / Look Wot You Dun** *(Mimed studio performances that are often mistaken as promo videos, instead they were originally made for this TV show. Repeated on Belgian TV as 'Music Unlimited' on 10-08-75, they were also released under the same title on official VHS tapes in the early '80s)*

13-04-72 – **'Pop Shop' (Belgium): Hear Me Calling / Comin' Home / Darling Be Home Soon / Coz I Luv You / Get Down and Get With It / Born To Be Wild** *(An excellent live performance filmed in black and white. Interestingly, Noddy introduces 'Comin' Home' as being from their forthcoming 'Slade Alive!' album, but when released this song wasn't actually included)*

17-05-72 – **'Entende Cordiale' (France): Look Wot You Dun** *(An interesting mimed performance, with Jim playing a grand piano)*

22-05-72 – 'Top Pop' (Holland): Take Me Back 'Ome

06-06-72 – 'Top Of The Pops' (UK): Take Me Bak 'Ome

13-06-72 – **'Set Of Six' (UK): Hear Me Calling / Look Wot You Dun / Darling Be Home Soon / Coz I Luv You / Get Down and Get With It / Born To Be Wild** *(One of the best live performances by Slade – or anyone else for that matter – ever captured on videotape, this features the same set-list as the earlier 'Pop Shop' with the exception of 'Comin' Home' being substituted by a tough, no-piano, version of 'Look Wot You Dun')*

15-06-72 – 'Top Of The Pops' (UK): Take Me Bak 'Ome

17-06-72 – **'2 G's And The Pop People' (UK): Take Me Bak 'Ome / Get Down and Get With It** *('Take Me Bak 'Ome' was a UK No. 1, also No. 4 in Ireland, No. 5 in Holland, No. 10 in Germany, No. 11 in Australia and No. 97 in the US, their first albeit minor US chart entry. Performing with live vocals, 'Take Me Bak 'Ome' very cleverly includes four female dancers, all dressed in similar clothes to each Slade member that they're dancing next to)*

28-06-72 – 'Lift Off With Ayshea' (UK): Take Me Bak 'Ome

29-06-72 – 'Top Of The Pops' (UK): Take Me Bak 'Ome

15-07-72 – 'It's Lulu, Not To Mention Dudley Moore' (UK)

17-08-72 – 'Pop Shop' (Belgium) *(This is probably a repeat of the 13-04-72 broadcast)*

24-08-72 – 'Top Of The Pops' (UK): Mama Weer All Crazee Now

31-08-72 – 'Top Of The Pops' (UK): Mama Weer All Crazee Now

07-09-72 – 'Top Of The Pops' (UK): Mama Weer All Crazee Now *(This is a repeat of an earlier performance)*

14-09-72 – 'Top Of The Pops' (UK): Mama Weer All Crazee Now *(This is a repeat of an earlier performance)*

21-09-72 – 'Top Of The Pops' (UK): Mama Weer All Crazee Now *(This is a repeat of an earlier performance)*

02-10-72 – **'Top Pop' (Holland): Mama Weer All Crazee Now** *(A mimed studio performance with interesting background effects, this is the earliest known surviving TV performance featuring Noddy in his iconic mirror top hat. 'Mama Weer All Crazee Now'* reached No. 1 in the UK and Ireland, No. 6 in Germany, No. 7 in Holland, No. 14 in Australia and No. 76 in the US)

00-11-72 – **Promo Video (UK): Gudbuy T'Jane** *(With a video largely filmed at a live concert, 'Gudbuy T'Jane' was A No. 2 UK hit, also hitting No. 2 in Ireland, No. 3 in Germany, No. 4 in Holland, No. 11 in Australia, No. 68 in the US and No. 72 in Canada)*

09-12-72 – **'Disco' (Germany): Mama Weer All Crazee Now** *(Another appearance on this German TV show)*

13-12-72 – **'Musikladen' (Germany): Gudbuy T'Jane / Mama Weer All Crazee Now** *('Musikladen' is pretty much 'Beat Club' under a new name, and again Slade turn in a particularly fine live performance, just as they did a year earlier. 'Mama Weer All Crazee Now' is an outtake that was not originally broadcast)*

14-12-72 – **'Top Of The Pops' (UK): Gudbuy T'Jane** *(Also broadcast on German TV's 'Disco' on 03-02-73, Noddy is hat-less here, and is easily upstaged by Dave in his metallic outfit)*

18-12-72 – **'Top Pop' (Holland): Gudbuy T'Jane** *(Another performance on Holland's top music TV show)*

20-12-72 – 'Lift Off With Ayshea' (UK): Mama Weer All Crazee Now / Gudbuy T'Jane

25-12-72 – 'Top Of The Pops' (UK): Take Me Bak 'Ome

28-12-72 – **'Top Of The Pops' (UK): Mama Weer All Crazee Now** *(With Noddy in his top hat, checked trousers and braces, Dave in a mirror covered black outfit and "Dr Who" type special effects, this is classic Slade)*

21-01-73 – 'They Sold A Million' (UK)

25-01-73 – 'Horizon: The Curtain Of Silence' (UK) *(In this current affairs programme, Slade played to deaf children)*

00-02-73 – Promo Video (Holland): Cum On Feel The Noize

05-02-73 – **'GTK' (Australia): Get Down and Get With It / Mama Weer All Crazee Now** *(These songs were taped at Randwick Racecourse, Sydney, on 28-01-73, though 'Mama Weer All Crazee Now' is overdubbed with the studio recording)*

22-02-73 – **'Top Of The Pops' (UK): Cum On Feel The Noize** *(This was also broadcast on 'Disco', German TV, on 28-04-73. 'Cum On Feel The Noize' got to No. 1 in both the UK and Ireland, No. 6 in Holland, No. 8 in Germany, No. 12 in Australia and No. 98 in the US)*

01-03-73 – 'Top Of The Pops' (UK): Cum On Feel The Noize

05-03-73 – 'Top Pop' (Holland): Cum On Feel The Noize

08-03-73 – **'Top Of The Pops' (UK): Cum On Feel The Noize** *(As well as Noddy in matching checked top hat, waist-coat and trousers, this performance also features Dave in his infamous "metal nun" outfit)*

10-03-73 – **'Pop Gala' (Holland): Coz I Luv You / Take Me Bak 'Ome** *(An electrifying live performance taped at the peak of Slade's success, other songs from 'Pop Gala' were originally broadcast on various episodes of 'Popzien', but these are all that have resurfaced so far since)*

15-03-73 – 'Top Of The Pops' (UK): Cum On Feel The Noize

16-03-73 – 'Crackerjack' (UK): Cum On Feel The Noize

16-03-73 – 'Popzien' (Holland): Gudbuy T'Jane / Move Over / Come On Feel The Noize / Get Down and Get With It *(This was taped at 'Pop Gala' on 10-03-73)*

22-03-73 – 'Top Of The Pops' (UK): Cum On Feel The Noize *(This is a repeat of an earlier performance)*

08-05-73 – 'GTK' (Australia)

11-05-73 – 'Popzien' (Holland): Keep On Rocking *(This was taped at 'Pop Gala', 10-03-73)*

25-05-73 – **'ABC In Concert' (USA): Cum On Feel The Noize / Move Over / Get Down and Get With It** *(The first of two US TV appearances in the space of a week, included here is a fabulous live version of Janis Joplin's 'Move Over')*

01-06-73 – **'The Midnight Special' (USA): Gudbuy T'Jane / Come On Feel The Noize** *(Another superb live performance for US TV)*

05-06-73 – **'Point Chaud' (France): Cum On Feel The Noize** *(This is exciting on-stage footage, albeit dubbed with the record)*

22-06-73 – 'Lift Off With Ayshea' (UK): Kill 'Em At The Hot Club Tonite / Skweeze Me, Please Me *(Performed here were both sides of Slade's new single, but unfortunately, like the majority of 'Lift Off With Ayshea' episodes, this is lost)*

22-06-73 – **'Top Of The Pops' (UK): Skweeze Me, Pleeze Me** *(Promoted here on 'Top Of The Pops', 'Skweeze Me, Pleeze Me' again got to No. 1 in the UK and Ireland, also No. 3 in Germany, No. 6 in Holland and No. 39 in Australia)*

29-06-73 – 'Top Of The Pops' (UK): Skweeze Me, Pleeze Me *(This 2nd 'Top Of The Pops' performance of Slade's latest single is lost. Following this, on 01-07-73, Slade did something that David Bowie failed to do months earlier, and that is sell out London's Earl's Court. The concert was filmed for US TV, with three songs broadcast there later in the year, see the 17-12-73 entry for more details. Unfortunately, on 04-07-73, Don Powell was involved in a horrific car accident, badly injuring himself and killing his girlfriend)*

13-07-73 – 'Top Of The Pops' (UK): Skweeze Me, Pleeze Me *(This is a repeat of the 29-06-73 performance)*

31-07-73 – 'Popzien' (Holland): Gudbuy T'Jane / Get Down and Get With It / Come On Feel The Noize / Keep On Rocking *(This was taped at 'Pop Gala' on 10-03-73)*

00-09-73 – **Promo Video (UK): My Frend Stan** *(Slade's 1st single following Don Powell's accident, 'My Frend Stan' got to No. 2 in the UK, No. 1 in Ireland, No. 5 in Germany, No. 10 in Holland and No. 44 in Australia. The video for this piano-led song shows the band recording the song in the studio)*

11-10-73 – **'Top Of The Pops' (UK): My Frend Stan** *(As well as a red suit and a purple hat, Noddy also wears a pair of over-sized Lennon-type granny glasses)*

15-10-73 – 'Top Pop' (Holland): My Frend Stan

04-11-73 – **'Dimanche Salvador' (France): My Frend Stan** *(A mimed studio performance with lots of quick zooms and fast edits, this is intercut with footage of a rather scary looking elderly gentleman – presumably "Stan")*

19-11-73 – **'Deutsche Wochenschau' (Germany): My Frend Stan / Mama Weer All Crazee Now** *(This short programme shown prior to movies at German cinemas, includes*

'My Frend Stand' mimed on the "Slade Express" plane, and live footage from the Musikhalle in Hamburg on 13-11-73, dubbed with the studio recording of 'Mama Weer All Crazee Now')

19-11-73 – 'Top Pop' (Holland): My Frend Stan

06-12-73 – 'Top Of The Pops' (UK): Merry Xmas Everybody

10-12-73 – 'Top Pop' (Holland): Merry Xmas Everybody

13-12-73 – 'Top Of The Pops' (UK): Merry Xmas Everybody

17-12-73 – **'Don Kirshner's Rock Concert' (USA): Skweeze Me, Pleeze Me / Get Down and Get With It / Mama Weer All Crazee Now** *(Taped at London's Earl's Court on 01-07-73, just days before Don's accident, this is Slade at their wildest and loudest)*

20-12-73 – **'Top Of The Pops' (UK): Merry Xmas Everybody** *(The greatest Christmas record of all time, 'Merry Xmas Everybody' topped the UK and Irish charts, as well as getting to No. 3 in Holland, No. 4 in Germany and No. 55 in Australia. The first of three surviving 'Top Of The Pops' appearances for this song – four if you include a 1983 performance – for this one Noddy wears a yellow shirt, red waistcoat and pink jacket)*

25-12-73 – **'Top Of The Pops' (UK): Cum On Feel The Noize / Merry Xmas Everybody** *(With Noddy wearing a black and white checked suit, the band reprise two of their biggest hits. For the 2nd song, Noddy dons his mirrored top-hat – and gets a custard pie in the face)*

26-12-73 – **'Sez Les Christmas Special' (UK): Merry Xmas Everybody** *(Slade was rarely off the screens during the Christmas of '73, and for this one Dave wears a futuristic-looking black and silver costume while playing his "Super Yob" guitar, and Noddy wears a green shirt with checked waist-coat and trousers)*

27-12-73 – 'Lift Off With Ayshea' (UK): Merry Xmas Everybody

03-01-74 – 'Top Of The Pops' (UK): Merry Xmas Everybody *(This is a repeat of an earlier performance)*

10-01-74 – 'Top Of The Pops' (UK): Merry Xmas Everybody *(This is a repeat of an earlier performance)*

15-02-74 – 'Crackerjack' (UK)

04-03-74 – 'GTK' (Australia)

28-03-74 – **'Top Of The Pops' (UK): Everyday** *(The first Slade single to feature a ballad on the A-side, 'Everyday' reached No. 3 in the UK, No. 4 in Ireland and Holland, No. 13 in Australia and No. 17 in Germany. For this first 'Top Of The Pop' performance, Noddy wears a plain suit and a long white scarf)*

29-03-74 – **'The Midnight Special' (USA): My Frend Stand / Do We Still Do It / Everyday** *(A return to US TV, this live performance is notable for the inclusion of the 'Old, New, Borrowed and Blue' album track 'Do We Still Do It')*

30-03-74 – **'Clunk Click' (UK): Everyday** *(More plugging of the latest single, this time on Jimmy Savile's precursor to 'Jim'll Fix It')*

11-04-74 – **'Top Of The Pops' (UK): Everyday** *(The more commonly-seen performance, this time Noddy wears a yellow checked suit)*

11-04-74 – '45' (UK): Everyday

29-04-74 – **'Top Pop' (Holland): Everyday** *(Another performance on Holland's popular music TV show, this one features interesting 3-way split-screen effects)*

01-07-74 – 'Lift Off With Ayshea' (UK): The Bangin' Man / My Frend Stan *('The Bangin' Man' peaked at No. 3 in the UK and Ireland, No. 7 in Germany, No. 18 in Holland and No. 48 in Australia. Due to industrial action at the BBC, 'Top Of The Pops' wasn't shown for several weeks, so this single didn't get as much promotion as Slade singles in the past)*

22-07-74 – 'Top Pop' (Holland): The Bangin' Man

00-10-74 – **Promo Video (UK): Far Far Away** *(From the forthcoming movie 'Slade in Flame', 'Far Far Away' got to No. 2 in both the UK and Ireland, No. 8 in Germany, No. 13 in Holland and No. 17 in Australia. The video features the band in the luminous white suits that they wore at the end of the movie, complete with simple but effective multi-image special effects)*

11-10-74 – 'Top Of The Pops' (UK): Far Far Away

17-10-74 – 'Top Of The Pops' (UK): Far Far Away

26-10-74 – **'Disco' (Germany): The Bangin' Man** *(This German show is notable for being the only surviving contemporary TV performance of 'The Bangin' Man')*

31-10-74 – 'Top Of The Pops' (UK): Far Far Away *(This is a repeat of an earlier performance)*

31-10-74 – '45' (UK): Far Far Away

05-11-74 – 'Lift Off With Ayshea' (UK): Far Far Away

08-11-74 – **'Top Pop' (Holland): Far Far Away** *(Slade wear their white suits again for this show)*

00-11-74 – **Copenhagen (Denmark): Hear Me Calling** *(Wearing their usual glam stage outfits, this footage features a tantalizing reprise of the 'Slade Alive!' classic, though annoyingly there are more shots of the audience than the band)*

25-12-74 – **'Top Of The Pops' (UK): Merry Xmas Everybody** *(Introduced by Jimmy Savile in a Santa outfit, the band reprise their giant hit, dressing-down for the occasion by wearing white suits with the occasional black trim or check)*

00-01-75 – **'Slade In Flame' Movie (UK): How Does It Feel** (opening titles) / **This Girl / Them Kinda Monkeys Can't Swing / Standin' On The Corner / How Does It Feel** (Instrumental) / **O.K. Yesterday Was Yesterday / Summer Song (Wishing You Were Here) / Far Far Away / How Does It Feel** (closing credits) *(Although this movie got a very mixed critical reaction at the time, it has rightly been revered since as an essential cinematic and musical document of the '70s, and the songs are strong throughout)*

01-02-75 – **'Disco' (Germany): Far Far Away** *(Another white-suited mimed performance)*

01-02-75 – 'Un Jour Future' (France)

06-02-75 – **'Top Of The Pops' (UK): How Does It Feel** *(From the 'Slade In Flame' movie, 'How Does It Feel', despite its classiness, stalled at No. 15 in the UK, as well as No. 11 in Ireland and No. 36 in Germany. Although not wearing the bright white suits used in the 'Far Far Away' promotion, the whole band are starting to dress a little more soberly now)*

07-02-75 – **'Russell Harty Plus' (UK): How Does It Feel** *(One of two surviving UK performances of the song besides 'Top Of The Pops', this features a live vocal from

Noddy)

08-02-75 – 'Un Jour Future' (France)

20-02-75 – 'Top Of The Pops' (UK): How Does It Feel

22-02-75 – 'Un Jour Future' (France)

06-03-75 – 'Top Of The Pops' (UK): How Does It Feel

07-03-75 – **'Crackerjack' (UK): How Does It Feel** *(More promotion for the new single, and another fine live vocal)*

07-03-75 – **'Top Pop' (Holland): How Does It Feel** *(Although mimed, this moodily-lit Dutch TV performance looks great visually thanks to the atmospheric blue lighting)*

00-05-75 – **Promo Video (UK): Thanks For The Memory (Wham Bam Thank You Mam)** *(With Noddy wearing a particularly loud yellow polka-dot jacket and Dave in a silver and black jacket plus a huge silver bow-tie, glam wasn't dead yet. The piano-led 'Thanks For The Memory (Wham Bam Thank You Mam)' peaked at No. 7 in the UK, No. 3 in Ireland, No. 13 in Germany and No. 16 in Holland. It was Slade's last top 10 hit of the decade)*

01-05-75 – 'Rock On With 45' (UK): Thanks For The Memory (Wham Bam Thank You Mam)

08-05-75 – 'Top Of The Pops' (UK): Thanks For The Memory (Wham Bam Thank You Mam)

22-05-75 – 'Top Of The Pops' (UK): Thanks For The Memory (Wham Bam Thank You Mam)

30-05-75 – 'Top Pop' (Holland): Thanks For The Memory (Wham Bam Thank You Mam)

02-06-75 – **'Shang-A-Lang' (UK): Thanks For The Memory (Wham Bam Thank You Mam)** *(Featuring a live vocal, Noddy and Dave both wear the same outfits they wore in the promo video)*

17-07-75 – 'GTK' (Australia)

04-08-75 – **Winterland Arena, San Francisco (USA): Them Kinda Monkeys Can't Swing / The Bangin' Man / Gudbuy T'Jane / Thanks For The Memory (Wham Bam Thank You**

Mam) / How Does It Feel / Just A Little Bit / Let The Good Times Roll – Feel So Good (Medley) / Get Down And Get With It / Mama Weer All Crazee Now *(From mid '75 until the beginning of '77, Slade relocated to the USA, only returning home for the occasional TV appearances. This show in San Francisco saw them playing a red-hot set to a lukewarm audience, who were far more interested in seeing headliners Ten Years After, though Noddy Holder, wearing his mirrored top-hat once again, doesn't seem overperturbed by the occasional boos and heckles)*

20-11-75 – 'Top Of The Pops' (UK): In For A Penny

20-11-75 – **'Supersonic' (UK): In For A Penny** *(Singing live, Noddy wears a French-styled beret, and starts the song playing the accordion though quickly switches to guitar. 'In For A Penny' got to No. 11 in the UK and No. 12 in Ireland)*

04-12-75 – 'Top Of The Pops' (UK): In For A Penny

19-12-75 – 'Top Pop' (Holland): In For A Penny

27-12-75 – **'Supersonic' (UK): In For A Penny** *(This is a repeat of the 20-11-75 performance)*

00-01-76 – **Promo Video (UK): Let's Call It Quits** *(Seen here in an interesting video incorporated mirrors and with the band clad in denim and leather, 'Let's Call It Quits' was again a No. 11 UK hit, the same as the last single)*

05-02-76 – 'Top Of The Pops' (UK): Let's Call It Quits

14-02-76 – **'Supersonic' (UK): The Bangin' Man / Let's Call It Quits** *(With live vocals, these are fine versions of the 18-month old 'The Bangin' Man' and the latest single)*

19-02-76 – 'Top Of The Pops' (UK): Let's Call It Quits

06-03-76 – **'Jim'll Fix It' (UK): Let's Call It Quits** *(For this performance the band all wear red noses, possibly not the best way to promote the new single)*

06-03-76 – **'Supersonic' (UK): Let's Call It Quits** *(This is a repeat of the 14-02-76 performance)*

Early 1976 – 'Top Pop' (Holland): Let's Call It Quits

00-04-76 – **Promo Video (UK): Nobody's Fool** *(A superb, soulful, record, with a great* video featuring female backing singers and interesting back-projected film, this was sadly Slade's first major flop since 1970. 'Nobody's Fool' peaked at just No. 53 in the UK charts)

19-05-76 – 'Point Chaud' (France)

17-01-77 – **'Blue Peter' (UK): Gypsy Road Hog** (Slade's last great single of the '70s, this sees the just-back-from-the-USA Slade miming in a car, albeit with a verse censored out. Only marginally more successful single than the last single, 'Gypsy Road Hog' was a UK No. 48)

20-01-77 – **'Top Of The Pops' (UK): Gypsy Road Hog** (With a superb live vocal, this was the band's first 'Top Of The Pops' appearance in nearly a year)

05-02-77 – **'Supersonic' (UK): Mama Weer All Crazee Now / Gypsy Road Hog** (Playing live, this was a timely reminder of just how great the band could still sound on stage. Not that it helped record sales)

09-07-77 – **'Hit Kwiss' (Germany): Burning In The Heat Of Love / Gudbuy T'Jane** (Many musicians had their hair cut shorter by 1977, but few went to the extreme of Dave Hill who now sported a shaved head! A hard-hitting slice of heavy metal, 'Burning In The Heat Of Love' was Slade's first single since they found fame that failed to chart)

Summer 1977– **'Szene '77' (Germany): Burning In The Heat Of Love / Gypsy Road Hog** (Now Noddy has joined the hair-cut brigade, sporting an unappealing mullet instead of the ribbon-in-hair look that he had on 'Hit Kwiss')

00-10-77 – **Promo Video (UK): My Baby Left Me – That's All Right (Medley)** (Recorded as a tribute to Elvis and seen here in a partly black and white video, this medley was a No. 32 UK hit, though unfortunately, it was to be their last until 1981)

27-10-77 – **'Top Of The Pops' (UK): My Baby Left Me – That's All Right (Medley)** (Slade's final 'Top Of The Pops' appearance of the '70s, they were undoubtedly the most exciting act on the show that evening)

10-12-77 – **'Disco' (Germany): My Baby Left Me – That's All Right (Medley)** (Promoting their latest single on this popular German TV show)

Late 1977 – **'Rund' (East Germany): Cum On Feel The Noize / Mama Weer All Crazee**

Now / Coz I Luv You / Gudbuy T'Jane / Gypsy Road Hog / The Bangin' Man / Far Far Away / When The Lights Are Out / My Baby Left Me – That's All Right (Medley) *(Interspersed with interviews, these songs are sung live over the records. 'When The Lights Go Out' is one of the few Slade songs where Jim Lea sings lead vocals)*

00-02-78 – **Promo Video (UK): Give Us A Goal** *(While there's nothing wrong with the video, filmed on a football pitch, the song is a far cry from their hits of old)*

14-03-78 – **'Get It Together' (UK): Give Us A Goal** *(With a live vocal, Noddy wears a black and yellow woolly hat on this)*

17-04-78 – **'Cheggers Plays Pop' (UK): Give Us A Goal** *(Another live vocal, with Noddy this time looking good in a red shirt and checked waist-coat)*

Summer 1979 – **Portland Studios, London (Belgium): Studio Jam / I'm A Rocker** *(Taped in the UK for Belgian TV broadcast – and thankfully featuring Dave growing back his hair – 'I'm A Rocker' is a fine version of a lesser-known Chuck Berry song)*

01-01-80 – **'Get It Together' (UK): Hokey Cokey / My Baby's Got It** *(Broadcast on New Year's Day in 1980 but taped in late 1979, the single 'Hokey Cokey' was the very nadir of their career, with the up-tempo 'My Baby's Got It' not much better)*

A triumphant performance at the 1980 Reading Rock Festival turned around Slade's declining fortunes and resulted in several more big hits over the next few years. These include 1981's 'We'll Bring The House Down' (No. 10), 1983's 'My Oh My' (No. 2), and 1984's 'Run Runaway' (No. 7) and 'All Join Hands' (No. 15). Both Noddy Holder and Jim Lea left the band in 1992, with Dave Hill and Don Powell recruiting new members to form Slade II.

MIDDLE OF THE ROAD

Early 1971 – **Unknown TV show (Europe): Chirpy Chirpy Cheep Cheep** *('Chirpy Chirpy Cheep Cheep' was a giant hit in most of continental Europe prior to topping the UK charts in the summer of '71, and first came out in Italy, where the Scottish band were based at the time. This black and white performance features singer Sally Carr with long same-length hair, prior to having her trade-mark fringe. Featuring the band miming on a multi-level flowered set, it comes from an unknown European TV show, as yet unidentified. 'Chirpy Chirpy Cheep Cheep' reached No. 1 in the UK, Switzerland and Norway, and No. 2 in Germany, Austria and Holland)*

25-05-71 – 'Top Pop' (Holland): Tweedle Dee, Tweedle Dum

26-05-71 – **'Hits A Go Go' (Switzerland): Chirpy Chirpy Cheep Cheep** *(Miming on Swiss TV without instruments, Sally wears white trousers and cropped-top, while the others can be seen in truly dreadful yellow, purple and beige outfits)*

24-06-71 – **'Top Of The Pops' (UK): Chirpy Chirpy Cheep Cheep** *(Singing live, Sally wears black hot pants with matching lace-up top and red thigh-high boots, yet somehow still looks classy. There are not many women who could equal Pan's People on 'Top Of The Pops' but Sally Carr was one of them)*

01-07-71 – **'Top Of The Pops' (UK): Chirpy Chirpy Cheep Cheep** *(This is a repeat of the 24-06-71 performance)*

07-07-71– 'Eddy Ready Go' (Holland): Tweedle Dee, Tweedle Dum

15-07-71 – **'Top Of The Pops' (UK): Chirpy Chirpy Cheep Cheep** *(This is a repeat of the 24-06-71 performance)*

14-08-71 – **'Disco' (Germany): Chirpy Chirpy Cheep Cheep** *(With Sally wearing the same outfit as on 'Top Of The Pops', the band appear on one of Germany's most popular music shows)*

00-09-71 – Promo Video (UK): Tweedle Dee, Tweedle Dum *(This was broadcast on 'Top Of The Pops' on 30-09-71)*

02-09-71 – 'Top Of The Pops' (UK): Tweedle Dee, Tweedle Dum

11-09-71 – **'Disco' (Germany): Tweedle Dee, Tweedle Dum** *(Another big hit, 'Tweedle Dee, Tweedle Dum' got to No. 2 in the UK, No. 6 in Norway, No. 7 in Holland and No. 15 in Germany. Here Sally looks good in skimpy cream hot-pants, checked shirt and silver boots, while the rest wear matching smart-casual outfits)*

23-09-71 – 'Top Of The Pops' (UK): Tweedle Dee, Tweedle Dum *(This is a repeat of the 02-09-71 performance)*

Late 1971 – **'London Line' (UK): Chirpy Chirpy Cheep Cheep / Tweedle Dee, Tweedle Dum** *(In black and white, and with Sally but not the others wearing different outfits for each song, this was taped in the UK for overseas broadcast in various Commonwealth countries)*

29-09-72 – 'Eddy Ready Go' (Holland): Soley Soley *(This was repeated on 06-06-73)*

14-10-71 – 'Top Of The Pops' (UK): Tweedle Dee, Tweedle Dum *(This is a repeat of the 02-09-71 performance)*

25-10-71 – **'Top Pop' (Holland): Soley Soley** *(With Sally wearing black boots, shorts and top with gold trim and silver belt, this is one of many appearances on Holland's top music show. 'Soley Soley' was a No. 5 UK hit, as well as No. 2 in Germany and No. 1 in Switzerland, Norway and Holland)*

Late 1971 – **'Top Pop' (Holland): On This Land** *(Although clearly taped on the same day and on the same studio set as 'Soley Soley', there is no record of 'On This Land' ever being broadcast. Therefore, it is probably an outtake that wasn't broadcast at the time. As for the song, this is a beautifully-sung piano-led ballad)*

11-11-71 – **'UNICEF In Het Zilver' ('A Concert For UNICEF') (Holland): Tweedle Dee, Tweedle Dum / Soley Soley** *(With Sally in a pink top, black shorts and white boots, this is a good live vocal performance)*

22-11-71 – **'Top Pop' (Holland): Soley Soley** *(This is a repeat of the 25-10-71 performance)*

02-12-71 – **'Top Of The Pops' (UK): Soley Soley** *(Sally, here wearing the same outfit as on the recent 'Top Pop' appearance, always looked good, and this time the men are at* least trying, wearing matching outfits of denim and silver. This performance was also broadcast on German TV's 'Disco' on 15-01-72)

16-12-71 – **'Top Of The Pops' (UK): Soley Soley** *(This is a repeat of the 02-12-71 performance)*

24-12-71 – 'Christmas Lift Off' (UK): Soley Soley

27-12-71 – **'Top Pop' (Holland): Soley Soley** *(This is a repeat of the 25-10-71 performance)*

Late 1971 – **Unknown TV show (Germany): Soley Soley** *(Wearing a colourful flowered hippy dress against a black and white projected background, this appears to be a Sally Carr solo appearance, as no other band members are seen)*

22-12-71 – 'Eddy Ready Go' (Holland): Sacramento (A Wonderful Town) *(This was repeated on 04-07-73)*

25-12-71 – 'Top Of The Pops' (UK): Chirpy Chirpy Cheep Cheep

16-01-72 – **'Tele Dimanche' (France): Samson and Delilah** *(A live vocal performance for French TV)*

21-01-72 – **'Midem' (France): Bottoms Up** *(Miming on the Cannes beach, the casually dressed band preview a song that was a big success in some European countries later in the year)*

22-01-72 – 'A La Maniere 2' (France)

31-01-72 – 'Top Pop' (Holland): Sacramento (A Wonderful Town)

25-02-72 – 'Grand Gala Du Disque' (Holland): Chirpy Chirpy Cheep Cheep / Soley Soley / Sacramento (A Wonderful Town)

28-02-72 – 'Top Pop' (Holland): Sacramento (A Wonderful Town)

20-03-72 – 'Top Pop' (Holland): Samson and Delilah

00-03-72 – **Promo Video (UK): Sacramento (A Wonderful Town)** *(Broadcast on German TV's 'Disco' on 08-04-72, this video features a casually-dressed band miming on a boat. With their UK popularity already in decline, 'Sacramento (A Wonderful Town)', with its*

'Get Back' rhythm, only got to No. 23, but was a No. 1 in Germany, Switzerland, Norway and Holland)

03-04-72 – 'Top Pop' (Holland): The Talk Of All The USA

06-04-72 – 'Top Of The Pops' (UK): Sacramento (A Wonderful Town)

13-04-72 – 'Top Of The Pops' (UK): Sacramento (A Wonderful Town) *(This is a repeat of the 06-04-72 performance)*

27-04-72 – **'Starparade' (Germany): Chirpy Chirpy Cheep Cheep** *(Reprising their most famous hit, Sally wears a shiny blue outfit remarkably similar to what Agnetha Fältskog wore in ABBA several years later, while the three male members of the group look smart but stuffy in tuxedos and bow-ties)*

29-04-72 – **'The Basil Brush Show' (UK): Sacramento (A Wonderful Town)** *(Promotion for their latest single on this popular family TV show)*

20-05-72 – **'Point Chaud' (France): Sacramento (A Wonderful Town)** *(A mimed performance in what looks like an empty discotheque)*

21-05-72 – **'Discorama' (France): The Talk Of All The USA / On This Land** *(A mimed performance in a bare-looking studio)*

Mid 1972 – **'Teatro 10' (Italy): Tweedle Dee Tweedle Dum / Sacramento (A Wonderful Town)** *(With live vocals, Sally wears denim flares and jacket)*

Mid 1972 – **'The Dave Cash Radio Programme' (UK): Soley Soley / Sacramento (A Wonderful Town)** *(Excellent outdoor videos, for 'Soley Soley' the band are outdoors with Sally reclining in a sun chair, while for 'Sacramento (A Wonderful Town)' they are in a railway carriage)*

06-06-72 – **'Set Of Six' (UK): Tweedle Dee, Tweedle Dum / Jesus Christ Superstar / Soley Soley / I Just Don't Know What To Do With Myself / Sacramento (A Wonderful Town) / The Talk Of All The USA / Samson and Delilah / Chirpy Chirpy Cheep Cheep** *(Featuring Sally in a white mini-dress, this is a fine live performance through-out, with Andrew Lloyd-Webber's 'Jesus Christ Superstar' and Dusty Springfield's 'I Just Don't Know What To Do With Myself' being particular highlights)*

24-06-72 – **'Disco' (Germany): The Talk Of All The USA / Samson and Delilah** *(With Sally* wearing an orange top with red bell-bottoms and the others in star-covered white jackets, for once the whole band looks good. Released as a double A-side, 'Samson and Delilah' b/w 'The Talk Of All The USA' was the group's final UK hit at No. 26, though it got to No. 1 in Holland, No. 2 in Germany, No. 3 in Switzerland and No. 11 in Norway)

Mid 1972 – **Unknown TV Show (Germany): Samson and Delilah** *(With the others casually dressed behind her, Sally looks particularly fine in a very short yellow tartan skirt and black top)*

20-07-72 – 'Top Of The Pops' (UK): Samson and Delilah

29-07-72 – **'Sez Les' (UK): Samson and Delilah** *(Surrounded by scantily-clad dancers, Sally and the band wear similar outfits to what they wore on 'Disco' a month earlier)*

10-08-72 – 'Top Of The Pops' (UK): Samson and Delilah *(This is a repeat of the 20-07-72 performance)*

18-09-72 – 'Top Pop' (Holland): Bottoms Up

06-12-72 – 'Lift Off With Ayshea' (UK): Bottoms Up

09-12-72 – **'Disco' (Germany): Bottoms Up** *(A return to this German show, with Sally in a short black mini-dress with yellow and red stripes, and the others in brightly coloured suits. 'Bottoms Up' was a No. 2 German hit, as well as No. 5 in Holland and No. 8 in Norway)*

19-02-73 – **'Top Pop' (Holland): Yellow Boomerang** *('Yellow Boomerang' got to No. 6 in Germany, No. 2 in Holland and Switzerland, No. 8 in Norway and No. 14 in Austria. The TV performance features Sally in a long black dress)*

31-03-73 – **'Disco' (Germany): Yellow Boomerang** *(A rare Sally Carr fashion faux pas, for this performance all four band members wear horrible yellow and purple outfits)*

02-04-73 – 'Top Pop' (Holland): On A Westbound Train

23-04-73 – **'Spotlight' (Austria): Medley: Chirpy Chirpy Cheep Cheep – Soley Soley – Samson and Delilah – Sacramento (A Wonderful Town) / Yellow Boomerang** *(The return of the yellow and purple outfits, while performing on a set that includes a carousel and a toy car)*

29-06-73 – 'Lift Off With Ayshea' (UK): Union Silver *(A very slow ballad, this wasn't a hit)*

Mid 1973 – 'Top Pop' (Holland): Union Silver

22-09-73 – **'Disco' (Germany): Kailakee Kailako** *(Performing while wearing country-ish outfits, 'Kailakee Kailako' is one of their weaker songs. It reached No. 29 in Germany, No. 19 in Holland and No. 5 in Switzerland)*

01-10-73 – 'Top Pop' (Holland): Samba D'Amour

20-12-73 – **'Starparade' (Germany): Samba D'Amour** *(With Sally now sporting a new silvery, wavy, hairstyle while wearing a long black dress, this is another mediocre song. 'Samba D'Amour was a No. 35 hit in Germany. The follow-up, 'Honey No', was a German No. 31 hit and got to No. 5 in Switzerland)*

31-12-73 – **'Spotlight' (Austria): Medley: Chirpy Chirpy Cheep Cheep – Soley Soley – Samson and Delilah – Sacramento (A Wonderful Town)** *(This is a repeat of the 23-04-73 performance)*

08-06-74 – **'Disco' (Germany): Rockin' Soul** *(Rightly feeling it was time for a change, in early 1974 Middle Of The Road recruited a 5th member in ex-The Bay City Rollers guitarist Neil Henderson, who also contributed songs, including this one. With all the band wearing leopard-skin outfits, including Sally in a cave-girl off-the-shoulder mini-dress, 'Rockin' Soul' is a song that would've been ideal for Suzi Quatro. Unfortunately, Sally is no Suzi, and she sounds completely out of her depth here. 'Rockin' Soul' got to No. 35 in Germany)*

18-10-74 – 'Mounties' (Holland): Bonjour Ca Va

21-12-74 – **'Disco' (Germany): Bonjour Ca Va** *(Featuring Sally in white tasselled shorts and crop-top and the rest of the band in leathers, 'Bonjour Ca Va' is a good compromise between the bubblegum of old and the glam of new. It wasn't a hit)*

09-06-75 – **'Shang-A-Lang' (UK): Hitchin' A Ride In The Moonlight** *(No doubt cashing in on their connections with The Bay City Rollers by guesting on their show, Sally looks surprisingly mumsy here in a casual pale blue jacket, cream trousers and polo-neck jumper. The forgettable song was not a hit)*

06-03-76 – **'Musikladen' (Germany): Everybody Loves A Winner** *(This time Sally goes all

Maddy Prior, dressing in a long hippy dress with headband while doing a rather embarrassing dance. Another so-so song, 'Everybody Loves A Winner' was a No. 43 hit in Germany)

27-03-76 – **'Disco' (Germany): Everybody Loves A Winner** *(Still a little hippy-ish, Sally is now wearing a long white and yellow pleated skirt with a frilly crop-top. Not that it improves the song)*

Sally Carr left the band in 1977, with drummer Ken Andrew quitting a year later, though the original 4-piece line-up reunited to record and promote a hits medley single in the early '80s. Today there are two groups: 'Middle Of The Road', featuring Ian McCredie plus various newer members, and the more authentic 'Middle Of The Road featuring Sally Carr', which also includes Ken Andrew. Eric McCredie died in 2007.

THE FACES

12-03-70 – 'Top Of The Pops' (UK): Flying *(The Faces' 1ˢᵗ single and 1ˢᵗ 'Top Of The Pops' appearance, the bluesy 'Flying' was not a hit)*

00-06-70 – **'London Rock' (UK): The Moaner / Nobody Knows** *('The Moaner' is a rehearsal by the two Ronnies – Lane and Wood – in Ronnie Lane's London flat, while 'Nobody Knows' is an outdoors acoustic performance featuring Rod Stewart and, unusually playing the guitar, Ian McLagan)*

03-12-70 – 'Top Of The Pops' (UK): Had Me A Real Good Time *(Another flop single and another lost 'Top Of The Pops' performance)*

15-01-71 – **'Swing In – The Faces Live at The Marquee' (Germany): Devotion / (You're My Girl) I Don't Want To Discuss It / Flying / Medley: Too Much Woman (For A Hen-Pecked Man) – Street Fighting Man / Maybe I'm Amazed / Gasoline Alley** *(Taped in London's Marquee on 07-12-70 for German TV broadcast, this is early proof of The Faces' live prowess)*

13-02-71 – **'Pop 2' (France): Maybe I'm Amazed** (part only) **/ Flying / Medley: Around The Plynth – Gasoline Alley / Love In Vain / It's All Over Now** *(This was taped at La Taverne De L'Olympia, Paris, on 26-01-71)*

22-04-71 – **'Disco 2' (UK): Tell Everyone / Sweet Lady Mary / Bad 'n' Ruin** *(A forerunner of 'The Old Grey Whistles Test', relatively little footage from 'Disco 2' survives, but fortunately this is amongst the few exceptions)*

29-04-71 – **'Top Of The Pops' (UK): Richmond / Bad 'n' Ruin** *(Taped on 28-04-71, this is more promotion for the band's 'Long Player' album)*

06-01-72 – **'Top Of The Pops' (UK): Stay With Me** *(This is an excerpt from 'Sounds For Saturday', taped on 26-1-71, and broadcast in full on 01-04-72)*

20-01-72 – **'Top Of The Pops' (UK): Stay With Me** *(This is a repeat of the 'Sounds For Saturday' excerpt)*

15-02-72 – **'The Old Grey Whistle Test' (UK): Stay With Me** *(This was taped live at The

Rainbow Theatre, London, on 10th, 11th or 12th of February 1972. The Faces' first hit single, 'Stay With Me' reached No. 6 in the UK and No. 17 in the US)

01-04-72 – **'Sounds For Saturday' (UK): Three Button Hand Me Down / Maybe I'm Amazed / Medley: Too Much Woman (For A Hen-Pecked Man) – Street Fighting Man / Miss Judy's Farm / Love In Vain / Stay With Me / (I Know) I'm Losing You** *(Capturing the band at their very peak – before they effectively became Rod Stewart's backing band – this stunning performance was taped at The Paris Theatre, London, on 26-10-71. '(I Know) I'm Losing You' was a US-only single, where it reached No. 24)*

06-05-72 – **The Roundhouse, London (UK): It's All Over Now / That's All You Need / Maggie May / Stay With Me / (I Know) I'm Losing You / I Feel So Good** *(Broadcast/released in various different edits, the above list features all known surviving songs from this performance)*

23-09-72 – 'Popzien' (Holland): Stay With Me / Bring It All Back Home / (I Know) I'm Losing You / Maggie May *(All songs were on film, with the original location and recording date unknown)*

08-02-73 – 'Top Of The Pops' (UK): Cindy Incidentally *(This was taped on 07-02-73)*

22-02-73 – 'Top Of The Pops' (UK): Cindy Incidentally *(This is a repeat of the 08-02-73 performance)*

24-02-73 – **'Russell Harty Plus' (UK): Cindy Incidentally** *(At last having a hit to rival Rod's solo singles, 'Cindy Incidentally' got to No. 2 in the UK charts, though it only reached No. 48 in the US, where it was the group's final hit)*

08-03-73 – 'Top Of The Pops' (UK): Cindy Incidentally *(This is a repeat of the 08-02-73 performance)*

10-03-73 – **'Pop Gala' (Holland): Memphis / True Blue / Cindy Incidentally / One Last Sweet Cheerio** *(While never really a glam rock band, by now both Rod Stewart and Ronnie Wood were often wearing glitter, bright colours and make-up. 'Pop Gala' was broadcast in several different edits on Dutch TV in 1973, though the above songs are all that definitely still survive)*

16-03-73 – 'Popzien' (Holland): Angel / You Wear It Well / Maggie May / Twisting The

Night Away *(All songs were taped at 'Pop Gala' on 10-03-73. 'You Wear It Well' and 'Maggie May' were repeated on 03-08-73)*

11-05-73 – 'Popzien' (Holland): Cindy Incidentally *(Taped at 'Pop Gala', 10-03-73)*

06-06-73 – **'Ooh La La' (UK): Cindy Incidentally / Angel / True Blue / I'd Rather Go Blind / Jealous Guy / You Wear It Well / Maggie May / Borstal Boys / Twistin' The Night Away / Memphis / We'll Meet Again** *(Increasingly disillusioned with the band and bored of performing Rod Stewart's solo material, Ronnie Wood decided to quit in the summer of '73, with this performance being his final appearance with The Faces. 'Maggie May' and 'Borstal Boys' were broadcast on 'Don Kirshner's Rock Concert' on 04-02-74)*

20-12-73 – **'Top Of The Pops' (UK): Pool Hall Richard** *(Taped on 18-12-73, this was The Faces first TV appearance with new bassist Tetsu Yamauchi. The Chuck Berry/The Rolling Stones-influenced 'Pool Hall Richard' was a No. 8 UK hit)*

03-01-74 – **'Top Of The Pops' (UK): Pool Hall Richard** *(This is a repeat of the 20-12-73 performance)*

00-02-74 – **'G.T.K.' (Australia): Pool Hall Richard / It's All Over Now / Twistin' The Night Away** *(These songs were taped at The Festival Hall, Melbourne, on 03-02-74)*

12-12-74 – **'Top Of The Pops' (UK): You Can Make Me Dance, Sing Or Anything** *(This was taped at The Odeon, Lewisham, on 15-11-74. 'You Can Make Me Dance, Sing Or Anything' got to No. 12 in the UK charts)*

23-12-74 – **'The Faces' Finale', Kilburn State Gaumont Theatre, London (UK): It's All Over Now / Take A Look At The Guy / Bring It On Home To Me / You Send Me / Sweet Little Rock 'N' Roller** [with Keith Richards] / **I'd Rather Go Blind** [with Keith Richards] / **Angel / I Can Feel The Fire / You Can Make Me Dance, Sing Or Anything / Twistin' The Night Away** [with Keith Richards] / **You Wear It Well / Maggie May / We'll Meet Again** *(With Ronnie Lane gone, Rod Stewart increasingly successful solo and Ronnie Wood becoming closer to Mick 'n' Keith, it was inevitable that they would split. This performance was broadcast, in edited form, on 'The Midnight Special' on 25-04-75, and broadcast uncut in the UK on 28-11-75)*

03-01-75 – 'Szene '75' (Germany): We'll Meet Again (filmed backstage) / Too Bad *(These songs were taped in Munich on 04-10-74)*

Following The Faces' 1975 split, Rod Stewart had continued success as a solo artist, Ronnie Wood joined The Rolling Stones and Kenney Jones joined The Who, while Ian McLagan and Ronnie Lane pursued more low key careers, the latter cruelly cut short by multiple sclerosis. There were one-off reunions in 1986 and 1993 (both featuring Bill Wyman on bass), and Ronnie Wood, Ian and Kenney (along with Mick Hucknall and Glen Matlock) reunited for concerts in 2010 – 2011. Ronnie Lane died in 1997 and Ian McLagan died in 2014.

ROD STEWART

02-11-65 – **'An Easter With Rod' (UK): Tiger In Your Tank / Up Above My Head** *(Taped in The Marquee, London, on 28-03-65, these songs are by John Baldry's band 'The Hoochie Coochie Men', with a youthful Rod Stewart as a featured vocalist. The documentary 'An Easter With Rod' is sometimes wrongly referred to as 'Rod The Mod')*

09-12-65 – **'Shindig! Goes To London (Part 2)' (USA): Lord Remember Me / I Feel Alright** *(This was taped at 'The 5th National Jazz and Blues Festival', Richmond, UK, on 08-08-65, with Stevie Winwood and Eric Burdon guesting on the 2nd song. Although generally credited as 'The Steampacket' for this performance, an advertisement for the show billed the band as 'The Steam Packet with The Brian Auger Trinity, Rod Stewart, Julie Driscoll and Long John Baldry'. Whatever they were called, Long John Baldry, Rod Stewart and Julie Driscoll made a formidable vocal trio. Surprisingly, this footage survives in colour, even though it was broadcast on 'Shindig!' in black and white)* – **STEAMPACKET**

27-04-67 – 'Top Of The Pops' (UK): Hi-Ho Silver Lining *(Despite appearing on 'Top Of The Pops' 4 times with The Jeff Beck Group, Rod Stewart wasn't the featured lead vocalist on any of them. 'Hi-Ho Silver Lining', featuring a rare Jeff Beck lead vocal, was a No. 14 UK hit in 1968, also getting to No. 17 when reissued in 1972)* – **THE JEFF BECK GROUP**

18-05-67 – 'Top Of The Pops' (UK): Hi-Ho Silver Lining – **THE JEFF BECK GROUP**

00-04-69 – **'Popside' (Sweden): Plynth (Water Down The Drain)** *(Considering their success, footage of the original The Jeff Beck Group is very thin on the ground, which makes this clip particularly special. Taped in a recording studio with producer Mickie Most, 'Plynth (Water Down The Drain)' was one of the highlights of The Jeff Beck Group's 2nd album 'Beck-Ola'. Shortly after this, the group imploded, with Rod and Ronnie joining ex-The Small Faces Ronnie Lane, Ian McLagan and Kenney Jones to form The Faces)* – **THE JEFF BECK GROUP**

10-07-69 – 'Top Of The Pops' (UK): Goo Goo Barabajagal (Love Is Hot) *(This time backing Donovan, 'Goo Goo Barabajagal (Love Is Hot)' got to No. 12 in the UK charts)* –

DONOVAN with THE JEFF BECK GROUP

31-07-69 – 'Top Of The Pops' (UK): Goo Goo Barabajagal (Love Is Hot) – ***DONOVAN with THE JEFF BECK GROUP*** *(This is a repeat of the 10-07-69 performance)*

Mid 1971 – **'Sympathy For The Devil' (Germany): Gasoline Alley / Lady Day** *(Both songs are acapella performances, taped outdoors in Berlin. This broadcast also features footage of The Faces in Hamburg, taped in April 1971)*

19-08-71 – 'Top Of The Pops' (UK): Maggie May *(This was taped on 18-08-71. As with all Rod Stewart 'Top Of The Pops' appearances during 1971 – 1972, he is backed by **THE FACES**)*

16-09-71 – 'Top Of The Pops' (UK): Maggie May *(This is a repeat of the 19-08-71 performance)*

30-09-71 – **'Top Of The Pops' (UK): Maggie May** *(Taped on 29-09-71, this joyful performance, featuring DJ John Peel self-consciously miming on mandolin and the band kicking around a football, remains one of the all-time great 'Top Of The Pops' appearances. 'Maggie May' topped the charts in the UK, US, Canada and Australia, while the flip-side, 'Reason To Believe' was a No. 24 Canadian hit)*

07-10-71 – 'Top Of The Pops' (UK): Maggie May *(This is a repeat of an earlier performance)*

14-10-71 – 'Top Of The Pops' (UK): Maggie May *(This is a repeat of an earlier performance)*

21-10-71 – 'Top Of The Pops' (UK): Maggie May *(This was taped on 20-10-71)*

28-10-71 – 'Top Of The Pops' (UK): Maggie May *(This is a repeat of an earlier performance)*

04-11-71 – 'Top Of The Pops' (UK): Maggie May *(This is a repeat of an earlier performance)*

27-12-71 – **'Top Of The Pops' (UK): Maggie May** *(This is a repeat of the 30-09-71 performance)*

17-08-72 – **'Top Of The Pops' (UK): You Wear It Well** *(Taped on 16-08-72, this is another* memorable performance by The Faces in all but name, and check out Rod's striped jacket and yellow trousers. 'You Wear It Well' was Rod Stewart's 2nd UK No. 1, also getting to No. 2 in Ireland, No. 7 in Canada, and No. 13 in both Australia and the US)

31-08-72 – **'Top Of The Pops' (UK): You Wear It Well** *(This is a repeat of the 17-08-72 performance)*

16-11-72 – **'Top Of The Pops' (UK): Angel** *(Taped on 15-11-72, this is a superior version of a Jimi Hendrix original, performed here with The Faces, minus Ronnie Lane who 'appears' as a cardboard cut-out, as he no longer wished to plug Rod's solo releases on 'Top Of The Pops'. A double A-side, 'Angel' b/w 'What's Made Milwaukee Famous (Has Made A Loser Out Of Me)' got to No. 4 in the UK, No. 11 in Germany and No. 71 in Australia)*

30-11-72 – **'Top Of The Pops' (UK): Angel** *(This is a repeat of the 16-11-72 performance)*

25-12-72 – **'Top Of The Pops' (UK): You Wear It Well** *(This is a repeat of the 17-08-72 performance)*

00-08-73 – **Promo Video (UK): Oh No Not My Baby** *(Which '70s act made the best videos? David Bowie? The Rolling Stones? Queen? No, it's Rod Stewart! While the others were making straight in-the-studio or on-stage performance videos, Rod more often than not had superb location videos to accompany his singles, with this one featuring him dressed in sparkling green trousers and tartan, while miming in the grounds of a stately home. 'Oh No Not My Baby' was a No. 6 UK hit, also reaching No. 8 in Ireland, No. 57 in Australia and No. 59 in the US)*

09-09-73 – **'Russell Harty Plus' (UK): Oh No Not My Baby** *(This is a fine live-vocal performance of Rod's current single, despite the fact that he was a little worse for wear through booze)*

13-09-73 – 'Top Of The Pops' (UK): Oh No Not My Baby *(Rod's first truly solo 'Top Of The Pops' appearance, this footage is lost)*

19-01-74 – **'Russell Harty Plus Pop' (UK): Oh No Not My Baby** *(This is a repeat of the 09-09-73 performance)*

05-05-74 – **Watford Stadium (UK): Country Comfort** [with Elton John] *(Performing one* of Elton's songs that Rod had also recorded, this footage is unfortunately greatly marred by Rod's voice being almost inaudible)

14-07-74 – **Kilburn Gaumont State Theatre, London (UK): If You Gotta Make A Fool Of Somebody / Mystifies Me / Take A Look At The Guy** [All song are with Ron Wood and Keith Richards] *(Although the Faces hadn't quite split up, their days were numbered, with Ronnie Wood also starting to pursue a career outside of the group. These three songs all feature Rod guesting on them, but for Ronnie's full set-list see The Rolling Stones section)*

00-09-74 – **Promo Video (UK): Farewell** *(Another fine song, and a fine video filmed on the banks of Loch Ness, 'Farewell' peaked at No. 7 in the UK, No. 11 in Ireland and No. 47 in Australia)*

18-10-74 – **'Russell Harty Plus' (UK): Medley: Bring It On Home To Me – You Send Me**

01-03-75 – **'Supersonic' (UK): Mine For Me / Sweet Little Rock 'N' Roller** *(Performing on the 'Supersonic' pilot show, 'Mine For Me' is a song written by Paul McCartney and exclusively recorded by Rod for his 'Smiler' album. It was released as a US single, where it became a minor hit)*

00-08-75 – **Promo Video #1 (UK): Sailing** *(There was not 1, not 2, but 3 completely different promo videos for 'Sailing'. This 1st version was shot by a 'Nationwide' camera crew on the dockside in Dublin. One of Rod's best-loved singles outside the USA, 'Sailing' got to No. 1 in the UK, Ireland and Holland, No. 2 in Australia, No. 4 in Germany and No. 58 in the US)*

00-08-75 – **Promo Video #2 (UK): Sailing** *(A 2nd video, shot on a US boat denoted by a US flag on it, probably outside New York)*

00-08-75 – **Promo Video #3 (UK): Sailing** *(This 3rd video was shot on a yacht called 'Synergy', possibly off the coast of the UK)*

00-11-75 – Promo Video? (UK): This Old Heart Of Mine *(Unseen since and now lost, an unknown video for this song was broadcast on 'Top Of The Pops' on 04-12-75. 'This Old Heart Of Mine' was a No. 4 UK hit, No. 3 in Ireland, No. 45 in Australia and No. 83 in the UK)*

08-11-75 – **'Disco' (Germany): Sailing** *(Rod's first of several appearances on this German TV show)*

00-05-76 – **Promo Video (UK): Tonight's The Night** *(A rather suggestive video, this features Rod seducing his then-girlfriend Britt Ekland in a cosy looking living room complete with roaring fire, and then taking her upstairs to the bedroom. 'Tonight's The Night' got to No. 5 in the UK, No. 1 in the US and Canada, No. 2 in Ireland, No. 3 in Australia, No. 5 in Holland and No. 26 in Germany)*

22-05-76 – **'Numero Un' (France): Sailing**

29-05-76 – **'Musikladen' (Germany): Tonight's The Night** *(As with Rod's appearance on 'Disco' a few months later, this includes Britt Ekland miming to her part on the record)*

19-06-76 – **'Top Pop' (Holland): Tonight's The Night** *(Specially made for this Dutch TV show and featuring Rod miming on a set with a pair of giant headphones, this is probably the most visually interesting of the various 'Tonight's The Night' TV performances, despite the lack of Britt Ekland)*

07-08-76 – **'The Sounds Of Scotland' (UK): Tonight's The Night / The Wild Side of Life / Sailing** *(A rarely seen live performance in this BBC Scotland TV series)*

00-08-76 – Promo Video? (UK): The Killing Of Georgie *(Another unknown video that is now lost, this was broadcast on 'Top Of The Pops' on 02-09-76)*

11-09-76 – **'Disco' (Germany): Tonight's The Night**

13-09-76 – **'Supersonic' (UK): The Killing Of Georgie / Pretty Flamingo** *(Performed here along with his revival of Manfred Mann's 'Pretty Flamingo', 'The Killing Of Georgie (Part 1 and II)' was a No. 2 UK hit, but didn't do so well elsewhere, getting to No. 30 in the US, No. 33 in Canada, No. 36 in Germany and No. 38 in Australia)*

23-09-76 – **'Top Of The Pops' (UK): Sailing** *(Often mistaken for a performance in the 'Top Of The Pops' studio, this is, in fact, an excerpt from 'The Sounds Of Scotland', broadcast earlier in the year on 07-08-76)*

26-09-76 – **'The Lively Arts: Rod The Mod Has Come Of Age' (UK): Sweet Little Rock 'N' Roller** *(A full-length rehearsal of this Chuck Berry classic is one of the many highlights of this lengthy documentary. It was repeated, in revised form, on 23-07-78)*

24-10-76 – **'A Night On The Town' (UK): Pretty Flamingo / The Killing Of Georgie / This Old Heart Of Mine / The Wild Side Of Life / The First Cut Is The Deepest / Tonight's The Night / Sailing** (Also featuring special guests Long John Baldry and Thin Lizzy, this excellent TV special helped promote the album of the same name. 'The Killing Of Geordie' and 'The First Cut Is The Deepest' were later broadcast on various 'Top Of The Pops' episodes)

13-11-76 – 'Multi-Coloured Swap Shop' (UK)

24-12-76 – **'The Old Grey Whistle Test', The Olympia, London (UK): Tonight's The Night / The Wild Side Of Life / This Old Heart Of Mine / Sweet Little Rock 'N' Roller / I Don't Want To Talk About It / The Killing Of Georgie / Maggie May / Get Back / (I Know) I'm Losing You / Sailing** (With a hot new band that includes Chuck Berry play-a-like Billy Peek on guitar, this was broadcast live, and repeated on 28-12-77 and 24-12-78. Released as a single, 'Get Back' peaked at No. 11 in the UK, No. 29 in Australia and No. 39 in Germany)

26-12-76 – **'Top Of The Pops' (UK): The Killing Of Georgie** (This is from the 'A Night On The Town' TV special)

27-12-76 – 'Swap Of The Pops' (UK) (This is a repeat of the 'Multi-Coloured Swap Shop' performance from 13-11-76)

26-01-77 – **'Samedi Est À Vous' (France): Tonight's The Night**

14-02-77 – **'Rod Stewart In Australia', Melbourne (Australia): Three Times Loser / Big Bayou / Tonight's The Night / The Wild Side Of Life / This Old Heart Of Mine / Sweet Little Rock 'N' Roller / I Don't Want To Talk About It / The Killing Of Georgie / Maggie May / You Keep Me Hangin' On / Get Back / (I Know) I'm Losing You / Sailing / Stay With Me / Twistin' The Night Away** (With a set-list that includes a couple of The Faces' classics, this is Rod Stewart at his peak)

00-04-77 – **Promo Video (UK): The First Cut Is The Deepest** (Looking at his best in white trousers and striped black and white jacket, this video sees Rod miming to the song while walking around a vast country garden. Released as a double A-side, 'I Don't Want To Talk About It' b/w 'The First Cut Is The Deepest' got to No. 1 in the UK, Germany and Holland, No. 11 in Canada, No. 19 in Australia and No. 21 in the US)

05-05-77 – **'Top Of The Pops' (UK): The First Cut Is The Deepest** *(This, and all subsequent repeats, are taken from the 'A Night On The Town' TV special)*

19-05-77 – **'Top Of The Pops' (UK): The First Cut Is The Deepest** *(This is a repeat of the 05-05-77 performance)*

26-05-77 – **'Top Of The Pops' (UK): The First Cut Is The Deepest** *(This is a repeat of the 05-05-77 performance)*

06-07-77 – **'Top Of The Pops' (UK): The First Cut Is The Deepest** *(This is a repeat of the 05-05-77 performance)*

09-06-77 – **'Top Of The Pops' (UK): The First Cut Is The Deepest** *(This is a repeat of the 05-05-77 performance)*

00-10-77 – **Promo Video (UK): You're In My Heart** *(With another memorable video featuring Rod in an empty restaurant, 'You're In My Heart' reached No. 3 in the UK, No. 1 in Australia and Canada, No. 2 in Ireland, No. 4 in the US and No. 8 in Holland)*

26-12-77 – **'Top Of The Pops' (UK): The First Cut Is The Deepest** *(This is a repeat of the 05-05-77 performance)*

00-01-78 – **Promo Video (UK): Hot Legs** *(For this video, 'Hot Legs' features Rod and the band outdoors in small-town USA, along with close-ups of some particularly hot-looking, though anonymous, legs. Another double A-side, 'Hot Legs' b/w 'I Was Only Joking' was a UK No. 5, No. 4 in Germany and Ireland, No. 8 in Holland, No. 22 in the US, No. 35 in Canada and No. 42 in Australia. The follow-up single in some countries was the football song 'Ole Ola (Mulher Brasileira)', which got to No. 4 in the UK and No. 44 in Australia)*

00-01-78 – **Promo Video (UK): I Was Only Joking** *(For once just a simple in-the-studio mimed performance, albeit with some nice double-image effects)*

23-01-78 – **'Disco' (Germany): Hot Legs**

00-11-78 – **Promo Video (UK): Da Ya Think I'm Sexy** *(With an on-stage video intercut with bar and bedroom scenes featuring Rod and Britt, 'Da Ya Think I'm Sexy' is a song that deeply divides fans. It was No. 1 in the UK, Ireland, Australia, the US and Canada, as well as No. 6 in Holland and No. 9 in Germany)*

06-12-78 – **The King's Hall, Manchester (UK): Hot Legs / Born Loose / Tonight's The**

Night / The Wild Side Of Life / Get Back / You're In My Heart / I Don't Want To Talk About It / Blondes Have More Fun / Da Ya Think I'm Sexy? / (If Loving You Is Wrong) I Don't Wana Be Right / The Killing Of Georgie / Maggie May / Sweet Little Rock 'N' Roller / Sailing / Twistin' The Night Away *(The hair is blonder and the trousers are tighter, but this is another fine concert. It was broadcast in two parts, on 02-06-79 and 09-06-79)*

30-12-78 – **'Rock-Pop' (Germany): Blondes (Have More Fun)**

00-01-79 – **Promo Video (UK): Ain't Love A Bitch** *(An on-stage mimed video, again with the double-image effects used in the 'I Was Only Joking' video. 'Ain't Love A Bitch' got to No. 11 in the UK, No. 4 in Germany, No. 5 in Ireland, No. 22 in the US, No. 29 in Holland and No. 44 in Australia)*

01-01-79 – **'The Didn't Quite Make It In Time For Christmas Video Show' (UK): Da Ya Think I'm Sexy / Maggie May**

13-01-79 – **'David Frost Presents The Gift Of Song' (UK): Da Ya Think I'm Sexy**

00-04-79 – **Promo Video (UK): Blondes (Have More Fun)** *(A simple but fun on-stage video, 'Blondes (Have More Fun)' was not released as a single in most countries, though did get to No. 63 in the UK and No. 23 in Ireland)*

01-06-79 – **The Forum, Los Angeles (USA): Hot Legs / Tonight's The Night / Da Ya Think I'm Sexy / I Just Wanna Make Love To You / Blondes Have More Fun / Maggie May / (If Loving You Is Wrong) I Don't Want To Be Right / The Wild Side Of Life / You're In My Heart / Sweet Little Rock 'N' Roller / Stay With Me / Twistin' The Night Away** *(Rod rocks L.A., with an unexpected highlight being a lengthy blues work-out on 'I Just Wanna Make Love To You')*

Rod Stewart went on to have many more huge UK hits, including 'Tonight I'm Yours (Don't Hurt Me)' (No. 8, 1981), 'Baby Jane' (No. 1, 1983), 'What Am I Gonna Do (I'm So In Love With You)' (No. 3, 1983), 'Every Beat Of My Heart' (No. 2, 1986), 'Downtown Train' (No. 10, 1989), 'It Takes Two' (with Tina Turner) (No. 5, 1990), 'Tom Traubert's

Blues (Waltzing Matilda)' (No. 6, 1992), 'Have I Told You Lately' (No. 5, 1993) and 'All For Love' (with Bryan Adams and Sting) (No. 2, 1993)

CHICORY TIP

05-08-71 – 'Top Of The Pops' (UK): Excuse Me Baby

07-09-71 – 'Lift Off' (UK): Excuse Me Baby

15-12-71 – 'Lift Off' (UK): I Love Onions

27-01-72 – **'Top Of The Pops' (UK): Son Of My Father** (Co-written by renowned Italian producer Giorgio Moroder, 'Son Of My Father' was Chicory Tip's 1st and only UK No. 1. Also broadcast on German TV's 'Disco' on 08-04-72, this is the most likely original broadcast date for this particular 'Top Of The Pops' performance. It was repeated in the UK on 28-12-72)

03-02-72 – 'Top Of The Pops' (UK): Son Of My Father

17-02-72 – 'Top Of The Pops' (UK): Son Of My Father *(This is a repeat of an earlier performance)*

24-02-72 – 'Top Of The Pops' (UK): Son Of My Father *(This is a repeat of an earlier performance)*

02-03-72 – 'Top Of The Pops' (UK): Son Of My Father *(This is a repeat of an earlier performance)*

20-03-72 – **'Top Pop' (Holland): Son Of My Father** *(Sometimes mistaken as an official Promo Video, this was taped outdoors at a UK seaside resort, especially for this Dutch TV show)*

10-05-72 – 'Lift Off With Ayshea' (UK): What's Your Name

11-05-72 – 'Top Of The Pops' (UK): What's Your Name

25-05-72 – 'Top Of The Pops' (UK): What's Your Name *(This is a repeat of the 11-05-72 performance)*

27-05-72 – **'Disco' (Germany): What's Your Name** *(The group never hit the heights of 'Son Of My Father' again, but 'What's Your Name' came closest, getting to No. 13 in the UK charts. Here the song is promoted on German TV)*

07-06-72 – 'Eddy Ready Go' (Holland): What's Your Name

08-06-72 – 'Top Of The Pops' (UK): What's Your Name *(This is a repeat of the 11-05-72 performance)*

28-09-72 – 'Top Of The Pops' (UK): The Future Is Past

28-12-72 – **'Top Of The Pops' (UK): Son Of My Father** *(This is a repeat of the 03-02-72 performance)*

27-04-73 – 'Top Of The Pops' (UK): Good Grief Christina *('Good Grief Christina' got to No. 17 in the UK, as well as No. 4 in Norway)*

07-05-73 – 'Top Pop' (Holland): Good Grief Christina

18-05-73 – 'Top Of The Pops' (UK): Good Grief Christina *(This is a repeat of the 27-04-73 performance)*

16-05-75 – 'Top Pop' (Holland): Survivor *(Chicory Tip's final single, 'Survivor' was not a hit)*

Led by original guitarist Rick Foster, a version of Chicory Tip still tours today, albeit without hit-era vocalist Peter Hewson.

GARY GLITTER

25-11-61 – 'Thank Your Lucky Stars' (UK): Tower Of Strength *(Before Gary Glitter, there was Paul Raven, Paul Monday and Rubber Bucket! Paul's/Gary's 3rd single, 'Tower Of Strength' lost out in the UK chart stakes to Frankie Vaughan, who had a No. 1 hit with the song. Paul Raven's single didn't chart, and neither did any other pre-Gary Glitter single. This performance on 'Thank Your Lucky Stars' no longer exists)* – **PAUL RAVEN**

22-06-72 – 'Top Of The Pops' (UK): Rock and Roll (Part 2) *(The first single as Gary Glitter, the semi-instrumental 'Rock and Roll (Part 2)' remains his most famous hit worldwide. It got to No. 2 in the UK, No. 1 in Australia, No. 4 in Ireland, Germany and Canada, and No. 7 in the US and Holland. Unfortunately, Gary Glitter's 'Top Of The Pops' debut and the two subsequent appearances in July are all lost)*

06-07-72 – 'Top Of The Pops' (UK): Rock and Roll (Part 2)

20-07-72 – 'Top Of The Pops' (UK): Rock and Roll (Part 2)

00-09-72 – **Promo Video (UK): I Didn't Know I Loved You (Till I Saw You Rock 'N' Roll)** *('I Didn't Know I Love You (Till I Saw You Rock 'N' Roll)' got to No. 4 in the UK, No. 5 in Ireland, No. 12 in Germany, No. 15 in Holland, No. 27 in Australia and No. 35 in the US. Although Gary Glitter would become increasingly popular elsewhere over the next couple of years, he wouldn't have another US hit. The earliest known surviving Gary Glitter footage, this simple studio promo video – which only survives in black and white – sees him in his trade-mark open-chest, shoulder-padded, silver outfit, backed by The Glitter Band)*

21-09-72 – **'Top Of The Pops' (UK): I Didn't Know I Loved You (Till I Saw You Rock 'N' Roll)** *(In colour and with plenty of 'Dr Who'-like special effects, one notable thing is how long The Glitter Band's hair is here)*

28-09-72 – **'Top Of The Pops' (UK): I Didn't Know I Loved You (Till I Saw You Rock 'N' Roll)** *(This is a repeat of the 21-09-72 performance)*

12-10-72 – **'Top Of The Pops' (UK): I Didn't Know I Loved You (Till I Saw You Rock 'N' Roll)** *(This is a repeat of the 21-09-72 performance)*

14-10-72 – **'Disco' (Germany): Rock and Roll (Part 2)** *(Making his German TV debut, this is the earliest surviving footage of Gary Glitter performing his 1st hit)*

23-10-72 – 'Top Pop' (Holland): I Didn't Know I Love You (Till I Saw You Rock 'N' Roll)

07-12-72 – **'Hits A Go Go' (Switzerland): I Didn't Know I Love You (Till I Saw You Rock 'N' Roll)**

28-12-72 – **'Top Of The Pops' (UK): Rock and Roll (Part 2)** *(A great live vocal for this reprise of his debut hit)*

25-01-73 – **'Top Of The Pops' (UK): Do You Wanna Touch Me (Oh Yeah)** *(Looking good in red glitter jacket with black trousers and shirt, this is another fine live vocal performance. 'Do You Wanna Touch Me (Oh Yeah)', got to No. 2 in the UK, No. 3 in Australia, No. 4 in Holland, No. 9 in Ireland and No. 16 in Germany)*

05-02-73 – 'Top Pop' (Holland): Do You Wanna Touch Me (Oh Yeah)

08-02-73 – **'Top Of The Pops' (UK): Do You Wanna Touch Me (Oh Yeah)** *(This is a repeat of the 25-01-73 performance)*

16-02-73 – 'Crackerjack' (UK): Do You Wanna Touch Me (Oh Yeah)

Early 1973 – **Unknown TV show (France): Do You Wanna Touch Me (Oh Yeah)** *(Singing live and alone without The Glitter Band, the sedate seated audience look more than bemused)*

16-03-73 – 'Popzien' (Holland): Honey Honey / Baby Please Don't Go / Do You Wanna Touch Me (Oh Yeah) / Rock and Roll *(All songs were taped at 'Pop Gala', Holland, on 10-03-73. In recent years footage of other acts on 'Pop Gala' – including Slade and The Faces – has surfaced, so it is probable that at least some of Gary Glitter's performance on the show also survives)*

00-03-73 – **Promo Video (UK): Hello! Hello! I'm Back Again** *(Seen here in another simple studio video, 'Hello! Hello! I'm Back Again' was a No. 2 hit in the UK and Ireland, as well as No. 6 in Australia, No. 10 in Germany and No. 19 in Holland)*

00-03-73 – **Promo Video (UK): Baby Please Don't Go** *(An interesting glam update of the old rhythm 'n' blues classic made famous by Them, this studio promo was taped on the same day as 'Hello! Hello! I'm Back Again')*

05-04-73 – 'Top Of The Pops' (UK): Hello! Hello! I'm Back Again

04-05-73 – 'Top Of The Pops' (UK): Hello! Hello! I'm Back Again *(This is a repeat of the 05-04-73 performance)*

14-05-73 – 'Top Pop' (Holland): Hello! Hello! I'm Back Again

13-07-73 – 'Top Of The Pops' (UK): I'm The Leader Of The Gang (I Am)

20-07-73 – 'Top Of The Pops' (UK): I'm The Leader Of The Gang (I Am) *(This is a repeat of the 13-07-73 performance)*

27-07-73 – 'Top Of The Pops' (UK): I'm The Leader Of The Gang (I Am) *(This is a repeat of the 13-07-73 performance)*

03-08-73 – 'Top Of The Pops' (UK): I'm The Leader Of The Gang (I Am) *(This is a repeat of the 13-07-73 performance)*

10-08-73 – 'Top Of The Pops' (UK): I'm The Leader Of The Gang (I Am) *(This is a repeat of the 13-07-73 performance)*

17-08-73 – 'Top Of The Pops' (UK): I'm The Leader Of The Gang (I Am) *(This is a repeat of the 13-07-73 performance)*

28-10-73 – **'Spotlight' (Austria): I'm The Leader Of The Gang (I Am) / Hello! Hello! I'm Back Again** *(A strong candidate for the most memorable hit of the Glam Rock era, 'I'm The Leader Of The Gang (I Am)' was No. 1 in the UK, No. 2 in Ireland and Australia, No. 6 in Germany and No. 12 in Holland. Here the song is performed for Austrian TV, along with his previous hit)*

14-11-73 – 'Lift Off With Ayshea' (UK): I Love You Love Me Love

15-11-73 – **'Top Of The Pops' (UK): I Love You Love Me Love** *('I Love You Love Me Love' was No. 1 in the UK, No. 2 in Ireland and Australia, No. 8 in Germany and No. 10 in Holland. For this first 'Top Of The Pops' performance of the song, Gary emerges from a huge silver heart while dressed in black glitter and silver boots)*

22-11-73 – **'Top Of The Pops' (UK): I Love You Love Me Love** *(This time Gary wears a blue outfit, similar to what his idol Elvis was wearing around this time, and starts the song reclining on a crescent moon prop)*

23-11-73 – **'Russell Harty Plus' (UK): I Love You Love Me Love**

29-11-73 – 'Top Of The Pops' (UK): I Love You Love Me Love

30-11-73 – **Sydney (Australia): Baby Please Don't Go** *(This live footage was broadcast on 'GTK', exact date(s) unknown)*

06-12-73 – 'Top Of The Pops' (UK): I Love You Love Me Love

17-12-73 – 'Top Pop' (Holland): I Love You Love Me Love

25-12-73 – **'Top Of The Pops' (UK): I'm The Leader Of The Gang (I Am)** *(Gary Glitter manages to hold his own on a strong show that also features Slade, The Sweet, Wizzard and Suzi Quatro)*

31-12-73 – **'Spotlight' (Austria): I'm The Leader Of The Gang (I Am)** *(This is a repeat of the 28-10-73 performance)*

02-02-74 – **'Disco' (Germany): I Love You Love Me Love**

Early 1974 – **'Remember Me This Way' movie (UK): I'm The Leader Of The Gang (I Am) / Sidewalk Sinner / Hello! Hello! I'm Back Again / I Love You Love Me Love / Remember Me This Way** *(All songs except the closing 'Remember Me This Way' were taped at The Rainbow Theatre, London, on 25-12-73. A documentary movie, this features live performances, interspersed with dramatic scenes, rehearsals, interviews, photo-shoots and press conferences)*

00-03-74 – **Promo Video (UK): Remember Me This Way** *(What was it about the spring of '74 that caused so many acts to go all melancholy? T. Rex released 'Teenage Dream', Slade had 'Everyday' and Elton John hit 'Candle In The Wind', yet none sounded quite so downbeat as Gary Glitter's 'Remember Me This Way', the title track of his new movie. His first hit with a ballad, this got to No. 3 in the UK, as well as No. 9 in Ireland, No. 31 in Australia and No. 50 in Germany)*

16-03-74 – **'Clunk Click' (UK): Remember Me This Way** *(Surviving in the BBC archives, the chances of them repeating a Gary Glitter performance on a Jimmy Savile hosted show are less than slim!)*

21-03-74 – **'Top Of The Pops' (UK): Remember Me This Way** *(Gary Glitter's only 'Top Of The Pops' performance of this song, this fortunately still survives)*

04-04-74 – **'Top Of The Pops' (UK): Remember Me This Way** *(This is a repeat of the 21-03-74 performance)*

04-04-74 – '45' (UK): Remember Me This Way

Early 1974 – **'Top Pop' (Holland): Remember Me This Way** *('Top Pop' always had great sets, and this one, featuring a staircase with huge wings on it, is no exception)*

00-06-74 – **Promo Video (UK): Always Yours** *(Another in-studio video, the upbeat 'Always Yours' was No. 1 in the UK and Ireland, No. 11 in Australia, No. 14 in Germany and No. 25 in Holland)*

06-06-74 – **'Top Of The Pops' (UK): Always Yours** *(The first of two surviving 'Top Of The Pops' performances for 'Always Yours', this one features Gary in a dark sleeveless outfit)*

13-06-74 – 'Top Of The Pops' (UK): Always Yours

14-11-74 – **'Top Of The Pops' (UK): Oh Yes! You're Beautiful** *('Oh Yes! You're Beautiful' reached No. 2 in the UK, No. 1 in Ireland, No. 10 in Australia and No. 28 in Germany. This performance sees Gary in white while The Glitter Band all wear blue)*

22-11-74 – **'Russell Harty Plus' (UK): Oh Yes! You're Beautiful**

28-11-74 – **'Top Of The Pops' (UK): Oh Yes! You're Beautiful** *(This is a repeat of the 14-11-74 performance)*

03-12-74 – 'Lift Off With Ayshea' (UK): Oh Yes! You're Beautiful

12-12-74 – 'Top Of The Pops' (UK): Oh Yes! You're Beautiful

27-12-74 – **'Top Of The Pops' (UK): Always Yours** *(A 2nd 'Top Of The Pops' performance for this song, with Gary in a silver glitter suit)*

01-03-75 – **'Supersonic' (UK): The Wanderer** *(Performing on a raised platform without The Glitter Band, this is a strong version of the Dion classic)*

24-04-75 – 'Top Of The Pops' (UK): Love Like You and Me

08-05-75 – 'Top Of The Pops' (UK): Love Like You and Me *(This is a repeat of the 24-04-75 performance)*

15-05-75 – 'Rock On With 45' (UK): Love Like You and Me

09-06-75 – **'Shang-A-Lang' (UK): Love Like You and Me** *(A so-so song that doesn't quite match up to his 1972-1974 singles, 'Love Like You and Me' peaked at No. 10 in the UK and No. 11 in Ireland, but just No. 100 in Australia, not doing much better elsewhere in the world)*

12-06-75 – **'Top Of The Pops' (UK): Doing Alright With The Boys** *(A far better song than the previous single, 'Doing Alright With The Boys' peaked at No. 6 in the UK and No. 3 in Ireland, though it was Gary Glitter's last top 10 hit of the '70s)*

26-06-75 – **'Top Of The Pops' (UK): Doing Alright With The Boys** *(This is a repeat of the 12-06-75 performance)*

23-10-75 – **'Supersonic' (UK): Papa Oom Mow Mow / Satan's Daughter** *(A dreadful version of a weak song, 'Papa Oom Mow Mow' peaked at a disastrous No. 38 in the UK, also getting to No. 20 in Ireland)*

06-11-75 – 'Top Of The Pops' (UK): Papa Oom Mow Mow

20-11-75 – **'Supersonic' (UK): Papa Oom Mow Mow**

22-11-75 – 'Saturday Scene: British Pop Awards' (UK): Basic Lady / Papa Oom Mow Mow

25-11-75 – **'Look Alive' (UK): Papa Oom Mow Mow**

13-03-76 – **'Supersonic' (UK): You Belong To Me** *(Although a tremendous single, 'You Belong To Me' reached just No. 40 in the UK charts, failing pretty much everywhere else)*

19-03-76 – 'Russell Harty Plus' (UK): You Belong To Me

10-04-76 – **'Goodbye Gary Glitter' (UK): Rock and Roll (Part 1) / I'm The Leader Of The Gang (I Am) / The Famous Instigator / Always Yours / Hello! Hello! I'm Back Again / Oh Yes! You're Beautiful / I Love You Love Me Love / You Belong To Me** *(Taped at The New London Victoria Theatre, London, on 14-03-76, this is Gary Glitter's 'retirement', though of course, he would resurface by the end of the year. Whatever, the full performance, including The Glitter Band's own warm-up set, is brilliant from beginning to end. See The Glitter Band section for details of their own songs from the show)*

25-12-76 – **'Supersonic' (UK): You Belong To Me / Medley: I'm The Leader Of The Gang (I Am) – Do You Wanna Touch – Hello! Hello! I'm Back Again / It Takes All Night Long (Part 1) / I Love You Love Me Love / You Belong To Me (Reprise) / We Wish You A**

Merry Christmas [Finale, with T. Rex, Guys and Dolls, Russell Harty and Joanna Lumley] *(Taped on 19-12-76 and now The Glitter Band-less, this was Gary's predicted "comeback" TV performance)*

00-01-77 – **Promo Video (UK): It Takes All Night Long (Part 1)** *('It Takes All Night Long (Part 1)' was Gary's biggest hit in 18 months, reaching No. 25 in the UK, No. 24 in Holland and No. 28 in Ireland)*

20-01-77 – **'Top Of The Pops' (UK): It Takes All Night Long (Part 1)** *(The first of two 'Top Of The Pops' performances for 'It Takes All Night Long (Part 1)', for this one Gary wears a silver suit with his collar up)*

03-02-77 – **'Top Of The Pops' (UK): It Takes All Night Long (Part 1)** *(Again wearing a silver suit, this time the collar is down)*

05-02-77 – **'Supersonic' (UK): It Takes All Night Long (Part 1) / You Belong To Me**

22-03-77 – **'Top Pop' (Holland): It Takes All Night Long (Part 1)**

28-05-77 – **'All You Need Is Love 16: Whatever Gets You Through The Night - Glitter Rock' (UK): Rock and Roll (Part 1)** *(Taped in late 1975, this performance is sometimes mistaken as a promo video)*

23-06-77 – **'Top Of The Pops' (UK): A Little Boogie Woogie In The Back Of My Mind** *(Later revived by Shakin' Stevens, 'A Little Boogie Woogie In The Back Of My Mind' was Gary Glitter's final hit of the decade at No. 31 in the UK charts. It's not a bad song, but the tuxedo-wearing band behind him look dreadful, a far cry from The Glitter Band)*

06-08-77 – **'Pop At The Mill' (UK): A Little Boogie Woogie In The Back Of My Mind / Rock and Roll (I Gave You The Best Years of My Life) / You Belong To Me** *(A live performance backed by an orchestra, 'Rock and Roll (I Gave You The Best Years Of My Life)' is a surprisingly good cover of the Kevin Johnson composed song)*

24-09-77 – 'Our Show' (UK) *(The most likely song performed here is 'Oh What A Fool I've Been', Gary Glitter's latest single at the time)*

19-12-79 – 'Live On Two' (UK)

Gary Glitter had numerous hits throughout the next decade and a half, with 1984's 'Another Rock and Roll Christmas' the most successful, at No.7 in the UK charts. He continued to tour, including acclaimed guest spots on The Who's 1996 'Quadrophenia' tour, as well as filming a cameo for The Spice Girls' 'Spice World' movie (which was subsequently edited out). Then, in 1997, he took his computer into a shop to be repaired... THE END!

THE ELECTRIC LIGHT ORCHESTRA

00-06-72 – **Promo Video (UK): 10538 Overture** (ELO's 1st single, this was a No. 9 UK hit. Incidentally, although often shortened to 'ELO', the group were almost always billed as 'The Electric Light Orchestra' on record during the '70s, and sometimes in the '80s too. The promo video is one of just three ELO performances to be filmed while Roy Wood was still part of the band)

04-06-72 – **'Festival Della Musica D'Avanguardia E Nuove Tendenze', Rome (Italy): 10538 Overture** (A lengthy but incomplete clip)

20-06-72 – **'Set Of 6' (UK): Queen Of The Hours / Jeff's Boogie #2 / Whisper In The Night / Great Balls Of Fire / 10538 Overture** (Taped on 09-05-72, this is a fascinating live performance capturing the group in their infancy, complete with Roy Wood playing guitar, bass, cello and saxophone, and singing 'Whisper In The Night')

09-07-72 – **'2Gs And The Pop People' (UK): 10538 Overture** (Also featured on this show is The Move, performing 'California Man', though oddly Roy Wood is not featured on '10538 Overture', suggesting that both band's appearances were taped at different times)

27-07-72 – 'Top Of The Pops' (UK): 10538 Overture

03-08-72 – 'Top Of The Pops' (UK): 10538 Overture (This is a repeat of the 27-07-72 performance)

17-08-72 – 'Top Of The Pops' (UK): 10538 Overture

00-01-73 – **Promo Video (UK): Roll Over Beethoven** (Seen here in a live promo video, 'Roll Over Beethoven' got to No. 6 in the UK, No. 19 in Holland, No. 22 in Germany, No. 42 in the US and No. 53 in Australia)

01-02-73 – **'Top Of The Pops' (UK): Roll Over Beethoven** (Although Roy Wood had left by now, Jeff continued to pursue a glam rock image for a while afterwards. Here he wears striped multi-coloured trousers and a pink boa, topped off with a silver wig)

15-02-73 – 'Top Of The Pops' (UK): Roll Over Beethoven

23-02-73 – 'Crackerjack' (UK): Roll Over Beethoven

29-06-73 – **'The Midnight Special' (USA): Roll Over Beethoven / Kuiama** *(Taped on 29-05-73, this is the first of many appearances on this influential live US TV show)*

21-07-73 – **'American Bandstand' (USA): Roll Over Beethoven**

17-08-73 – 'In Concert' (USA): Roll Over Beethoven

17-08-73 – **'The Midnight Special' (USA): Roll Over Beethoven** *(This is a repeat of the 29-06-73 performance)*

00-09-73 – **Promo Video (UK): Showdown** *('Showdown' was a No. 12 hit in the UK, also getting to No. 25 in Holland and No. 53 in the US. The video was filmed in London near the River Thames)*

11-10-73 – **'Top Of The Pops' (UK): Showdown**

29-10-73 – 'Top Pop' (Holland): Showdown

01-11-73 – **'Top Of The Pops' (UK): Showdown** *(This is a repeat of the 11-10-73 performance)*

07-11-73 – **'The Mike Douglas Show' (USA): Roll Over Beethoven / Showdown**

23-11-73 – **'The Midnight Special' (USA): Showdown / Ma-Ma-Ma Belle** *(This was taped on 20-11-73. 'Showdown' was repeated on 08-02-74 and 17-09-76. 'Ma-Ma-Ma Belle' got to No. 22 in the UK charts, but didn't do much elsewhere)*

08-02-74 – **'The Midnight Special' (USA): Bluebird Is Dead / Showdown** *('Showdown' is a repeat of the 23-11-73 performance. Both songs were also broadcast on 07-06-74)*

14-02-74 – **'Top Pop' (Holland): Can't Get It Out Of My Head** *(Sometimes mistaken for an official Promo Video, this was taped in a Birmingham rehearsal studio especially for this Dutch TV show. Although a flop in the UK, this ballad got to No. 9 in the US, No. 20 in Holland, No. 25 in Canada and No. 59 in Australia)*

14-03-74 – 'Top Of The Pops' (UK): Ma-Ma-Ma Belle

21-03-74 – 'Top Of The Pops' (UK): Ma-Ma-Ma Belle

15-04-74 – 'The Mike Douglas Show' (USA): Ma-Ma-Ma Belle / possibly other songs

20-04-74 – **'Don Kirshner's Rock Concert' (USA):** Medley: New World Rising - Ocean Breakup Reprise / Dreaming Of 4000 / Ma-Ma-Ma Belle

19-07-74 – **'In Concert' (USA):** In The Hall Of The Mountain King / Great Balls Of Fire *(This performance was taped at The Rainbow Theatre, London, for USA broadcast)*

11-10-74 – **'Szene '74' (Germany):** Daybreaker / Showdown / Day Tripper / Medley: Mik's Violin Solo – Orange Blossom Special / Ma-Ma-Ma Belle / In The Hall Of The Mountain King / Great Balls Of Fire / Roll Over Beethoven *(This live performance was taped on 04-10-74, and later rebroadcast as 'Rockpalast')*

Late 1974 – 'Top Pop' (Holland): Day Tripper

07-11-74 – **'The Mike Douglas Show' (USA):** Poor Boy (The Greenwood) / Can't Get It Out Of My Head

17-01-75 – **'The Midnight Special' (USA):** In The Hall Of The Mountain King / Great Balls Of Fire / Eldorado Overture / Can't Get It Out Of My Head / Medley: Mik's Violin Solo - Orange Blossom Special / Laredo Tornado / Medley: Hugh's Cello Solo - Flight Of The Bumblebee / Roll Over Beethoven *(Parts of this performance were repeated on 28-03-75 and 09-01-76)*

18-07-75 – 'Top Pop' (Holland): Poor Boy (The Greenwood)

04-12-75 – **'Supersonic' (UK):** Evil Woman *('Evil Woman' was a No. 10 hit in the UK, the US and Ireland, also getting to No. 6 in Canada, No. 21 in Holland and No. 23 in Australia)*

05-12-75 – **'Top Pop' (Holland):** Evil Woman *(Often mistaken for an official Promo Video, like 'Can't Get It Out Of My Head', this was taped especially for 'Top Pop', on a Birmingham concert stage)*

Late 1975 – **'Pop 75' (Germany):** Evil Woman

08-01-76 – **'Top Of The Pops' (UK):** Evil Woman

22-01-76 – **'Top Of The Pops' (UK):** Evil Woman *(This is a repeat of the 08-01-76 performance)*

31-01-76 – **'Top Of The Pops' (UK):** Evil Woman *(This is a repeat of the 08-01-76* performance)

12-02-76 – **'Top Of The Pops' (UK): Evil Woman** *(This is a repeat of the 08-01-76 performance)*

05-03-76 – **'The Midnight Special' (USA): Evil Woman / Nightrider / Strange Magic** *(Parts of this performance were repeated on 23-04-76 and 25-06-76)*

29-04-76 – **'Top Of The Pops' (UK): Nightrider** *(Despite promotion on this and other TV shows, 'Nightrider' didn't chart in any major territories)*

14-08-76 – **'Fusion' (UK): Poker / Nightrider / Showdown / Eldorado Overture / Can't Get It Out Of My Head / Poor Boy (The Greenwood) / Illusions In G Major / Strange Magic / Medley: 10538 Overture - Do Ya / Evil Woman / Ma-Ma-Ma Belle / Roll Over Beethoven** *(This was taped on 20-06-76. Released as a single, 'Strange Magic' got to No. 38 in the UK and No. 85 in Australia, though did much better stateside at No. 14 in the US and No. 20 in Canada)*

00-10-76 – **Promo Video (UK): Livin' Thing** *(Returning ELO to the UK top 10 for the first time since early '73, 'Livin' Thing' was a No. 4 hit in the UK and Holland, as well as No. 2 in Australia, No. 5 in Germany, No. 6 in Ireland, No. 8 in Canada and No. 13 in the US. From this record onwards, ELO's singles would nearly always hit the UK top 10 right up until the end of the decade)*

04-12-76 – 'Multi-Coloured Swap Shop' (UK): Livin' Thing

11-12-76 – 'The Basil Brush Show' (UK): Livin' Thing

Late 1976 – **Promo Video (UK): Tightrope**

31-01-77 – **'American Music Awards' (USA): Livin' Thing**

00-02-77 – **Promo Video (UK): Rockaria!** *(A non-US single, 'Rockaria!' got to No. 9 in the UK charts, No. 10 in Australia and No. 23 in Holland. Two different edits of this video are available)*

00-02-77 – **Promo Video (UK): Do Ya** *(Not issued as a single in the UK, 'Do Ya' got to No. 13 in Canada, No. 24 in the US and No. 42 in Germany)*

18-02-77 – **'The Midnight Special' (USA): Livin' Thing / Do Ya / Telephone Line /

Look Wot They Dun!

Rockaria! / **Livin' Thing** (Reprise) *(Parts of this performance were repeated on 01-04-77, 29-04-77, 12-08-77, 21-10-77 and 17-02-78)*

00-05-77 – **Promo Video (UK): Telephone Line** *('Telephone Line' reached No. 8 in the UK, No. 1 in Canada, No. 7 in the US, No. 10 in Australia and No. 32 in Germany)*

04-06-77 – **'All You Need Is Love: The Story Of Popular Music' (UK): Can't Get It Out Of My Head** *(This was taped in late 1975)*

00-10-77 – **Promo Video (UK): Turn To Stone** *('Turn To Stone' was a relative UK flop compared to most ELO singles in the latter half of the '70s, peaking at No. 18. It also got to No. 9 in Canada, No. 13 in the US, No. 17 in Australia, No. 23 in Holland and No. 32 in Germany)*

00-01-78 – **Promo Video (UK): Mr Blue Sky** *(Perhaps the ultimate ELO single, 'Mr Blue Sky' got to No. 6 in the UK, No. 8 in Holland, No. 27 in Germany and Canada, No. 35 in the US and No. 87 in Australia)*

00-02-78 – **Promo Video #1 (UK): Sweet Talkin' Woman**

00-05-78 – **Promo Video (UK): Wild West Hero** *('Wild West Hero' got to No. 6 in the UK and No. 9 in Ireland)*

10-07-78 – **'Electric Light Orchestra Live at Wembley' (UK): Standin' In The Rain / Night In The City / Turn To Stone / Tightrope / Telephone Line / Rockaria! / Wild West Hero / Showdown / Sweet Talkin' Woman /Mr Blue Sky / Do Ya / Livin' Thing / Roll Over Beethoven** *(This was taped at Wembley Arena, London, on 02-06-78, and remains the most widely-seen ELO filmed concert)*

00-09-78 – **Promo Video #2 (UK): Sweet Talkin' Woman** *(Dissatisfied with the 1st video, a 2nd one was made when 'Sweet Talkin' Woman' was issued as a single. It must've helped, as it got to No. 6 in the UK, Ireland and Canada, as well as No. 17 in the US, No. 24 in Holland and No. 38 in Australia)*

00-10-78 – **Promo Video (UK): It's Over** *(Another non-UK single, 'It's Over' was a No. 75 hit in the US)*

01-03-79 – **'Top Of The Pops' (UK): Clog Dance** *(A spin-off group featuring ELO member Mik Kaminski and ex-ELO member Mike De Albuquerque, 'Clog Dance' was a No. 17 UK hit. This is the first of two 'Top Of The Pops' appearances by the band, and features Mik in a silver jacket while the rest of the band wear tuxedos) – **VIOLINSKI**

15-03-79 – **'Top Of The Pops' (UK): Clog Dance** *(Again featuring Mik in a silver jacket, the rest of the band this time wear more casual clothing)* – **VIOLINSKI**

00-05-79 – **Promo Video #1 (UK): Shine A Little Love** *(Another song which had two distinctly different promo videos made for it, the disco-flavoured 'Shine Little Love' was No. 6 in the UK, No. 1 in Canada, No. 4 in Ireland, No. 8 in the US, No. 14 in Australia, No. 17 in Holland and No. 30 in Germany)*

00-06-79 – **Promo Video #2 (UK): Shine A Little Love** *(Although still mostly mimed-in-the-studio performances, the 1979 'Discovery' videos also feature special effects and cartoon inserts)*

00-06-79 – **Promo Video (UK): The Diary Of Horace Wimp** *('The Diary Of Horace Wimp' was a UK No. 8 hit, also reaching No. 10 in Ireland, No. 48 in Australia and No. 52 in Germany)*

00-06-79 – **Promo Video (UK): Don't Bring Me Down** *(The band's biggest US hit, 'Don't Bring Me Down' got to No. 3 in the UK, No. 1 in Canada, No. 4 in the US, No. 5 in Germany and Holland, and No. 6 in Ireland and Australia. Two different edits of this video are available)*

00-06-79 – **Promo Video (UK): Confusion** *(Released as a double A-side, 'Confusion' b/w 'Last Train To London' was a UK No. 8 hit, also getting to No. 5 in Holland, No. 6 in Germany, No. 9 in Ireland and No. 37 in the US)*

00-06-79 – **Promo Video (UK): Last Train To London**

00-06-79 – **Promo Video (UK): Need Her Love**

00-06-79 – **Promo Video (UK): Midnight Blue**

00-06-79 – **Promo Video (UK): On The Run**

00-06-79 – **Promo Video (UK): Wishing**

After a few more big hits (including 'I'm Alive', 'Xanadu' [with Olivia Newton-John], 'All Over The World', 'Hold On Tight' and 'Rock 'N' Roll Is King'), ELO disbanded in 1986. Bev Bevan, Mik Kaminski, Hugh McDowell, and Kelly Groucutt were all part of the band ELO Part II from 1992 to 2000, while Jeff Lynne and Richard Tandy put together new line-ups of ELO in 2001 and from 2014 onwards. Kelly Groucutt died in 2009, as did Mike Edwards in 2010, Wilfred Gibson in 2014 and Hugh McDowell in 2018.

MOTT THE HOOPLE

17-04-67 – **'Diamoci Del Tu' (Italy): My Babe** *(Three of 'The Doc Thomas Group' went on to form Mott The Hoople, namely Mick Ralphs on guitar, Overend Watts on bass and Dale Griffin on drums. Here, along with singer Stan Tippins, they mime to an excellent version of The Righteous Brothers' 'My Babe')* – **THE DOC THOMAS GROUP**

13-07-68 – **'Beat Club' (Germany): I Can't Drive / Great Balls Of Fire** *(An early showcase for the Jerry Lee Lewis-influenced Freddie "Fingers" Lee, a shades-less Ian Hunter plays bass and sings backing vocals)* – **AT LAST THE 1958 SHOW**

28-03-70 – **'Beat Club' (Germany): You Really Got Me (Instrumental) / At The Crossroads** *(Taped on 24-03-70 and performing live, this excellent performance is the earliest known footage of the band. 'You Really Got Me' was intercut with non-related interview footage on the original broadcast, but also circulates in un-cut form)*

10-10-70 – 'Disco 2' (UK) *(Their debut UK TV performance, none of Mott The Hoople's two 'Disco 2' performances survive, and details of songs performed appear to be lost in the midst of time)*

07-04-71 – **'GTK' (Australia): Keep-A-Knockin' / What'd I Say** *(Taped at The Big Brother Club, Greenford, UK, on 20-01-71, also featured on the broadcast is a backstage interview)*

15-04-71 – 'Disco 2' (UK)

22-07-71 – 'Top Of The Pops' (UK): Midnight Lady *(Their 'Top Of The Pops' debut, 'Midnight Lady' was not a hit)*

06-11-71 – **'Pop 2' (France): The Moon Upstairs / Walkin' With A Mountain / Rock 'n' Roll Queen / Keep A-Knockin'** *(This live performance was taped in Paris on 29-09-71)*

20-10-71 – **'GTK' (Australia): Midnight Lady** *(This was taped in the UK)*

00-07-72 – **Promo Video (UK): All The Young Dudes** *(Wiping the floor with any version by the song's composer David Bowie, 'All The Young Dudes' was Mott The Hoople's 1st and biggest hit, getting to No. 3 in the UK and No. 37 in the USA)*

03-08-72 – 'Top Of The Pops' (UK): All The Young Dudes

10-08-72 – 'Top Of The Pops' (UK): All The Young Dudes

24-08-72 – 'Top Of The Pops' (UK): All The Young Dudes *(This is a repeat of an earlier performance)*

00-05-73 – **Promo Video (UK): Honaloochie Boogie** *(Seen here in an interesting promo video that sees Ian Hunter leaning on a jukebox, 'Honaloochie Boogie' was a No. 12 UK hit)*

08-06-73 – 'Top Of The Pops' (UK): Honaloochie Boogie

24-06-73 – **'Hits A Go Go' (Switzerland): Drivin' Sister / Honaloochie Boogie** *(An enthusiastic performance for Swiss TV)*

29-06-73 – 'Top Of The Pops' (UK): Honaloochie Boogie

24-07-73 – 'Tienerklanken' (Belgium)

20-09-73 – 'Top Of The Pops' (UK): All The Way From Memphis

28-09-73 – **'ABC In Concert' (USA): All The Young Dudes / Sweet Angeline / Drivin' Sister** *(By now with original organist Verden Allen replaced by ex-Love Affair's Morgan Fisher and guitarist Mick Ralphs replaced by Ariel Bender, this is the first of four late 1973 performances for US TV)*

09-10-73 – 'Iltatahti' (Finland)

16-10-73 – **'Don Kirshner's Rock Concert' (USA): Drivin' Sister / All The Young Dudes / All The Way From Memphis / Sweet Angeline** *('All The Way From Memphis' got to No. 10 in the UK charts)*

19-10-73 – **'The Midnight Special' (USA): All The Way From Memphis / Rose**

15-11-73 – **'Top Of The Pops' (UK): Roll Away The Stone** *(Backed by the female vocal trio 'Thunderthighs', this memorable performance helped propel 'Roll Away The Stone' to No. 8 in the UK charts)*

29-11-73 – **'Top Of The Pops' (UK): Roll Away The Stone** *(This is a repeat of the 15-11-73 performance)*

07-12-73 – **'The Midnight Special' (USA): Drivin' Sister / Hymn For The Dudes**

13-12-73 – 'Top Of The Pops' (UK): Roll Away The Stone

02-03-74 – **'Disco' (Germany): Roll Away The Stone** *(German TV promotion for the recent UK hit single)*

00-03-74 – **Promo Video (UK): The Golden Age Of Rock 'N' Roll** *(Seen here in a simple mimed-in-the-studio promo video, the shouty 'The Golden Age Of Rock 'N' Roll' was a No. 16 UK hit, as well as a minor success in the US)*

21-03-74 – 'Top Of The Pops' (UK): The Golden Age Of Rock 'N' Roll

04-04-74 – **'Top Of The Pops' (UK): The Golden Age Of Rock 'N' Roll** *(Although there's no doubting Mott The Hoople's glam credentials, they were never a pretty sight, nor was their look quite as memorable as that of David Bowie, Slade and The Sweet, as seen here)*

18-04-74 – 'Top Of The Pops' (UK): The Golden Age Of Rock 'N' Roll *(This is a repeat of an earlier performance)*

02-09-74 – 'Top Pop' (Holland): Foxy Foxy *('Foxy Foxy' got to No. 33 in the UK charts, while the follow-up 'Saturday Gigs' – featuring new guitarist Mick Ronson on guitar – stalled at No. 41. Soon afterwards, both Ian Hunter and Mick Ronson quit the band, with the others recruiting new members and carrying on first as 'Mott' and then, with ex-Medicine Head's John Fiddler – British Lions)*

24-07-76 – **'So It Goes' (UK): Shouting and Pointing –** *MOTT*

09-05-78 – **'The Old Grey Whistle Test' (UK): One More Chance To Run –** *BRITISH LIONS*

Mid 1978 – **'Musikladen Extra' (Germany): One More Chance To Run / Fork Talking Man / Come On / International Heroes / My Life In Your Hands / Wild In The Streets / Booster / Wild One / Eat The Rich–** *BRITISH LIONS*

26-04-79 – 'Top Pop' (Holland): Standing In My Light – *IAN HUNTER*

18-06-79 – **Agora Ballroom, Cleveland, Ohio (USA): Once Bitten, Twice Shy / Life After Death / Just Another Night / Standin' In My Light / Bastard / All The Way From Memphis / Cleveland Rocks / All The Young Dudes –** *THE IAN HUNTER BAND* *('Once*

Bitten, Twice Shy' was released as a single in 1975, when it reached No. 14 in the UK charts)

19-09-79 – **'The New Music', Ryerson Theatre, Toronto (Canada): Life After Death / Just Another Night / The Golden Age Of Rock 'N' Roll / Standin' In My Light / Bastard / Cleveland Rocks / All The Young Dudes / When The Daylight Comes –** *THE IAN HUNTER BAND*

00-07-79 – **The Roxy Theatre, Hollywood (USA): Once Bitten Twice Shy –** *THE IAN HUNTER BAND*

All five original members (with the addition of Martin Chambers from The Pretenders helping out an ailing Dale Griffin) reunited for UK dates in 2009, and again in 2011. Dale Griffin died in 2016, and Overend Watts died in 2017. At the time of writing, a version of the group that includes Ian Hunter, Morgan Fisher and Ariel Bender are touring.

10cc

00-07-70 – **Promo Video (UK): Neanderthal Man** *(Featuring three future members of 10cc in Eric Stewart, Kevin Godley and Lol Creme, Hotlegs' 'Neanderthal Man' was a No. 2 UK hit. This studio promo is quite nicely intercut with footage of women dancing on a beach while wearing leopard skin bikinis and white boots)* – **HOTLEGS**

16-07-70 – 'Top Of The Pops' (UK): Neanderthal Man – **HOTLEGS**

30-07-70 – 'Top Of The Pops' (UK): Neanderthal Man – **HOTLEGS**

13-08-70 – 'Top Of The Pops' (UK): Neanderthal Man *(This is a repeat of an earlier performance)* – **HOTLEGS**

26-12-70 – 'Top Of The Pops' (UK): Neanderthal Man – **HOTLEGS**

28-04-71 – **'Hits A Go Go' (Switzerland): Desperate Dan / Run Baby Run** *(Besides taking far too long to follow-up their smash hit, when they did the songs were mediocre at best, so Hotlegs never had another hit)* – **HOTLEGS**

08-05-71 – **'Disco' (Germany): Desperate Dan** – **HOTLEGS**

00-08-72 – **Promo Video (UK): Donna** *(Now joining forces with Graham Gouldman, the quartet formed 10cc, and issued the doo-wop styled 'Donna' as their debut single. This got to No. 2 in the UK, Ireland and Holland, as well as No. 53 in Australia. Although this performance is usually listed as a promo video, it looks more like a TV performance, origins unknown)*

28-09-72 – 'Top Of The Pops' (UK): Donna

12-10-72 – 'Top Of The Pops' (UK): Donna

18-10-72 – 'Lift Off With Ayshea' (UK): Donna

26-10-72 – 'Top Of The Pops' (UK): Donna

04-12-72 – **'Top Pop' (Holland): Donna** *(This features the band miming while accompanied by wild-haired 'Top Pop' dancer Penney De Jager)*

00-12-72 – Promo Video (UK): Johnny Don't Do It *(10cc's 2nd single, 'Johnny Don't Do It' failed to chart)*

27-12-72 – 'Lift Off With Ayshea' (UK): Johnny Don't Do It

17-01-73 – 'Eddy Ready Go' (Holland): Donna

04-05-73 – 'Top Of The Pops' (UK): Rubber Bullets

04-05-73 – 'Lift Off With Ayshea' (UK): Rubber Bullets

25-05-73 – 'Top Of The Pops' (UK): Rubber Bullets

04-06-73 – 'Lift Off With Ayshea' (UK): Rubber Bullets

08-06-73 – 'Top Of The Pops' (UK): Rubber Bullets

22-06-73 – **'Top Of The Pops' (UK): Rubber Bullets** *('Rubber Bullets' got to No. 1 in the UK and Ireland, No. 3 in Australia, No. 18 in Germany, No. 73 in the US and No. 76 in Canada. This 'Top Of The Pops' appearance is actually a repeat of an earlier performance, date unknown.)*

10-08-73 – 'Top Of The Pops' (UK): The Dean and I

25-08-73 – **'Disco' (Germany): Rubber Bullets**

31-08-73 – **'Top Of The Pops' (UK): The Dean and I** *('The Dean and I' was a UK No. 10, as well as No. 1 in Ireland and No. 61 in Australia)*

13-09-73 – 'Top Of The Pops' (UK): The Dean and I

07-10-73 – **'Hits A Go Go' (Switzerland): The Dean and I**

25-12-73 – **'Top Of The Pops' (UK): Rubber Bullets** *(A reprise of their biggest hit to date on this Christmas edition of 'Top Of The Pops')*

09-01-74 – 'Lift Off With Ayshea' (UK): The Worst Band In The World

25-02-74 – **'Top Pop' (Holland): The Worst Band In The World** *('The Worst Band In The World' was also one of 10cc's worst-selling singles, failing to chart anywhere)*

26-02-74 – **'The Old Grey Whistle Test' (UK): Old Wild Men** *(This song was taped at The Hard Rock, Manchester. See also the entry for 27-04-74)*

21-04-74 – **'See You Sunday' (UK): Fresh Air For My Momma / The Wall Street Shuffle** *('The Wall Street Shuffle' was a UK No. 10, No. 2 in Holland, No. 9 in Ireland, No. 38 in Germany and No. 87 in Canada)*

27-04-74 – **'Don Kirshner's Rock Concert' (USA): Sand In My Face / The Dean and I / Fresh Air for My Mama / Headline Hustler / Rubber Bullets** *(All songs were taped at The Hard Rock, Manchester, UK)*

30-05-74 – 'Top Of The Pops' (UK): The Wall Street Shuffle

29-07-74 – 'Top Pop' (Holland): The Wall Street Shuffle

21-08-74 – **'In Concert' (UK): Silly Love / The Wall Street Shuffle / Baron Samedi / Old Wild Men / Oh Effendi / Fresh Air For My Momma / Rubber Bullets** *(A fabulous performance that proves just how good both vocally and instrumentally each member of 10cc was)*

05-09-74 – **'Top Of The Pops' (UK): Silly Love** *('Silly Love' peaked at No. 24 in the UK, also getting to No. 7 in Holland)*

19-09-74 – '45' (UK): Silly Love / The Sacro-Iliac

27-09-74 – 'Top Of The Pops' (UK): Silly Love

18-10-74 – 'Top Pop' (Holland): Silly Love

00-00-74 – 'Top Pop' (Holland): Rubber Bullets

27-12-74 – 'Top Pop' (Holland): Wall Street Shuffle *(This is probably a repeat of the 29-07-74 performance)*

00-03-75 – **Promo Video (UK): Life Is A Minestrone** *('Life Is A Minestrone' was a No. 7 hit in both the UK and Ireland, No. 12 in Holland and No. 48 in Australia)*

27-03-75 – 'Top Of The Pops' (UK): Life Is A Minestrone

10-04-75 – **'Top Of The Pops' (UK): Life Is A Minestrone**

11-04-75 – 'Top Pop' (Holland): Life Is A Minestrone

24-04-75 – 'Top Of The Pops' (UK): Life Is A Minestrone

00-05-75 – **Promo Video (UK): I'm Not In Love** *(10cc's biggest hit, 'I'm Not In Love' was*

No. 1 in the UK, Ireland and Canada, No. 2 in the US, No. 3 in Australia, No. 5 in Holland and No. 8 in Germany)

29-05-75 – **'Top Of The Pops' (UK): I'm Not In Love**

12-06-75 – **'Top Of The Pops' (UK): I'm Not In Love** *(This is a repeat of the 29-05-75 performance)*

20-06-75 – 'Top Pop' (Holland): I'm Not In Love

26-06-75 – 'Top Of The Pops' (UK): I'm Not In Love

03-07-75 – 'Top Of The Pops' (UK): I'm Not In Love

20-08-75 – **'Musikladen' (Germany): I'm Not In Love**

00-11-75 – **Promo Video (UK): Art For Art's Sake** *(A far smaller hit than its predecessor, 'Art For Art's Sake', peaked at No. 5 in the UK, No. 4 in Ireland, No. 61 in Australia, No. 69 in Canada and No. 83 in the US)*

04-12-75 – 'Top Of The Pops' (UK): Art For Art's Sake

18-12-75 – 'Top Of The Pops' (UK): Art For Art's Sake *(This is a repeat of the 04-12-75 performance)*

25-12-75 – **'Top Of The Pops' (UK): I'm Not In Love** *(This is a repeat of the 04-12-75 performance)*

15-01-76 – 'Top Of The Pops' (UK): Art For Art's Sake

21-02-76 – **'Don Kirshner's Rock Concert' (USA): Art For Art's Sake / I'm Not In Love / Don't Hang Up / Head Room**

00-03-76 – **Promo Video (UK): I'm Mandy Fly Me** *(The final single to feature the classic 4-piece line-up, 'I'm Mandy Fly Me' got to No. 6 in the UK, No. 3 in Ireland, No. 50 in Holland, No. 60 in the US and No. 62 in Canada)*

28-05-76 – 'Iltatahti' (Finland) (on film)

21-08-76 – **'Knebworth Fair', Knebworth Park (UK): I'm Not In Love / Rubber Bullets** *(Un-broadcast footage that circulates unofficially, 10cc's support set to The Rolling Stones was their last show to feature all four members. After this, Godley and Creme *formed a duet, while Stewart and Gouldman carried on as 10cc)*

00-12-76 – **Promo Video (UK): The Things We Do For Love** *('The Things We Do For Love' was a No. 6 UK hit, No. 1 in Canada, No. 2 in Ireland, No. 5 in Australia and the US and No. 13 in Holland)*

07-12-76 – 'Top Pop' (Holland): The Things We Do For Love

01-01-77 – '10cc' (Holland): The Wall Street Shuffle / People In Love / Modern Man Blues / Good Morning Judge / The Things We Do For Love / I'm Not In Love

00-04-77 – **Promo Video (UK): Good Morning Judge** *('Good Morning Judge' got to No. 5 in the UK, No. 7 in Australia, No. 12 in Holland, No. 23 in Germany and No. 69 in the US. Unlike all their earlier promo videos, this one features a bit of a storyline)*

18-06-77 – **The Hammersmith Odeon, London (UK): The Second Sitting For The Last Supper / The Wall Street Shuffle / People In Love / Marriage Bureau Rendezvous / Good Morning Judge / Feel The Benefit / The Things We Do For Love / I'm Not In Love / Modern Man Blues** *(A show that was first issued as an official VHS tape in 1980, the band are on fine form, though inevitably they lack the versatility of the earlier quartet)*

00-08-77 – **Promo Video (UK): People In Love** *(The McCartney-like 'People In Love' didn't chart in the UK, but it did get to No. 40 in the US, No. 74 in Australia and No. 90 in Canada. This video was broadcast on 'Marc' on 31-08-77)*

19-08-77 – **'Szene '77' (Germany): Good Morning Judge**

22-12-77 – 'Top Of The Pops' (UK): 5 0'Clock In The Morning *(Godley and Crème's 1st single since they left 10cc, '5 0'Clock In The Morning' didn't chart, and neither did the follow-up, 'Sandwiches Of You')* – **GODLEY and CREME**

01-04-78 – 'Top Pop' (Holland): 5 0'Clock In The Morning – **GODLEY and CREME**

00-07-78 – **Promo Video (UK): Dreadlock Holiday** *(With a great promo video that no doubt helped sales, 'Dreadlock Holiday' got to No. 1 in the UK and Holland, No. 2 in Ireland and Australia, No. 11 in Germany, No. 30 in Canada and No. 44 in the US. Unfortunately, it was 10cc's final UK hit, with 'For You and I', 'Reds In My Bed' and 'From Rochdale to Ocho Rios' failing in the UK and not doing much better elsewhere)*

17-08-78 – **'Top Of The Pops' (UK): Dreadlock Holiday**

31-08-78 – **'Top Of The Pops' (UK): Dreadlock Holiday** *(This is a repeat of the 17-08-78 performance)*

14-09-78 – **'Top Of The Pops' (UK): Dreadlock Holiday** *(This is a repeat of the 17-08-78 performance)*

21-09-78 – **'Top Of The Pops' (UK): Dreadlock Holiday** *(This is a repeat of the 17-08-78 performance)*

03-11-78 – **'Szene '78' (Germany): Dreadlock Holiday**

24-12-78 – **'The Old Grey Whistle Test' (UK)** *(This featured a live concert, taped at London's Wembley Arena earlier in the year)*

15-07-79 – 'Kenny's TV Show' (Sweden)

21-08-79 – 'Flimra' (Norway)

15-10-79 – **'Top Pop' (Holland): I'm Not In Love** *(A reprise of 10cc's big 1975 hit, it looks a bit odd seeing the band miming to this without Lol and Kevin)*

00-10-79 – **Promo Video (UK): An Englishman In New York** *(Another chart failure for the duo in the UK, 'An Englishman In New York' reached No. 7 in Holland, No. 17 in Australia and No. 25 in Germany, though the song was later a UK success for Sting. The promo video is excellent, and is clearly a forerunner of the ground-breaking work that they'd do for other artists in the '80s) – **GODLEY and CREME***

In the early to mid-'80s, Godley and Creme had major chart success, with such hits as 'Under Your Thumb', 'Wedding Bells' and 'Cry'. Eric Stewart and Graham Gouldman carried on as 10cc with little success until 1983, with the pair reuniting from 1991 to 1995. Since 1999 10cc has continued, though with Graham Gouldman as the only original member.

BLACKFOOT SUE

10-08-72 – 'Top Of The Pops' (UK): Standing In The Road

17-08-72 – 'Top Of The Pops' (UK): Standing In The Road

31-08-72 – 'Top Of The Pops' (UK): Standing In The Road

11-11-72 – **'Disco' (Germany): Standing In The Road** *(With a sound midway between John Kongos and Slade, 'Standing In The Road' was Blackfoot Sue's biggest hit, reaching No. 4 in the UK charts. Here the song is mimed on German TV)*

07-12-72 – 'Top Of The Pops' (UK): Sing Don't Speak

01-02-73 – **'Hits A Go Go' (Switzerland): Sing Don't Speak** *(Performed here on Swiss TV, 'Sing Don't Speak' was the band's only other UK hit, deserving far better than its No. 36 chart peak)*

21-04-79 – **'Rock-Pop' (Germany): Keep Reaching Out For Love** *(Looking much the same but sounding very different, in 1979 Blackfoot Sue reinvented themselves as soft-rock group Liner. The first of two minor hits, 'Keep Reaching Out For Love' got to No. 49 in the UK charts)* – **LINER**

24-09-79 – **'Top Of The Pops' (UK): You and Me** *(Marginally more successful than the previous hit, 'You and Me' was a UK No. 44)* – **LINER**

Following the demise of Liner, brothers Tom and Dave Farmer formed the band Outside Edge, recording four albums under that name. By 1993 the band had renamed themselves Blackfoot Sue, performing their final gig in 1999.

ROXY MUSIC

00-06-72 – **Promo Video (UK): Re-make/Re-model** (*Taped at The Royal College Of Art, this highlights just how original early Roxy Music were*)

20-06-72 – **'The Old Grey Whistle Test' (UK): Ladytron** / Re-make/Re-model (*'Ladytron' was repeated on 26-12-72, and is the only song that survives from this performance*)

24-08-72 – **'Top Of The Pops' (UK): Virginia Plain** (*Songs like 'Remake/Remodel' and 'Ladytron' didn't stand a hope in hell of selling in the singles charts, so singer and pianist Bryan Ferry came up with this. Roxy Music's 1st and best single, 'Virginia Plain' was a UK No. 1, as well as No. 18 in Holland, No. 20 in Germany and No. 99 in Australia*)

07-09-72 – **'Top Of The Pops' (UK): Virginia Plain** (*This is a repeat of the 24-08-72 performance*)

25-11-72 – **'Full House' (UK): Re-make/Re-model** / **For Your Pleasure** / **Ladytron** / **Grey Lagoons** (*Performing a couple of songs apiece from their first two albums, this captures the early band at their best*)

16-12-72 – **'Pop Deux' (France): Would You Believe** / **If There Is Something** / **Sea Breezes** / **Virginia Plain** (*This was taped at the Bataclan, Paris, on 26-11-72*)

13-03-73 – 'Point Chaud' (France)

15-03-73 – 'Top Of The Pops' (UK): Pyjamarama (*'Pyjamarama' got to No. 10 in the UK and No. 96 in Australia*)

03-04-73 – **'The Old Grey Whistle Test' (UK): Do The Strand** / **In Every Dream Home A Heartache** (*Strangely not a single in the UK, 'Do The Strand' was a No. 23 hit in Holland and a No. 41 hit in Germany*)

05-04-73 – 'Top Of The Pops' (UK): Pyjamarama

29-04-73 – **'The Montreux Jazz Festival' (Switzerland): Editions Of You** / **Ladytron**

01-05-73 – **'JT Nuit' (France): Re-make/Re-model**

28-05-73 – 'Top Pop' (Holland): Do The Strand

30-05-73 – **'Musikladen' (Germany): Virginia Plain / Do The Strand / Editions Of You / In Every Dream Home A Heartache / Re-make/Re-model** *(Performing live on German TV, this is one of the last Roxy Music TV appearances to feature flamboyant keyboardist Brian Eno, who would soon quit. By now the whole band, and particularly Bryan Ferry, was fast moving away from their early glam rock image, with him wearing a white suit here)*

00-09-73 – **Promo Video (UK): A Hard Rain's A-Gonna Fall** *(Bryan Ferry's 1st solo single, this excellent cover of Bob Dylan's 'A Hard Rain's A-Gonna Fall' got to No. 10 in the UK, No. 23 in Australia and No. 42 in Germany)* – **BRYAN FERRY**

00-09-73 – **Promo Video (UK): These Foolish Things** *(Around the same time that David Bowie did a similar thing with 'Pin Ups', Bryan Ferry released a debut solo album of cover versions. This is the title track)* – **BRYAN FERRY**

04-10-73 – 'Top Of The Pops' (UK): A Hard Rain's A-Gonna Fall – **BRYAN FERRY**

18-10-73 – 'Top Of The Pops' (UK): A Hard Rain's A-Gonna Fall – **BRYAN FERRY**

22-11-73 – **'Top Of The Pops' (UK): Street Life** *('Street Life' peaked at No. 9 in the UK and No. 40 in Germany)*

06-12-73 – **'Top Of The Pops' (UK): Street Life** *(This is a repeat of the 22-11-73 performance)*

07-01-74 – 'Top Pop' (Holland): Street Life

23-01-74 – **'Musikladen' (Germany): A Hard Rain's A-Gonna Fall** – **BRYAN FERRY**

23-02-74 – **'Cilla!' (UK): These Foolish Things / It's My Party** [with Cilla Black] – **BRYAN FERRY**

Early 1974 – **'Musikladen Extra' (Germany): Street Life / Pyjamarama / Mother Of Pearl / Amazona / Psalm**

16-08-74 – **'In Concert' (USA): Editions Of You / A Song For Europe / Do The Strand** *(This was taped in London's The Rainbow Theatre for US TV broadcast)*

29-08-74 – 'Top Of The Pops' (UK): Smoke Gets In Your Eyes – **BRYAN FERRY**

13-09-74 – **'Top Of The Pops' (UK): Smoke Gets In Your Eyes** *(Still remembered by many* people as the 'Esso Blue' song, 'Smoke Gets In Your Eyes' peaked at No. 17 in the UK and No. 99 in Australia) – **BRYAN FERRY**

04-10-74 – **'Top Of The Pops' (UK): All I Want Is You** *('All I Want Is You' was a No. 12 UK hit, but didn't do much elsewhere. One of their better songs, but Bryan takes the non-glam image to extremes here, appearing in faded T-shirt and jeans)*

11-10-74 – **'Russell Harty Plus' (UK): It Ain't Me Babe** – **BRYAN FERRY**

17-10-74 – **'Top Of The Pops' (UK): All I Want Is You** *(This is a repeat of the 04-10-74 performance)*

17-10-74 – **'Twiggs' (UK): Smoke Gets In Your Eyes / What A Wonderful World** [with Twiggy] *(This was repeated on 01-05-75)* – **BRYAN FERRY**

07-11-74 – **'Top Of The Pops' (UK): All I Want Is You** *(For this 2nd 'Top Of The Pops' performance Bryan tries a little harder, wearing beige trousers, white shirt and a tie. The result is him looking like an estate agent as opposed to the painter and decorator of a month previously)*

13-11-74 – **'Musikladen' (Germany): All I Want Is You / Out Of The Blue / If It Takes All Night** *('Out Of The Blue' and 'If It Takes All Night' are outtakes that were not originally broadcast)*

09-05-75 – **'The Midnight Special' (USA): Out Of The Blue / The Thrill Of It All / A Really Good Time**

00-06-75 – **Promo Video (UK): You Go To My Head** *('You Go To My Head' stalled at No. 33 in the UK charts)* – **BRYAN FERRY**

03-07-75 – 'Top Of The Pops' (UK): You Go To My Head – **BRYAN FERRY**

10-07-75 – **'Top Pop' (Holland): All I Want Is You**

00-10-75 – **Promo Video (UK): Love Is The Drug** *(Taped at Wembley Arena, London. 'Love Is The Drug' got to No. 2 in the UK, No. 3 in Canada, No. 9 in Holland, No. 18 in Australia, No. 30 in the US and No. 39 in Germany)*

00-10-75 – **Promo Video (UK): Both Ends Burning** *(Taped at Wembley Arena, London. Roxy Music's last single before a three-year hiatus, 'Both Ends Burning' reached No. 25 in* the UK charts)

09-10-75 – **'Supersonic' (UK): Love Is The Drug / Both Ends Burning** *(By now featuring female backing singers that look like they've just stepped off one of Roxy Music's infamous album covers, the band look and sound very different from three years earlier)*

23-10-75 – 'Top Of The Pops' (UK): Love Is The Drug

23-10-75 – **'Supersonic' (UK): Love Is The Drug** *(This is a repeat of the 09-10-75 performance)*

06-11-75 – 'Top Of The Pops' (UK): Love Is The Drug *(This is a repeat of the 23-10-75 performance)*

18-12-75 – **'Supersonic' (UK): Both Ends Burning** *(This is a repeat of the 09-10-75 performance)*

25-12-75 – **'The Supersonic Christmas Show' (UK): Love Is The Drug / Both Ends Burning** *(This is a repeat of the 09-10-75 performance)*

27-01-76 – **Konserthuset, Stockholm (Sweden): The Thrill Of It All / Mother Of Pearl / Nightingale / Out Of The Blue / Street Life / Diamond Head / Wild Weekend / The "In" Crowd / Virginia Plain / A Hard Rain's A-Gonna Fall** *(Featuring Bryan Ferry sporting what looks like a dead caterpillar above his top lip, shortly after this the band temporarily split, and it wouldn't be until the spring of 1979 that they would release a new studio recording. Meanwhile, Bryan continued his successful solo career)*

00-05-76 – **Promo Video (UK): Let's Stick Together** *(Bryan Ferry's most successful single, 'Let's Stick Together' got to No. 4 in the UK, No. 1 in Australia, No. 5 in Ireland and No. 47 in Germany)* – ***BRYAN FERRY***

00-08-76 – **Promo Video (UK): The Price Of Love** *(Another big seller, 'The Price Of Love' reached No. 7 in the UK, No. 9 in Australia and No. 12 in Ireland)* – ***BRYAN FERRY***

00-01-77 – **Promo Video (UK): This Is Tomorrow** *('This Is Tomorrow' peaked at No. 9 in the UK and No. 6 in Australia)* – ***BRYAN FERRY***

Early 1977 – **'Les Visiteurs Du Mercredi' (France): This Is Tomorrow** – ***BRYAN FERRY***

00-06-77 – **Unknown TV Show (Australia): Tokyo Joe** *('Tokyo Joe' got to No. 15 in the*

UK and No. 30 in Australia) – **BRYAN FERRY**

09-06-77 – **'The Young Music Show' (Japan): Let's Stick Together / Shame, Shame, Shame / In Your Mind / Casanova / Love Me Madly Again / Love Is The Drug / Tokyo Joe / This Is Tomorrow / A Hard Rain's A-Gonna Fall / The Price Of Love** *(This is the only known filmed full length Bryan Ferry concert from the '70s)* – **BRYAN FERRY**

20-10-77 – **'Top Of The Pops' (UK): Virginia Plain** *(This is a repeat of the 24-08-72 performance)*

10-11-77 – **'Top Of The Pops' (UK): Virginia Plain** *(This is a repeat of the 24-08-72 performance)*

00-04-78 – **Promo Video (UK): What Goes On** *('What Goes On' peaked at only No. 67 in the UK and No. 73 in Australia)* – **BRYAN FERRY**

20-04-78 – **'Top Of The Pops' (UK): What Goes On** – **BRYAN FERRY**

03-07-78 – **'The Kenny Everett Video Show' (UK): Sign Of The Times** – **BRYAN FERRY**

08-09-78 – **'Szene '78' (Germany): Sign Of The Times** – **BRYAN FERRY**

00-02-79 – **Promo Video (UK): Trash** *(Roxy Music's 'comeback' single, 'Trash' stalled at No. 40 in both the UK and Holland)*

13-03-79 – **'Plattenkuche' (UK): Trash**

Early 1979 – **Unknown TV show (France): Trash**

00-04-79 – **Promo Video (UK): Dance Away** *(A more sophisticated and polished sound than of old, 'Dance Away' got to No. 2 in the UK, No. 8 in Holland, No. 30 in Germany, No. 44 in the US, No. 75 in Canada and No. 92 in Australia)*

16-04-79 – **'ABBA In Switzerland' (UK): Dance Away** *(Taped in Switzerland in February 1979 for Swedish and UK TV broadcast, 'Dance Away' from this show was also broadcast on 'Top Of The Pops' on 10-05-79, 24-05-79 and 07-06-79)*

12-05-79 – **'On The Road' (UK): Manifesto / A Song For Europe / Still Falls The Rain / Mother Of Pearl / In Every Dream Home A Heartache / Ain't That So / Love Is The Drug / Editions Of You / Re-make/Re-model / Virginia Plain** *(This was taped at The Apollo, Manchester)*

19-06-79 – **'Plattenkuche' (UK): Dance Away**

00-06-79 – **'Ohne Maulkorb' (Germany): Ain't That So / Love Is The Drug / Ladytron / Editions Of You** *(This was taped in Munich)*

00-08-79 – **Promo Video (UK): Angel Eyes** *(Roxy Music approached the new decade sounding more contemporary than just about any other glam era artist with the possible exception of David Bowie. 'Angel Eyes' peaked at No. 4 in the UK charts, as well as No. 13 in Holland and No. 89 in Australia)*

00-08-79 – **Promo Video (UK): Angel Eyes** [extended 12" version]

00-00-79 – **Promo Video (UK): Ain't That So**

15-08-79 – 'Countdown' (Holland)

22-09-79 – **'Numero Un' (France): Angel Eyes**

24-10-79 – **'Studio 3' (France): Angel Eyes**

05-11-79 – **'Disco' (Germany): Angel Eyes**

Late 1979 – **'Aplauso' (Spain): Dance Away / Angel Eyes**

25-12-79 – **'Top Of The Pops' (UK): Dance Away**

31-12-79 – **'Will Kenny Everett Make It To 1980?' (UK): The Midnight Hour**

After Roxy Music split in 1983, Bryan Ferry had continued success as a solo artist, while other members pursued various solo projects. Bryan Ferry, Phil Manzanera, Andy Mackay and Paul Thompson all reunited Roxy Music in 2001, with further occasional reunions until 2011.

LIEUTENANT PIGEON

27-07-72 – 'Eddy Ready Go' (Holland): Mouldy Old Dough *(This was repeated on 04-07-73)*

21-09-72 – 'Top Of The Pops' (UK): Mouldy Old Dough

05-10-72 – 'Top Of The Pops' (UK): Mouldy Old Dough

12-10-72 – 'Top Of The Pops' (UK): Mouldy Old Dough *(This is a repeat of an earlier performance)*

19-10-72 – 'Top Of The Pops' (UK): Mouldy Old Dough

23-10-72 – **'Top Pop' (Holland): Mouldy Old Dough** *(A spin-off from the non-hit band Stavely Makepeace, Lieutenant Pigeon's 'Mouldy Old Dough' topped the UK charts in late '72. Here the song is mimed in a Dutch TV studio, with everyone apart from pianist Hilda Woodward looking the very epitome of Glam)*

24-10-72 – 'Lift Off With Ayshea' (UK): Mouldy Old Dough

26-10-72 – 'Top Of The Pops' (UK): Mouldy Old Dough

31-10-72 – 'Lift Off With Ayshea' (UK): Mouldy Old Dough

02-11-72 – 'Top Of The Pops' (UK): Mouldy Old Dough *(This is a repeat of an earlier performance)*

24-12-72 – **'Christmas Company' (UK): Desperate Dan** *(The band's only other UK hit, 'Desperate Dan' reached No. 17)*

28-12-72 – **'Top Of The Pops' (UK): Mouldy Old Dough** *(With drummer and vocalist' Nigel Fletcher wearing an 18th Century military costume, this is the only known surviving Lieutenant Pigeon 'Top Of The Pops' performance)*

03-01-73 – 'Lift Off With Ayshea' (UK): Desperate Dan *(The band's only other UK hit, 'Desperate Dan' reached No. 17)*

04-01-73 – 'Top Of The Pops' (UK): Desperate Dan

18-01-73 – 'Top Of The Pops' (UK): Desperate Dan

02-02-73 – 'Crackerjack' (UK): Desperate Dan

31-10-73 – 'Lift Off With Ayshea' (UK): Creativity

22-03-74 – 'Crackerjack' (UK): I'll Take You Home Again, Kathleen

01-04-75 – **'Shang-A-Lang' (UK): I'll Take You Home Again, Kathleen** *(Not a hit in the UK, this was a surprise No. 3 in Australia)*

08-06-76 – **'The Arrows' (UK): Good-bye (From The Horse Inn)** *(Yet more in the same mould as their No. 1 hit, by now the formula had exhausted its appeal)*

Although the band initially stopped touring in 1978, a version of Lieutenant Pigeon continues to this day. Pianist Hilda Woodward died in 1999.

GEORDIE

09-11-72 – 'Top Of The Pops' (UK): Don't Do That *(Closer to Led Zeppelin than glam rock, Geordie's 1st single, 'Don't Do That', got to No. 32 in the UK charts)*

20-12-72 – 'Eddy Ready Go' (Holland): Don't Do That

19-01-73 – 'Popzien' (Holland): Don't Do That

29-03-73 – 'Top Of The Pops' (UK): All Because Of You *(Sounding like a no-thrills Slade, 'All Because Of You' was Geordie's biggest UK hit at No. 6)*

13-04-73 – 'Crackerjack' (UK): All Because Of You

09-05-73 – 'Eddy Ready Go' (Holland): All Because Of You

11-05-73 – 'Lift Off With Ayshea' (UK): All Because Of You

15-06-73 – 'Top Of The Pops' (UK): Can You Do It *(Even more Slade-like than the last single, 'Can You Do It' reached No. 13 in the UK charts)*

15-06-73 – 'Lift Off With Ayshea' (UK): Can You Do It

15-05-73 – **'Hits A Go Go' (Switzerland): All Because Of You** *(The earliest known surviving Geordie footage, this sees the band promoting their biggest hit on Swiss TV)*

29-06-73 – 'Top Of The Pops' (UK): Can You Do It

16-07-73 – 'GTK' (Australia)

17-08-73 – **'Top Of The Pops' (UK): Electric Lady** *(Not as strong as the previous singles, the band's final UK hit 'Electric Lady' got to No. 32. This is their 5th and final 'Top Of The Pops' appearance, and the only one known to still survive)*

15-09-73 – 'Top Pop' (Holland): Don't Do That / Can You Do it / Keep On Rocking / All Because Of You / Roll Over Beethoven *(All songs were taped at 'Top Pop Festival')*

17-10-73 – 'Lift Off With Ayshea' (UK)

00-11-73 – **Promo Video (UK): Black Cat Woman** *(With a song less commercial sounding and not unlike Deep Purple, this video features the band in a studio interspersed with* *special effect close-ups of a woman)*

12-12-73 – 'Lift Off With Ayshea' (UK): Black Cat Woman

12-02-74 – 'Iltatahti' (Finland)

13-02-74 – **'GTK' (Australia): Medley: Long Tall Sally-Whole Lotta Shakin' Goin' On** *(This was taped live in Sydney, and shows how Geordie, and in particular Brian Johnson, could rock as hard as anyone. The 'GTK' broadcasts on 19-02-74 and 25-02-74 are probably repeats)*

19-02-74 – 'GTK' (Australia)

25-02-74 – 'GTK' (Australia)

25-04-74 – '45' (UK)

06-07-74 – **'Kussrock' Festival (Finland): Going Down / Mercenary Man** *(Live footage from a Finnish rock festival)*

12-07-74 – 'Iltatahti' (Finland)

00-08-74 – **Promo Video (UK): She's A Teaser** *(Another simple studio promo, if it wasn't for the horns this would sound as near as damn it to AC/DC)*

26-08-74 – 'Lift Off With Ayshea' (UK): She's A Teaser

02-11-74 – **'The Geordie Scene' (UK)** *(The first of two performances on a TV show that was not named after the band)*

15-11-74 – **'Hits A Go Go' (Switzerland): She's A Teaser** *(A return to Swiss TV to plug their latest single)*

19-11-74 – 'Lift Off With Ayshea' (UK): Ride On Baby

21-11-74 – **'45' (UK): Ride On Baby** *(Another hard rockin' single – another flop)*

28-12-74 – **'Point Chaud' (France): All Because Of You** *(A belated French TV performance of their biggest hit)*

23-01-75 – 'Iltatahti' (Finland)

27-03-75 – **'The Geordie Scene' (UK): She's A Lady / You've Gotta Help Me / Medley:**

Blue Suede Shoes – Long Tall Sally [with Fogg]

27-09-75 – **'Pop '75' (Germany): Goodbye Love** *(Geordie goes disco! Well almost, as this, the band's final single, is certainly far more dance orientated than anything else they did)*

Singer Brian Johnson quit Geordie in 1980 to replace the late Bon Scott in AC/DC, with the rest of the band subsequently splitting, though they regrouped with new singer Rob Turnbull from 1982 to 1985. In 2001, during a brief break from AC/DC duties, Brian Johnson reformed Geordie for a short UK tour.

WIZZARD

12-02-72 – 'It's Cliff Richard!' (UK): Songs Of Praise – **ROY WOOD**

12-04-72 – 'Lift Off With Ayshea' (UK): When Grandma Plays The Banjo *(Roy Wood's 1st solo single, 'When Grandma Plays The Banjo' did not chart)* – **ROY WOOD**

00-11-72 – **Promo Video (UK): Ball Park Incident** *(Wizzard's 1st single, seen here in an in-studio promo video, 'Ball Park Incident' was a No. 6 UK hit, also getting to No. 8 in Ireland)*

15-11-72 – 'Lift Off With Ayshea' (UK): Ball Park Incident

14-12-72 – 'Top Of The Pops' (UK): Ball Park Incident

21-12-72 – 'Top Of The Pops' (UK): Ball Park Incident

11-01-73 – 'Top Of The Pops' (UK): Ball Park Incident

18-01-73 – 'Top Of The Pops' (UK): Ball Park Incident

00-04-73 – **Promo Video (UK): See My Baby Jive** *('See My Baby Jive' was Wizzard's 1st chart-topper, reaching No. 1 in both the UK and Ireland. With Roy Wood in war paint and blue hair while wearing tartan trousers and a floor-length scarf and the others in various other bizarre costumes, this video is quintessential Wizzard)*

27-04-73 – 'Top Of The Pops' (UK): See My Baby Jive

27-04-73 – 'Lift Off With Ayshea' (UK): See My Baby Jive

04-05-73 – 'Top Of The Pops' (UK): See My Baby Jive

11-05-73 – 'Top Of The Pops' (UK): See My Baby Jive

18-05-73 – 'Top Of The Pops' (UK): See My Baby Jive

25-05-73 – 'Top Of The Pops' (UK): See My Baby Jive

28-05-73 – 'Top Pop' (Holland): See My Baby Jive

01-06-73 – 'Top Of The Pops' (UK): See My Baby Jive *(This is a repeat of an earlier*

performance)

08-06-73 – 'Top Of The Pops' (UK): See My Baby Jive *(This is a repeat of an earlier performance)*

00-07-73 – **Promo Video (UK): Angel Fingers (A Teen Ballad)** *('Angel Fingers (A Teen Ballad)' was Wizzard's 2nd and last UK number, also getting to No. 7 in Ireland. By Wizzard standards, Roy Wood is dressed down for this, with hair tied back and a leopard-skin teddy boy jacket)*

24-07-73 – 'Tienerklanken' (Belgium)

Mid 1973 – **'The Dave Cash Radio Programme' (UK): Dear Elaine** *('Dear Elaine' was Roy Wood's 1st solo hit, reaching No. 18 in the UK charts. This video, made especially for 'The Dave Cash Radio Programme', was filmed outdoors in a vast stately home garden)* – **ROY WOOD**

03-08-73 – 'Top Of The Pops' (UK): Dear Elaine – **ROY WOOD**

05-08-73 – **'Russell Harty Plus' (UK): Angel Fingers (A Teen Ballad) / Do The Locomotive / See My Baby Jive** *('See My Baby Jive' was repeated on 'Russell Harty Plus Pop' on 19-01-74, as well as shown in black and white on 'GTK' in Australia)*

24-08-73 – 'Top Of The Pops' (UK): Dear Elaine – **ROY WOOD**

25-08-73 – **'Disco' (Germany): See My Baby Jive**

31-08-73 – **'Top Of The Pops' (UK): Angel Fingers (A Teen Ballad)** *(This was Wizzard's 10th 'Top Of The Pops' appearance – 12th if you include Roy's solo performances – yet it is the first to survive)*

13-09-73 – 'Top Of The Pops' (UK): Angel Fingers (A Teen Ballad)

20-09-73 – 'Top Of The Pops' (UK): Angel Fingers (A Teen Ballad)

24-10-73 – 'Lift Off With Ayshea' (UK): Angel Fingers (A Teen Ballad) / Forever *(the 2nd song is by **ROY WOOD** only)*

00-11-73 – **Promo Video (UK): I Wish It Could Be Christmas Everyday** *(Glam Rock's 2nd most famous Christmas single, this got to No. 4 in the UK charts and No. 6 in Ireland. The video is filmed against a backdrop of a children's Disney-like castle, and features all the* band at their most colourful)

06-12-73 – **'Top Of The Pops' (UK): I Wish It Could Be Christmas Everyday** *(Repeated a couple of weeks later, this is probably Wizzard's most seen TV appearance)*

20-12-73 – **'Top Of The Pops' (UK): Forever** *(Roy Wood's biggest solo hit, the Beach Boys influenced 'Forever' got to No. 8 in the UK charts. The follow-up, 'Goin' Down The Road', peaked at No. 13. This 'Top Of The Pops' performance sees Roy accompanied by Rick Price, with both sans make-up, casually dressed and seated)* – **ROY WOOD**

20-12-73 – **'Top Of The Pops' (UK): I Wish It Could Be Christmas Everyday** *(This is a repeat of the 06-12-73 performance)*

25-12-73 – **'Top Of The Pops' (UK): See My Baby Jive** *(This is Wizzard's contribution to the 1973 Christmas edition of 'Top Of The Pops', a strong candidate for the best TOTP episode ever)*

27-12-73 – **'Top Of The Pops' (UK): Ball Park Incident / Angel Fingers (A Teen Ballad)** *(A special 10th-anniversary edition, Wizzard close the show with these two songs, though the 2nd one is faded over the credits)*

03-01-74 – **'Top Of The Pops' (UK): Forever** *(This is a repeat of the 20-12-73 performance)* – **ROY WOOD**

09-01-74 – 'Lift Off With Ayshea' (UK): Forever – **ROY WOOD**

17-01-74 – 'Top Of The Pops' (UK): Forever – **ROY WOOD**

19-01-74 – **'Russell Harty Plus Pop' (UK): See My Baby Jive** *(This is a repeat of the 05-08-73 performance)*

18-04-74 – 'Top Of The Pops' (UK): Rock 'N' Roll Winter (Loony's Tune)

02-05-74 – **'Top Of The Pops' (UK): Rock 'N' Roll Winter (Loony's Tune)** *('Rock 'N' Roll Winter (Loony's Tune)' was a No. 6 hit in the UK and No. 13 hit in Ireland. Here the band are at their looniest best / worst, depending on your point of view, with rainbow hair, gorilla costumes, and someone with a face drawn on his knee, among other things)*

16-05-74 – 'Top Of The Pops' (UK): Rock 'N' Roll Winter (Loony's Tune)

Spring 1974 – 'Top Pop' (Holland): Rock 'N' Roll Winter (Loony's Tune)

17-09-74 – 'Lift Off With Ayshea' (UK): This Is The Story Of My Love (Baby) *('This Is The Story Of My Love (Baby)' peaked at just No. 34 in the UK charts, while the follow-up, 'You Got Me Running' didn't chart at all)*

22-11-74 – **'The Midnight Special' (USA): Brand New '88 / Ball Park Incident** *(The first of several live performances on US TV, unfortunately, it didn't change their lack of chart success there)* –

12-12-74 – **'Top Of The Pops' (UK): Are You Ready To Rock** *(Basically Bill Haley with bagpipes, 'Are You Ready To Rock' reached No. 8 in both the UK and No. 8 in Ireland, though it was to be their final hit. This first of two 'Top Of The Pops' performances features a blonde-haired Roy Wood with a couple of glove puppets)*

02-01-75 – **'Top Of The Pops' (UK): Are You Ready To Rock** *(Again with glove puppets, though this time Roy has a carrot growing out of the top of his bald head)*

10-01-75 – **'Crackerjack' (UK): Are You Ready To Rock**

11-01-75 – **'Don Kirshner's Rock Concert' (USA): But She'll Be Gone / Angel Fingers (A Teen Ballad) / Forever / Goin' Down The Road / This Is The Story Of My Love / Unknown Instrumental**

16-01-75 – 'Top Of The Pops' (UK): Are You Ready To Rock *(This is a repeat of an earlier performance)*

14-03-75 – **'Top Pop' (Holland): Are You Ready To Rock**

22-05-75 – 'Top Of The Pops' (UK): Oh What A Shame – **ROY WOOD**

05-06-75 – **'Top Of The Pops' (UK): Oh What A Shame** *(Roy's final solo hit at No. 13, this performance sees him seated on top of a sports car while miming the song)* – **ROY WOOD**

30-10-75 – **'Supersonic' (UK): Rattlesnake Roll** *(Despite this TV appearance, 'Rattlesnake Roll' didn't chart, with the same fate befalling the follow-up, Wizzard's final single 'Indiana Rainbow')*

26-12-75 – **'The Midnight Special' (USA): This Is The Story Of My Love (Baby) / Forever**

31-01-76 – **'Supersonic' (UK): Look Thru' The Eyes Of A Fool** *(As with Wizzard's*

'Rattlesnake Roll' a couple of months earlier, 'Look Thru' The Eyes Of A Fool' failed to chart) – **ROY WOOD**

02-04-77 – **'Sight and Sound In Concert' (UK): Life Is Wonderful / Waiting At The Door / French Perfume / California Man / I Should Have Known / Another Wrong Night / Are You Ready To Rock / Sneakin' Round The Corner / Another Wrong Night** (Reprise) – **ROY WOOD'S WIZZO BAND**

11-06-79 – **'Cheggers Plays Pop' (UK): (We're) On The Road Again** – **ROY WOOD'S ROCK BRIGADE**

Roy Wood largely concentrated on live work during the subsequent decades, touring under such names as Roy Wood's Helicopters, The Roy Wood Big Band and Roy Wood's Rock & Roll Band. Former Wizzard member Mike Burney died in 2014, while Wizzard / Electric Light Orchestra member Hugh McDowell died in 2018.

MUD

00-00-68 – 'The Basil Brush Show' (UK) *(Mud made their TV debut on 'The Basil Brush Show' in 1968, and, according to some sources, followed this with an appearance on 'Crackerjack'. Broadcast dates and songs performed are unknown)*

24-06-69 – 'Pop Scotch' (UK)

03-08-70 – 'Opportunity Knocks' (UK)

06-09-70 – **'South Bank Summer' (UK): Vehicle** *(Taped on 28-07-70, this is a competent version of a song originally done by The Ides of March, though the band's dungaree costumes are less impressive)*

04-11-70 – 'Lift Off' (UK)

07-11-70 – **'Ed and Zed!' (UK): Love Grows (Where My Rosemary Goes) / Up Around The Bend / Jumping Jehosephat** *('Jumping Jehosephat' was Mud's 4th single and 4th chart failure)*

00-01-73 – **Promo Video (UK): Crazy** *(The band had to wait over two years before they released another single, but they finally got in the charts with 'Crazy', a No. 12 UK hit. Accompanied by dancers, the band are dressed smart, in a C&A kind of way)*

29-03-73 – 'Top Of The Pops' (UK): Crazy

30-03-73 – 'Crackerjack' (UK): Crazy

13-04-73 – 'Popzien' (Holland): Crazy

27-04-73 – 'Top Of The Pops' (UK): Crazy *(This is a repeat of the 29-03-73 performance)*

Early 1973 – **'Hits A Go Go' (Switzerland): Crazy** *(Wearing similarly outfits to the promo video, the shades-less Les Gray has also added a heavy dollop of mascara)*

13-07-73 – 'Top Of The Pops' (UK): Hypnosis *(A sound-a-like follow-up, 'Hypnosis' got to just No. 16, but after this, they'd have continuous top 10 hits for the next two years)*

27-07-73 – 'Top Of The Pops' (UK): Hypnosis

10-08-73 – 'Top Of The Pops' (UK): Hypnosis

20-08-73 – 'GTK' (Australia)

00-10-73 – **Promo Video (UK): Dyna-Mite** *(The first of nine UK top 10 hits, 'Dyna-Mite' peaked at No. 4.)*

18-10-73 – 'Top Of The Pops' (UK): Dyna-Mite

01-11-73 – 'Top Of The Pops' (UK): Dyna-Mite

21-11-73 – 'Lift Off' (UK): Dyna-Mite

22-11-73 – **'Top Of The Pops' (UK): Dyna-Mite**

00-01-74 – **Promo Video (UK): Tiger Feet** *(With a video featuring the group in yellow drapes, 'Tiger Feet' was Mud's 1st UK No. 1 hit)*

01-01-74 – 'Iltatahti' (Finland)

03-01-74 – 'Top Of The Pops' (UK): Tiger Feet

04-01-74 – 'Crackerjack' (UK): Tiger Feet

14-01-74 – **'Top Pop' (Holland): Dyna-Mite**

17-01-74 – 'Top Of The Pops' (UK): Tiger Feet

24-01-74 – 'Top Of The Pops' (UK): Tiger Feet

31-01-74 – **'Top Of The Pops' (UK): Tiger Feet** *(This first surviving 'Top Of The Pops' performance of 'Tiger Feet' features the band in red)*

07-02-74 – 'Top Of The Pops' (UK): Tiger Feet

14-02-74 – 'Top Of The Pops' (UK): Tiger Feet

Early 1974 – **'Hits A Go Go' (Switzerland): Tiger Feet**

05-03-74 – 'GTK' (Australia)

10-03-74 – 'Spotlight' (Austria): Dyna-Mite / Tiger Feet

11-03-74 – 'Top Pop' (Holland): Tiger Feet

04-04-74 – 'Top Of The Pops' (UK): The Cat Crept In

11-04-74 – **'Top Of The Pops' (UK): The Cat Crept In** *('The Cat Crept In' just missed the UK top spot at No. 2)*

06-05-74 – **'Top Pop' (Holland): The Cat Crept In** *(At least one 'Top Pop' performance of this song survives, however, it is not certain if this is from 06-05-74 or 20-05-74)*

16-05-74 – 'GTK' (Australia)

20-05-74 – 'Top Pop' (Holland): The Cat Crept In *(See 06-05-74 entry)*

00-07-74 – **Promo Video (UK): Rocket** *(With Les Gray doing his best Elvis voice, 'Rocket' got to No. 6 in the UK charts. It wouldn't be the last time he'd impersonate Elvis)*

12-07-74 – 'Iltatahti' (Finland)

29-07-74 – **'Top Pop' (Holland): Rocket**

05-08-74 – 'Lift Off' (UK): Rocket

08-08-74 – **'Top Of The Pops' (UK): Rocket**

31-08-74 – **'Disco' (Germany): The Cat Crept In**

05-09-74 – 'Iltatahti' (Finland)

12-10-74 – **'The Geordie Scene' (UK): Rocket / The End Of The World / Shake, Rattle and Roll / See You Later Alligator** *(As well as their current hit and a couple of rock 'n' roll classics, Mud turn in a great version of Skeeter Davis' 'The End Of The World')*

00-11-74 – **Promo Video (UK): Lonely This Christmas** *(Along with the previous year's seasonal offerings by Slade and Wizzard, Mud's 'Lonely This Christmas' complete the holy trinity of classic Glam era Christmas songs. The song was Mud's 2nd UK No. 1)*

07-11-74 – **'45' (UK): Shake, Rattle and Roll / Hippy Hippy Shake / See You Later Alligator / Blue Moon**

22-11-74 – **'Top Pop' (Holland): Lonely This Christmas**

05-12-74 – **'Top Of The Pops' (UK): Lonely This Christmas** *(The first of four surviving 'Top Of The Pops' performances for this song, this one sees them all wearing white suits with red trim while performing the song in a somewhat serious fashion)*

19-12-74 – 'Top Of The Pops' (UK): Lonely This Christmas

25-12-74 – **'Top Of The Pops' (UK): Lonely This Christmas** *(This time they all wear different clothes from each other while Les Gray plays the piano)*

25-12-74 – '45' (UK): Lonely This Christmas

27-12-74 – **'Top Of The Pops' (UK): Tiger Feet** *(For this performance of 'Tiger Feet' the band are in pink and are accompanied by several roadies for the dance routine)*

31-12-74 – 'Spotlight' (Austria): Dyna-Mite *(This is a repeat of the 10-03-74 performance)*

02-01-75 – **'Top Of The Pops' (UK): Lonely This Christmas** *(Although wearing the same outfits as the 05-12-74 performance, this time they play it for laughs by featuring a ventriloquist's dummy for the spoken part)*

09-01-75 – 'Top Of The Pops' (UK): Lonely This Christmas

13-02-75 – 'Top Of The Pops' (UK): The Secrets That You Keep

14-02-75 – **'Top Pop' (Holland): The Secrets That You Keep** *(Again featuring Les Gray's best Elvis impersonation, 'The Secrets That You Keep' was a No. 3 UK hit)*

27-02-75 – **'Top Of The Pops' (UK): The Secrets That You Keep**

06-03-75 – 'Rock On With 45' (UK): The Secrets That You Keep

Early 1975 – **'Never Too Young To Rock' movie (UK): The Cat Crept In / Tiger Feet / Dyna-Mite / Rocket / Never Too Young To Rock** [finale, with The Rubettes and The Glitter Band]

Early 1975 – **'Side By Side' movie (UK): Side By Side** [with Hello]

17-04-75 – 'Top Of The Pops' (UK): Oh Boy *(A slowed-down, almost acapella, treatment of the Buddy Holly classic, 'Oh Boy' was Mud's 3rd and final UK No. 1)*

25-04-75 – 'Top Pop' (Holland): Oh Boy

01-05-75 – 'Top Of The Pops' (UK): Oh Boy

08-05-75 – 'Top Of The Pops' (UK): Oh Boy

19-06-75 – **'Top Of The Pops' (UK): Moonshine Sally** *('Moonshine Sally' was a UK No. 10)*

27-06-75 – 'Top Pop' (Holland): Moonshine Sally

03-07-75 – 'Top Of The Pops' (UK): Moonshine Sally

02-08-75 – **'Disco' (Germany): Oh Boy**

15-08-75 – 'Top Pop' (Holland): One Night *('One Night' stalled at No. 32)*

00-09-75 – **Promo Video (UK): L-L-Lucy** *(Back to the top 10, 'L-L-Lucy' peaked at No. 10 in the UK charts)*

18-09-75 – 'Top Of The Pops' (UK): L-L-Lucy

26-09-75 – 'Top Pop' (Holland): L-L-Lucy

02-10-75 – 'Top Of The Pops' (UK): L-L-Lucy

02-10-75 – **'Supersonic' (UK): L-L-Lucy** *(The first of two performances of 'L-L-Lucy' on the show, this one features the band wearing yellow shirts while miming to the song)*

14-10-75 – **'Look Alive' (UK): L-L-Lucy**

16-10-75 – 'Top Of The Pops' (UK): L-L-Lucy

30-10-75 – **'Supersonic' (UK): L-L-Lucy** *(This time the band wear blue shirts and play live)*

13-11-75 – 'Supersonic' (UK): Show Me You're A Woman

17-11-75 – **'Musikladen' (Germany): L-L-Lucy**

27-11-75 – 'Top Of The Pops' (UK): Show Me You're A Woman

27-11-75 – **'Supersonic' (UK): Show Me You're A Woman** *('Show Me You're A Woman' was a No. 8 UK hit)*

05-12-75 – **'Top Pop' (Holland): Show Me You're A Woman**

11-12-75 – 'Top Of The Pops' (UK): Show Me You're A Woman

20-12-75 – 'Saturday Scene' (UK): L-L-Lucy *(This is probably a repeat of an earlier performance)*

23-12-75 – **'Top Of The Pops' (UK): Oh Boy**

25-12-75 – **'Top Of The Pops' (UK): Lonely This Christmas** *(The fourth surviving 'Top Of*

The Pops' performance of the song, this sees them all with white shirts plus dark jackets and waistcoats)

25-12-75 – **'Supersonic' (UK): L-L-Lucy** *(This is a repeat of the 02-10-75 performance)*

31-01-76 – **'Disco' (Germany): L-L-Lucy**

06-05-76 – **'Top Of The Pops' (UK): Shake It Down** *('Shake It Down' peaked at No. 12 in the UK charts. The first of three performances of the song on 'Top Of The Pops', this sees the band in green trousers with white jackets while Rob plays a sunburst Fender Stratocaster guitar)*

07-05-76 – 'Top Pop' (Holland): Shake It Down

20-05-76 – **'Top Of The Pops' (UK): Shake It Down** *(This time the band wear blue trousers with their white jackets)*

03-06-76 – **'Top Of The Pops' (UK): Shake It Down** *(This is a repeat of the 20-05-76 performance)*

17-06-76 – **'Top Of The Pops' (UK): Shake It Down** *(Wearing the same clothes as on 06-05-76, this time Rob plays a blue and white guitar)*

05-10-76 – **'Top Pop' (Holland): Nite On The Tiles**

11-10-76 – **'Supersonic' (UK): Nite On The Tiles / Dyna-Mite** *(Hot, live versions, with 'Dyna-Mite' being a particularly explosive performance. 'A Nite On The Tiles', one of Mud's best rockers, didn't chart)*

16-10-76 – **'The Basil Brush Show' (UK): Nite On The Tiles**

06-11-76 – 'Multi-Coloured Swap Shop' (UK): Lean On Me / It Don't Mean A Thing

18-11-76 – 'Top Of The Pops' (UK): Lean On Me

22-11-76 – **'Supersonic' (UK): Beating Around The Bush / Lean On Me** *(Mud's cover of Bill Withers' 'Lean On Me' was their final hit, reaching No. 7 in the UK charts)*

02-12-76 – 'Top Of The Pops' (UK): Lean On Me

06-12-76 – 'Plattenkuche' (Germany): Nite On The Tiles

16-12-76 – **'Top Of The Pops' (UK): Lean On Me**

27-12-76 – 'Swap Of The Pops' (UK): Lean On Me *(This is a repeat from the 06-11-76 edition of 'Multi-Coloured Swap Shop')*

29-12-76 – 'Iltatähti' (Finland)

08-01-77 – **'Supersonic' (UK): Lean On Me** *(This is a repeat of the 22-11-76 performance)*

Early 1977 – **'Top Pop' (Holland): Lean On Me**

Early 1977 – **'Szene '77' (Germany): Lean On Me / It Don't Mean A Thing**

00-02-77 – **Promo Video (UK): A Groovy Kind Of Love** *(Les Gray's 1st solo single, 'A Groovy Kind Of Love' was a UK No. 32 hit. He released two follow-ups, but they didn't chart)* – **LES GRAY**

17-02-77 – **'Top Of The Pops' (UK): A Groovy Kind Of Love** – **LES GRAY**

19-03-77 – **'Supersonic' (UK): A Groovy Kind Of Love** – **LES GRAY**

25-04-77 – 'The Little and Large Telly Show' (UK): Slow Talking Boy

03-05-77 – **'Top Pop' (Holland): Slow Talking Boy** *(Mud's final seven singles were all chart flops. 'Slow Talking Boy' was the first of these)*

11-05-77 – **'Get It Together' (UK): Slow Talking Boy**

12-05-77 – **'Top Of The Pops' (UK): Slow Talking Boy**

20-08-77 – 'Pop At The Mill' (UK)

31-08-77 – **'Marc' (UK): Just Try (A Little Tenderness)** *('Just Try (A Little Tenderness)' failed to chart, as did the follow-up, 'Beating Around The Bush'. This performance was repeated on 'The Best of Marc' on 03-09-80)*

30-03-78 – **'Top Of The Pops' (UK): Cut Across Shorty** *(Another single, another 'Top Of The Pops' appearance, and another flop)*

24-04-78 – **'Cheggers Plays Pop' (UK): Cut Across Shorty**

12-06-78 – **'Cheggers Plays Pop' (UK): Drift Away** *('Drift Away' did not chart)*

01-12-78 – **'Crackerjack' (UK): Why Do Fools Fall In Love?** *(Mud's final single to feature*

Les Gray, 'Why Do Fools Fall In Love?' was not a hit)

19-12-78 – **'Get It Together' (UK): Why Do Fools Fall In Love? / Book Of Love** (This was the last time the classic line-up of Les Gray, Rob Davis, Ray Stiles and Dave Mount performed on TV together)

11-06-79 – **'Cheggers Plays Pop' (UK): Drop Everything and Run** (After Les Gray quit for a solo career, the others briefly replaced him with female singer Margo Buchanan, recording just this one single. 'Drop Everything and Run' isn't bad, but it was never going to succeed under Mud's name, and didn't chart)

02-07-79 – **'Oh Boy!' (UK): New Orleans / A Night At Daddy Gee's** (While the rest of Mud were attempting to establish themselves with a new line-up, Les Gray appeared alongside Alvin Stardust, Joe Brown and Shakin' Stevens in this revival of Jack Good's '50s TV show) – **LES GRAY**

09-07-79 – **'Oh Boy!' (UK): Splish Splash / Shout** [with Lulu and Alvin Stardust] – **LES GRAY**

16-07-79 – **'Oh Boy!' (UK): Buzz, Buzz, Buzz / Shake, Rattle and Roll** [with Alvin Stardust, Joe Brown and Don Lang] – **LES GRAY**

23-07-79 – **'Oh Boy!' (UK): Rockin' Robin / Leave My Woman Alone / Teen Angel / Wake Up Little Susie** (Some sources state that this episode was postponed until a later date due to industrial action) – **LES GRAY**

06-08-79 – **'Oh Boy!' (UK): Rock Around The Clock / Stagger Lee** – **LES GRAY**

Following the short-lived line-up featuring Margo Buchanan on vocals, Mud split in late 1979. Les Gray formed Les Gray's Mud, Rod Davis briefly joined Darts before moving into songwriting and production, Ray Stiles joined The Hollies and Dave Mount left the music business. Following Les Gray's death in 2004, the remaining members of Les Gray's Mud became 'Mud II'. Dave Mount died in 2006.

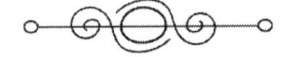

SUZI QUATRO

00-04-73 – **Promo Video (UK): Can The Can** *(Suzi Quatro's 2nd single, 'Can The Can' was a No. 1 in the UK, Germany and Australia, also getting to No. 5 in Ireland and No. 56 in the US)*

11-05-73 – 'Top Of The Pops' (UK): Can The Can

01-06-73 – 'Top Of The Pops' (UK): Can The Can

15-06-73 – 'Top Of The Pops' (UK): Can The Can

00-07-73 – **Promo Video (UK): 48 Crash** *('48 Crash' peaked at No. 3 in the UK, No. 1 in Australia and No. 2 in Germany)*

20-07-73 – 'Top Of The Pops' (UK): 48 Crash

27-07-73 – 'Top Of The Pops' (UK): 48 Crash

10-08-73 – 'Top Of The Pops' (UK): 48 Crash

25-08-73 – **'Disco' (Germany): Can The Can**

00-10-73 – **Promo Video (UK): Daytona Demon** *(Although stalling at No. 14 in the UK charts, 'Daytona Demon' was a German No. 2 and an Australian No. 4)*

08-10-73 – 'Top Pop' (Holland): 48 Crash

31-10-73 – **'Musikladen' (Germany): 48 Crash** *(Performing live, this is early proof of little Suzi's prowess, both as a singer and a musician, and with a great band too)*

01-11-73 – 'Top Of The Pops' (UK): Daytona Demon

08-11-73 – 'Top Of The Pops' (UK): Daytona Demon

24-11-73 – **'Disco' (Germany): 48 Crash**

10-12-73 – 'Top Pop' (Holland): Daytona Demon

25-12-73 – **'Top Of The Pops' (UK): Can The Can**

00-01-74 – **Promo Video (UK): Devil Gate Drive** *('Devil Gate Drive' was a No. 1 in the UK,*

Ireland and Australia, and No. 2 in Germany)

29-01-74 – 'Top Of The Pops' (UK): Devil Gate Drive

02-02-74 – **'Disco' (Germany): Daytona Demon**

07-02-74 – **'Top Of The Pops' (UK): Devil Gate Drive**

12-02-74 – 'GTK' (Australia)

21-02-74 – 'Top Of The Pops' (UK): Devil Gate Drive *(This is a repeat of an earlier performance)*

28-02-74 – 'Top Of The Pops' (UK): Devil Gate Drive *(This is a repeat of an earlier performance)*

18-03-74 – 'Top Pop' (Holland): Devil Gate Drive

14-05-74 – 'GTK' (Australia)

00-06-74 – **Promo Video (UK): Too Big** *('Too Big' got to No. 14 in the UK, No. 6 in Germany, No. 12 in Ireland and No. 13 in Australia)*

07-06-74 – **'The Midnight Special' (USA): All Shook Up / Glycerine Queen** *(A US-only single, 'All Shook Up' was a No. 85 hit)*

05-08-74 – 'Top Pop' (Holland): Too Big

11-08-74 – 'Pop Scene' (Switzerland)

00-10-74 – **Promo Video (UK): The Wild One** *('The Wild One' was a UK No. 7 hit, also reaching No. 2 in Australia, No. 11 in Ireland and No. 15 in Germany)*

11-10-74 – 'ABC In Concert' (USA): 48 Crash / All Shook Up

31-10-74 – 'Top Of The Pops' (UK): The Wild One

01-11-74 – 'Top Pop' (Holland): The Wild One

14-11-74 – 'Top Of The Pops' (UK): The Wild One

21-11-74 – 'GTK' (Australia)

28-11-74 – 'Top Of The Pops' (UK): The Wild One *(This is a repeat of an earlier performance)*

27-12-74 – **'Top Of The Pops' (UK): Devil Gate Drive** *(This is a repeat of the 07-02-74 performance)*

00-01-75 – **Promo Video (UK): Your Mamma Won't Like Me** *('Your Mamma Won't Like Me' peaked at No. 31 in the UK, No. 14 in Australia and No. 27 in Germany)*

30-01-75 – **'Top Of The Pops' (UK): Your Mamma Won't Like Me**

00-04-75 – **Promo Video (UK): I Bit Off More Than I Could Chew** *('I Bit Off More Than I Could Chew' got to just No. 54 in the UK and No. 34 in Germany)*

12-05-75 – **'The Mike Douglas Show' (USA)**

14-08-75 – **'Top Of The Pops' (UK): I May Be Too Young**

04-09-75 – **'Supersonic' (UK): I May Be Too Young** *(Another low-placing hit, 'I May Be Too Young' got to No. 52 in the UK and No. 50 in Australia. It would be almost 18 months before she released another UK single)*

00-10-75 – **Unknown live concert (Japan): I May Be Too Young / Your Mamma Won't Like Me / Jailhouse Rock / Glycerine Queen / Can The Can / Devil Gate Drive** *(Suzie rocks Japan!)*

06-11-75 – **'Supersonic' (UK): I May Be Too Young** *(This is a repeat of the 04-09-75 performance)*

18-09-76 – **'Musikladen' (Germany): Tear Me Apart** *(Although it wouldn't be released in the UK until around five months later, 'Tear Me Apart' got to No. 27 in the UK, No. 17 in Germany and No. 25 in Australia. After being away for the best part of a year, here Suzi returns with a rather unflattering and thankfully short-lived perm)*

04-12-76 – **'Disco' (Germany): Tear Me Apart**

Early 1977 – **Unknown TV show (Germany): Wake Up Little Suzie / 48 Crash / Heartbreak Hotel / Can The Can / Honky Tonk Downstairs / Make Me Smile (Come Up and See Me) / The Wild One / Half As Much As Me / Too Big / Tear Me Apart / Devil Gate Drive** *(Miming in a TV studio, this performance also includes tour bus interviews)*

29-01-77 – **'Hit Kwiss' (Germany): Make Me Smile (Come Up and See Me) / 48 Crash**

00-02-77 – **Promo Video (UK): Tear Me Apart**

12-02-77 – **'Supersonic' (UK): The Wild One / Tear Me Apart**

17-02-77 – **'Top Of The Pops' (UK): Tear Me Apart** *(The first of two 'Top Of The Pops' appearances for 'Tear Me Apart', Suzi wears a light tasselled outfit)*

26-02-77 – 'Multi-Coloured Swap Shop' (UK) *(Includes Swap Show Supergroup with Leo Sayer, Suzi Quatro, John Miles, John Christie, Kenney Jones)*

05-03-77 – 'Saturday Night At The Mill' (UK): Tear Me Apart

17-03-77 – **'Top Of The Pops' (UK): Tear Me Apart** *(This time Suzi is wearing a black leather jacket)*

03-04-77 – **'Countdown' (Australia): Tear Me Apart** *(This was taped in London, UK, for Australian TV broadcast)*

09-05-77 – 'The Little and Large Telly Show' (UK): Tear Me Apart

19-05-77 – **'Top Of The Pops' (UK): Roxy Roller** *(Despite this 'Top Of The Pops' appearance, 'Roxy Roller' didn't chart in the UK, nor anywhere else)*

14-07-77 – **Festival Hall, Melbourne (Australia): The Wild One / The Honky Tonk Downstairs / Heartbreak Hotel / Half As Much As Me / Cat Size / Make Me Smile (Come Up and See Me) / Devil Gate Drive / Tear Me Apart / Keep-A-Knockin'** *(Suzi rocks Australia!)*

08-11-77 – **'Happy Days' (USA): Cat Size / All Shook Up** *(Not really known in the USA until now, Suzy found her biggest fame there via occasional cameos in this retro comedy TV series. This episode was broadcast in the UK on 04-03-78)*

15-11-77 – **'Happy Days' (USA): Heartbreak Hotel / Devil Gate Drive** *(This was broadcast in the UK on 11-03-78)*

24-01-78 – **'Happy Days' (USA): I May Be Too Young** *(This was broadcast in the UK on 13-05-78)*

31-01-78 – **'Happy Days' (USA): Believe** *(This was broadcast in the UK on 20-05-78)*

00-02-78 – **Promo Video (UK): If You Can't Give Me Love** *(A superb country-rock number, 'If You Can't Give Me Love' reached No. 4 in the UK, No. 2 in Ireland, No. 5 in Germany, No. 10 in Australia and No. 45 in the US)*

03-03-78 – **'Crackerjack' (UK): If You Can't Give Me Love**

11-03-78 – 'Our Show' (UK): If You Can't Give Me Love

16-03-78 – **'Top Of The Pops' (UK): If You Can't Give Me Love** *(The first of two 'Top Of The Pops' performances, for this Suzi wears a cream outfit)*

23-03-78 – **'Musikladen' (Germany): If You Can't Give Me Love**

30-03-78 – **'Top Of The Pops' (UK): If You Can't Give Me Love** *(This time Suzi is dressed in red and pink)*

10-04-78 – **'Cheggers Plays Pop' (UK): If You Can't Give Me Love**

13-04-78 – **'Top Of The Pops' (UK): If You Can't Give Me Love** *(This is a repeat of the 30-03-78 performance)*

17-04-78 – **'Disco' (Germany): If You Can't Give Me Love**

21-04-78 – **'Szene' (Germany): If You Can't Give Me Love**

23-05-78 – **'Happy Days' (USA): Johnny B. Goode** *(This was also broadcast in the UK, date unknown)*

00-06-78 – **Promo Video (UK): The Race Is On** *('The Race Is On' only got to No. 43 in the UK, but did get to No. 11 in Ireland, No. 15 in Germany and No. 28 in Australia)*

13-06-78 – **'Musikladen' (Germany): If You Can't Give Me Love** *(This is a repeat of the 23-03-78 performance)*

13-07-78 – **'Top Of The Pops' (UK): The Race Is On**

17-07-78 – 'The Kenny Everett Video Show' (UK): The Race Is On

19-08-78 – **'Revolver' (Germany): The Race Is On / Devil Gate Drive** *(Although 'Revolver' is largely regarded in retrospect as a punk / new wave show, Suzi Quatro goes down a storm here)*

26-09-78 – **'Get It Together' (UK): The Race Is On**

28-09-78 – **'Pop '78' (Germany): The Race Is On**

02-10-78 – **'Disco' (Germany): The Race Is On** *(This was repeated on 23-07-79)*

26-10-78 – **'What's On' (UK): If You Can't Give Me Love**

Late 1978 – **'Ein Kessel Buntes' (Germany): The Race Is On / If You Can't Give Me Love**

00-11-78 – **Promo Video (UK): Stumblin' In** [with Chris Norman] *('Stumblin' In' stalled at No. 41 in the UK, yet got to No. 2 in Germany and Australia, and, more significantly, No. 4 in the US, as well as No. 13 in Ireland. Along with her cameos in 'Happy Days' Suzi Quatro is known in the US for 'Stumblin' In' above any other song)*

27-11-78 – **'Disco' (Germany): Stumblin' In** [with Chris Norman] *(This was repeated on 23-07-79)*

05-12-78 – **'Get It Together' (UK): Stumblin' In** [with Chris Norman]

30-01-79 – **'Happy Days' (USA): Moonlight Love / Do The Fonzie** *(This was also broadcast in the UK, date unknown)*

Early 1979 – **Prague (Czechoslovakia): The Wild One / Don't Change My Luck / Breakdown / Suicide / Evie / Glycerine Queen / What's It Like To Be Loved – Bass Solo / Stumblin' In / If You Can't Give Me Love** *(This stunning live performance features Suzi at her very best, showing total command of the stage. On keyboards at this time was former and future member of The Rubettes Bill Hurd, who duets with Suzi on 'Stumblin' In')*

21-04-79 – **'Rock-Pop' (Germany): Breakdown / Evie** *('Breakdown' is Suzi's excellent cover of a Tom Petty song)*

17-05-79 – **'Musikladen' (Germany): Don't Change My Luck** *(Despite being one of her best songs, 'Don't Change My Luck' was not released in the UK, though it did reach No. 72 in Australia)*

Mid 1979 – **Unknown TV show (East Germany): Evie / Don't Change My Luck / The Race Is On**

08-06-79 – 'Kenny's TV Show' (Sweden)

20-07-79 – **'The Midnight Special' (USA): Stumblin' In / Evie / If You Can't Give Me Love / Breakdown / Non-Citizen**

07-08-79 – 'The Merv Griffin Show' (USA): If You Can't Give Me Love

12-10-79 – **'Crackerjack' (UK): She's In Love With You** *('She's In Love With You' got to No. 11 in the UK, No. 5 in Ireland, No. 8 in Germany, No. 30 in Australia and No. 41 in the US)*

18-10-79 – **'Musikladen' (Germany): She's In Love With You**

18-10-79 – **'Top Of The Pops' (UK): She's In Love With You** *(The first of two 'Top Of The Pops' performances, this features Suzi in a white T-shirt and a black waistcoat)*

00-10-79 – **'Banned BBC Xmas Tape' (UK): He's A Sports PA** *(Clearly taped on the same day as the 18-10-79 'Top Of The Pops' broadcast, here Suzi changes the words of her current hit especially for an in-house BBC compilation tape)*

01-11-79 – **'Top Of The Pops' (UK): She's In Love With You** *(This time Suzi wears a black T-shirt with a white waistcoat)*

05-11-79 – **'Top Pop' (Holland): She's In Love With You**

15-11-79 – **'Top Of The Pops' (UK): She's In Love With You** *(This is a repeat the 01-11-79 performance)*

31-12-79 – **'Disco' (Germany): She's In Love With You**

31-12-79 – **'Will Kenny Everett Make It To 1980 Show?' (UK): Don't Change My Luck**

Suzi Quatro had a few more minor hits in the early '80s (including 'Mama's Boy', 'I've Never Been In Love', 'Rock Hard' and 'Heart Of Stone'), won the 1982 'Rear of The Year' award, branched into acting (in such shows as 'Minder', 'Dempsey and Makepeace' and 'Annie Get Your Gun'), and has hosted her own radio shows on BBC Radio 2. She continues to record and tour.

Peter Checksfield

BARRY BLUE

08-06-73 – 'Popzien' (Holland): Dancing (On A Saturday Night)

03-08-73 – 'Top Of The Pops' (UK): Dancing (On A Saturday Night)

10-08-73 – 'Top Of The Pops' (UK): Dancing (On A Saturday Night)

24-08-73 – 'Top Of The Pops' (UK): Dancing (On A Saturday Night)

20-10-73 – **'Hits A Go Go' (Switzerland): Dancing (On A Saturday Night)** *(Co-written with Lynsey De Paul, 'Dancin' (On A Saturday Night)' got to No. 2 in the UK and Australia, No. 9 in Germany and No. 11 in Holland. None of Barry's three 'Top Of The Pops' performances of the song is known to survive, but this Swiss TV performance, featuring him in a blue satin suit with strategically-placed 'B's on it, more than compensates)*

07-11-73 – 'Lift Off With Ayshea' (UK): Do You Wanna Dance

08-11-73 – **'Top Of The Pops' (UK): Do You Wanna Dance** *(Seen here wearing a white jacket and trousers while backed by a blue satin wearing band, 'Do You Wanna Dance' was a No. 7 UK hit)*

22-11-73 – **'Top Of The Pops' (UK): Do You Wanna Dance** *(This is a repeat of the 08-11-73 performance)*

24-11-73 – 'Disco' (Germany): Dancing (On A Saturday Night) *(Unusually for the almost-intact 'Disco' archives, this song is missing, presumed lost)*

25-11-73 – **'Spotlight' (Austria): Dancing (On A Saturday Night)** *(Barry is dressed in black and white for this Austrian TV show)*

17-12-73 – 'Top Pop' (Holland): Do You Wanna Dance

02-03-74 – **'Disco' (Germany): Do You Wanna Dance** *(German TV promotion for his recent UK hit)*

07-03-74 – 'Top Of The Pops' (UK): School Love *('School Love' reached No. 11 in the UK, No. 3 in Denmark and No. 31 in Australia)*

21-03-74 – 'Top Of The Pops' (UK): School Love *(This is a repeat of the 07-03-74 performance)*

18-04-74 – '45' (UK): School Love

22-07-74 – 'Lift Off With Ayshea' (UK): Miss Hit and Run *('Miss Hit and Run' was a No. 26 UK hit)*

26-08-74 – 'Top Pop' (Holland): Miss Hit and Run

11-10-74 – 'Top Of The Pops' (UK): Hot Shot *('Hot Shot' got to No. 23 in the UK, and was a No. 1 in Sweden)*

15-10-74 – 'Lift Off With Ayshea' (UK): Hot Shot

31-10-74 – 'Top Of The Pops' (UK): Hot Shot *(This is a repeat of the 11-10-74 performance)*

Barry Blue has continued to have major success in the music industry, albeit as a songwriter and producer for artists including Heatwave, Bananarama and Toto Coelo, rather than as a performer.

DAVID ESSEX

11-01-66 – 'The Five O' Clock Club' (UK) *(The most likely song performed here is David Essex's second single, 'Can't Nobody Love You', which was released the previous month)*

23-08-66 – 'The Five O' Clock Club' (UK)

23-09-66 – 'The Five O' Clock Club' (UK)

08-11-68 – 'The Discotheque' (UK)

05-07-69 – 'Set 'Em Up Joe' (UK): That Takes Me Back

07-10-70 – 'Lift Off' (UK): Time Of Our Life [as 'David and Rozaa']

02-04-72 – 'Godspell' (UK) *(It was David Essex's performance in this musical that first brought him fame, though it would be a while longer before he finally had a hit single)*

29-04-73 – **'The John Denver Show' (UK): One More Time / Buddy Holly Medley** [with John Denver] *(Thanks to his 'Godspell' fame, David received an invite to appear on this show, despite the fact that he hadn't released a record in years)*

00-07-73 – **Promo Video (UK): Rock On** *(After 11 other singles over an 8-year period, David Essex finally made it! 'Rock On' is a song that's heard, but not performed, in the movie 'That'll Be The Day', and got to No. 3 in the UK, No. 5 in the US and No. 8 in Australia. It was to remain his only major US hit)*

31-08-73 – **'Top Of The Pops' (UK): Rock On**

02-09-73 – **'Russell Harty Plus' (UK): On and On**

13-09-73 – 'Top Of The Pops' (UK): Rock On

29-10-73 – 'Top Pop' (Holland): Rock On

31-10-73 – **'Musikladen' (Germany): Rock On**

00-11-73 – **Promo Video (UK): Lamplight** *('Lamplight' reached No. 7 in the UK, No. 53 in Australia and No. 71 in the US)*

15-11-73 – **'Top Of The Pops' (UK): Lamplight**

23-11-73 – 'The Midnight Special' (USA): Rock On / Lamplight

06-12-73 – **'Top Of The Pops' (UK): Lamplight** *(This is a repeat of the 15-11-73 performance)*

26-12-73 – **'That's Christmas Sez Les!' (UK): Lamplight**

19-01-74 – 'Russell Harty Plus Pop' (UK): On and On *(This is a repeat of the 02-09-73 performance)*

08-02-74 – **'The Midnight Special' (USA): Rock On / Streetfight**

29-03-74 – **'The Midnight Special' (USA): Rock On / Lamplight / On and On**

30-03-74 – 'American Bandstand' (USA): Rock On / Lamplight

20-04-74 – 'Don Kirshner's Rock Concert' (USA): Rock On

Mid 1974 – **Unknown TV show (France): America** *(Performed here with a live vocal, the disappointing 'America' got to No. 32 in the UK charts)*

Mid 1974 – **'Stardust' movie (UK): Dea Sancta** *('Stardust' was the sequel to 'That'll Be The Day')*

12-07-74 – **'The Midnight Special' (USA): Rock On / Streetfight** *(This is probably a repeat of the 08-02-74 performance)*

19-07-74 – **'Top Pop' (Holland): Stardust**

01-10-74 – 'Lift Off With Ayshea' (UK): Gonna Make You A Star

03-10-74 – **'Twiggs' (UK): America / Don't Stop Me Rockin' / On and On** [with Twiggy] *(This was repeated on 24-04-75)*

04-10-74 – **'Top Of The Pops' (UK): Gonna Make You A Star** *('Gonna Make You A Star' was a UK No. 1 and an Australian No. 4. The first of four surviving 'Top Of The Pops' performances for this song, this first one features mostly full-length shots of him without fancy effects)*

04-10-74 – **'Russell Harty' (UK): There's Something About You Baby**

17-10-74 – 'Top Of The Pops' (UK): Gonna Make You A Star

17-10-74 – '45' (UK): Gonna Make You A Star

31-10-74 – 'Top Of The Pops' (UK): Gonna Make You A Star

14-11-74 – 'Top Of The Pops' (UK): Gonna Make You A Star *(This is a repeat of an earlier performance)*

21-11-74 – **'Top Of The Pops' (UK): Gonna Make You A Star** *(Featuring an ever-changing vivid colour background, this includes a brief but amusing cameo from Paul McCartney and Wings)*

23-11-74 – **'The Sound Of Petula: Off To The Movies' (UK): Stardust / Medley** [with Petula Clark and Michael York] *(From the movie of the same name, 'Stardust' was a No. 7 UK hit)*

28-11-74 – **'Top Of The Pops' (UK): Gonna Make You A Star** *(A repeat of an earlier performance from either 17-10-74 or 31-1-74, this one features lots of close-ups and includes a star-shaped special effect)*

19-12-74 – 'Top Of The Pops' (UK): Stardust

25-12-74 – **'Top Of The Pops' (UK): Gonna Make You A Star** *(Surrounded by Christmas trees, this performance includes a cameo by Tony Blackburn and The Rubettes)*

26-12-74 – **'Cilla!' (UK): Stardust / And I Love Her** [with Cilla Black] **/ A Night To Remember** [with Cilla Black and Gerald Harper]

09-01-75 – 'Top Of The Pops' (UK): Stardust

18-01-75 – **'In Concert' (UK): Rock On / Gonna Make You A Star / Good Ole Rock 'N Roll / I Know / There's Something About You Baby / America / Lamplight / On and On / Stardust / Street Fight / Rock On (Reprise)**

18-02-75 – 'Dinah!' (USA): Rock On

19-02-75 – 'The Merv Griffin Show' (USA)

01-03-75 – **'Disco' (Germany): Gonna Make You A Star**

Early 1975 – **'Top Pop' (Holland): Gonna Make You A Star**

Early 1975 – 'Top Pop' (Holland): Stardust

Look Wot They Dun!

29-03-75 – 'Don Kirshner's Rock Concert' (USA): Stardust / Gonna Make You A Star

Early 1975 – **Unknown TV show (France): Stardust / Good Ol' Rock 'N' Roll**

19-04-75 – 'American Bandstand' (USA): Stardust / Gonna Make You A Star

00-06-75 – **Promo Video (UK): Rolling Stone** *('Rolling Stone' reached No. 5 in the UK charts)*

03-07-75 – 'Top Of The Pops' (UK): Rolling Stone

17-07-75 – 'Top Of The Pops' (UK): Rolling Stone *(This is a repeat of the 03-07-75 performance)*

00-09-75 – **Promo Video (UK): Hold Me Close** *('Hold Me Close' got to No. 1 in the UK and No. 2 in Australia)*

04-09-75 – **'Supersonic' (UK): Won't Get Burned Again / Hold Me Close**

11-09-75 – 'Top Of The Pops' (UK): Hold Me Close

25-09-75 – 'Top Of The Pops' (UK): Hold Me Close *(This is a repeat of the 11-09-75 performance)*

01-10-75 – **'Twiggy' (UK): Hold Me Close / If I Could / Send In The Clowns** [with Twiggy]

02-10-75 – 'Top Of The Pops' (UK): Hold Me Close *(This is a repeat of the 11-09-75 performance)*

02-10-75 – **'Supersonic' (UK): Hold Me Close** *(This is a repeat of the 04-09-75 performance)*

09-10-75 – 'Top Of The Pops' (UK): Hold Me Close

16-10-75 – 'Top Of The Pops' (UK): Hold Me Close

16-10-75 – **'Supersonic' (UK): All The Fun Of The Fair**

26-10-75 – 'Late Night Special: All The Fun Of The Fair' (UK) *(This was repeated on 03-01-76)*

11-11-75 – 'The Merv Griffin Show' (USA)

21-11-75 – **'The Midnight Special' (USA): Rock On / All The Fun Of The Fair / Won't Get

Burned Again

30-11-75 – **'Cher' (USA): The Long and Winding Road** [with Cher] / **Hold Me Close**

04-12-75 – 'Top Of The Pops' (UK): If I Could

04-12-75 – **'Supersonic' (UK): If I Could / Here It Comes Again** *('If I Could' reached No. 13 in the UK charts but just No. 83 in Australia)*

12-12-75 – **'Don Kirshner's Rock Concert' (USA): All The Fun Of The Fair / Rock On / Good Ol' Rock 'N' Roll / Here It Comes Again / All The Fun Of The Fair** (reprise)

18-12-75 – 'Top Of The Pops' (UK): If I Could

25-12-75 – **'Top Of The Pops' (UK): Hold Me Close**

27-12-75 – **'Supersonic Christmas Special' (UK): If I Could / Here It Comes Again** *(This is a repeat of the 04-12-75 performance)*

00-03-76 – **Promo Video (UK): City Lights** *('City Lights' was a UK No. 24 and an Australian No. 4)*

18-03-76 – 'Top Of The Pops' (UK): City Lights

Early 1976 – 'Top Pop' (Holland): City Lights

21-05-76 – 'Szene '76' (Germany)

00-09-76 – **Promo Video (UK): Coming Home** *('Coming Home' got to No. 24 in the UK and No. 57 in Australia, but the follow-up, 'Ooh Love', didn't chart)*

04-10-76 – **'Supersonic' (UK): Rock On / Coming Home**

14-10-76 – **'Top Of The Pops' (UK): Coming Home**

23-10-76 – **'The Basil Brush Show' (UK): Coming Home**

27-01-77 – **'The British Rock and Pop Awards 1976' (UK): Good Loving Gone Bad / Run With The Pack**

01-09-77 – **'Top Of The Pops' (UK): Cool Out Tonight** *('Cool Out Tonight' reached No. 23 in the UK and No. 57 in Australia. The first of two 'Top Of The Pops' performances, this features David in a checked shirt without a jacket)*

06-09-77 – **'David Essex' (UK)** *(Tonight's guests are The Small Faces and Hot Gossip. This was repeated on 17-10-78)*

13-09-77 – **'David Essex' (UK)** *(Tonight's guest is Ronnie Spector. This was repeated on 24-10-78)*

20-09-77 – **'David Essex' (UK)** *(Tonight's guests are The Real Thing. This was repeated on 31-10-78 and 03-01-79)*

27-09-77 – **'David Essex' (UK): Rock On / Yesterday in Old LA / All The Fun Of The Fair / Back Street Crawler / Walkin' In the Sand / There's Something About You Baby** *(Tonight's guest is Denny Laine. This was repeated on 07-11-78)*

29-09-77 – **'Top Of The Pops' (UK): Cool Out Tonight** *(A second 'Top Of The Pops' performance, this time David wears a dark shirt with a jacket)*

04-10-77 – **'David Essex' (UK)** *(Tonight's guest is Twiggy. This was repeated on 14-11-78)*

11-10-77 – **'David Essex' (UK)** *(Tonight's guests are the reunited original London cast of 'Godspell' and Marti Webb. This was repeated on 21-11-78)*

23-03-78 – **'Top Of The Pops' (UK): Stay With Me Baby** *(Despite this TV appearance, 'Stay With Me Baby' stalled at No. 45 in the UK charts)*

01-04-78 – 'Saturday Night At The Mill' (UK)

07-05-78 – **'Blue Jean' (France): Stay With Me Baby**

14-08-78 – **'The Kenny Everett Video Show' (UK): Let It Flow**

00-08-78 – **Promo Video (UK): Oh What A Circus** *(At long last, after 3 years, David Essex had another top 10 UK hit. 'Oh What A Circus' peaked at No. 3 in the UK, also getting to No. 72 in the Australian charts. The follow-up, 'Brave New World', got to No. 55 in the UK)*

23-11-78 – **'Top Of The Pops' (UK): Goodbye First Love** *(Despite appearances on 'Top Of The Pops' and 'Get It Together', 'Goodbye First Love' didn't chart)*

12-12-78 – **'Get It Together' (UK): Goodbye First Love**

00-02-79 – **Promo Video (UK): Imperial Wizard** *(Drummer Kenney Jones guests in this* *video, but all that are seen are his hands! 'Imperial Wizard' was a UK No. 32 hit)*

19-02-79 – **'The Kenny Everett Video Show' (UK): Imperial Wizard / 20 Flights Up**
(Released as a single, '20 Flights Up' did not chart, and neither did the follow-up, 'World')

01-03-79 – **'Top Of The Pops' (UK): Imperial Wizard**

Early 1979 – **'Aplauso' (Spain): Imperial Wizard**

01-04-79 – **'On The Road' (UK)**

01-12-79 – **'The Year Of The Child Concert' (UK): Rock On / World**

David Essex went on to have more than a dozen hits during the '80s and '90s, including 1980's 'Silver Dream Machine' (No. 4), 1982's 'A Winter's Tale' (No. 2) and 1983's 'Tahiti' (No. 8). He has continued to tour regularly, as well as act on TV, most notably as the character Alfie Moon in 'Eastenders'.

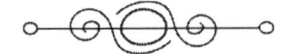

ALVIN STARDUST

31-10-73 – 'Lift Off With Ayshea' (UK): My Coo-Ca-Choo *(The released 45 of 'My Coo-Ca-Choo' was actually sung by singer-songwriter Peter Shelley, but when the song became a hit he didn't want to be the public face of "Alvin Stardust", so the task was handed to the former Shane Fenton, real name Bernard Jewry. However, he couldn't make this first TV appearance featuring the single, so Peter Shelley – the singer on the record – was also "Alvin Stardust" on TV for the one and only time. It was Shane Fenton/Bernard Jewry who came up with the leather-clad image that everyone remembers; instead, Peter's image for this featured him wearing a blue and pink clown's outfit, complete with half of his face painted pink and the other half blue! Sadly, this performance is lost)*

00-11-73 – **Promo Video (UK): My Coo-Ca-Choo** *('My Coo Ca Choo' was a UK No. 2 hit, and this video sees Bernard Jewry already installed as the face of Alvin Stardust)*

15-11-73 – **'Top Of The Pops' (UK): My Coo-Ca-Choo** *(This 1st 'Top Of The Pops' appearance sees Alvin Stardust in his trademark black leather outfit, complete with rings on his gloves, though the effect is spoiled somewhat by the scruffy backing band behind him)*

22-11-73 – **'Top Of The Pops' (UK): My Coo-Ca-Choo** *(This time Alvin dispenses with the on-screen band, quite wisely appearing solo)*

13-12-73 – 'Top Of The Pops' (UK): My Coo-Ca-Choo

17-01-74 – 'Top Of The Pops' (UK): My Coo-Ca-Choo

14-02-74 – **'Top Of The Pops' (UK): Jealous Mind** *(Alvin Stardust's first and only UK chart-topper, this 1st 'Top Of The Pops' performance of 'Jealous Mind' unusually sees him playing the guitar)*

18-02-74 – 'Top Pop' (Holland): My Coo-Ca-Choo

14-02-74 – **'Top Of The Pops' (UK): Jealous Mind** *(This is a repeat of the 14-02-74 performance)*

02-03-74 – **'Disco' (Germany): My Coo-Ca-Choo**

07-03-74 – 'Top Of The Pops' (UK): Jealous Mind

09-03-74 – **'Russell Harty Plus' (UK): Jealous Mind**

00-04-74 – **Promo Video (UK): Red Dress** *(A little weaker than the first two singles, 'Red Dress' was still a UK No. 7 hit)*

11-04-74 – '45' (UK): Red Dress

15-04-74 – 'Spotlight' (Austria): My Coo-Ca-Choo

02-05-74 – **'Top Of The Pops' (UK): Red Dress**

02-05-74 – '45' (UK): Red Dress

11-05-74 – **'Disco' (Germany): Jealous Mind**

13-05-74 – 'Top Pop' (Holland): Jealous Mind

16-05-74 – 'Top Of The Pops' (UK): Red Dress

11-07-74 – **'Van Oekel's Discoheok' (Holland): Red Dress** *(This bizarre TV appearance sees the leather-clad Alvin singing at the bottom of a middle-aged couple's bedroom, with a portly negligee-clad woman sitting on the bed looking at him adoringly and her husband doing his best to ignore him. All very strange)*

13-07-74 – **'Top Pop' (Holland): Red Dress** *(This sees Alvin Stardust against a '50s jukebox backdrop while wearing his leathers and a black and red cape, making him look like a biker vampire)*

20-06-74 – **'Arnaud Leys Melody' (France): Dressed In Black / My Coo-Ca-Choo / You're My Everything / Red Dress / Jealous Mind** *(A superb live vocal performance for this French TV show)*

00-08-74 – **Promo Video (UK): You You You** *(His 4th top 10 UK hit in a row, 'You You You' got to No. 6)*

19-08-74 – 'Lift Off With Ayshea' (UK): You You You

05-09-74 – 'Top Of The Pops' (UK): You You You

12-09-74 – '45' (UK): You You You

13-09-74 – 'Top Of The Pops' (UK): You You You

16-09-74 – 'Top Pop' (Holland): You You You

27-09-74 – **'Top Of The Pops' (UK): You You You** *(This is a repeat of an earlier performance, date unknown, and sees Alvin now in red leather)*

01-10-74 – **'Van Oekel's Discoheok' (Holland): You You You** *(Another appearance on this Dutch TV show, though now Alvin has moved to the lounge and the woman is nowhere to be seen)*

05-10-74 – 'Point Chaud' (France)

21-11-74 – **'Top Of The Pops' (UK): Tell Me Why** *('Tell Me Why' was a No. 16 UK hit)*

23-11-74 – **'Disco' (Germany): You You You**

26-11-74 – 'Lift Off With Ayshea' (UK): Tell Me Why

05-12-74 – 'Top Of The Pops' (UK): Tell Me Why

05-12-74 – '45' (UK): Tell Me Why

19-12-74 – 'Top Of The Pops' (UK): Tell Me Why

Late 1974 – 'Top Pop' (Holland): Tell Me Why

27-12-74 – **'Top Of The Pops' (UK): Jealous Mind** *(Unlike the earlier 'Top Of The Pops' performance of this song, Alvin is guitar-less, so instead, he twirls the microphone stand Gene Vincent-style)*

30-01-75 – **'Top Of The Pops' (UK): Good Love Can Never Die** *(Wearing his black leathers including gloves, this sees Alvin singing to a little silver statue that he's wearing on his finger, while backed by a glammy looking band in red. The Buddy Holly-styled 'Good Love Can Never Die' got to No. 11 in the UK charts)*

06-02-75 – 'Rock On With 45' (UK): Good Love Can Never Die

13-02-75 – 'Top Of The Pops' (UK): Good Love Can Never Die

22-02-75 – **'The Wheeltappers and Shunters Social Club' (UK): Medley: My Coo-Ca-Choo – Jealous Mind / Come On, Come On** *(Around this time Alvin Stardust did some cabaret dates, and this TV appearance probably gives a taste of his shows. Wearing a* *loud George Melly-style checked suit with leather gloves and bare chest, he sounds far better than he looks, and 'Come On, Come On' is a strong rocker)*

28-02-75 – **'Russell Harty Plus' (UK): Good Love Can Never Die**

01-03-75 – **'Supersonic' (UK): Good Love Can Never Die**

26-06-75 – 'Rock On With 45' (UK): Sweet Cheatin' Rita

03-07-75 – 'Top Of The Pops' (UK): Sweet Cheatin' Rita

12-07-75 – 'Jim'll Fix It' (UK): Sweet Cheatin' Rita

04-08-75 – **'Shang-A-Lang' (UK): Sweet Cheatin' Rita** *(Alvin Stardust's final hit of the '70s, 'Sweet Cheatin' Rita' got no higher than No. 37 in the UK charts)*

04-09-75 – **'Supersonic' (UK): Move It / Come On, Come On**

25-09-75 – 'Top Of The Pops' (UK): Move It

25-09-75 – **'Supersonic' (UK): Come On, Come On**

28-10-75 – **'Look Alive' (UK): Move It**

22-11-75 – 'Saturday Scene: British Pop Awards' (UK): Angel From Hamburger Heaven

27-11-75 – **'Supersonic' (UK): Angel From Hamburger Heaven**

12-12-75 – **'Russell Harty' (UK): Angel From Hamburger Heaven**

20-12-75 – 'Saturday Scene' (UK): Angel From Hamburger Heaven *(This is probably a repeat of the 22-11-75 performance)*

25-12-75 – **'Supersonic' (UK): Angel From Hamburger Heaven** *(This is a repeat of the 27-11-75 performance)*

03-03-76 – **'Sez Les' (UK): It's Better To Be Cruel Than Be Kind**

08-04-76 – 'International Pop Proms' (UK): My Coo-Ca-Choo / Stardust

18-05-76 – **'The Arrows' (UK): It's Better To Be Cruel Than Be Kind**

30-07-76 – 'Late Night Stardust' (UK)

13-09-76 – **'Supersonic' (UK): The Word Is Out / Can't Go**

18-11-76 – 'Tienerklanken' (Holland)

02-04-77 – **'Supersonic' (UK): Growing Up / Sweet Little Rock 'n' Roller** [with T-Rex, Dave Edmunds, Ray Davies, Alvin Stardust, Elkie Brooks, Gloria Jones and John Lodge] *(This was taped on 29-03-77)*

20-04-77 – **'Get It Together' (UK): Growing Up**

20-08-77 – 'Pop At The Mill' (UK)

19-11-77 – **'The Basil Brush Show' (UK)**

02-07-79 – **'Oh Boy!' (UK): Mack The Knife / He's Got The Whole World In His Hands**
(Alvin Stardust closed the '70s by appearing regularly on the revived 'Oh Boy!', something that also helped revive his career)

09-07-79 – **'Oh Boy!' (UK): Say Mama / Shout** [with Lulu and Les Gray]

16-07-79 – **'Oh Boy!' (UK): Shakin' All Over / Shake, Rattle and Roll** [with Les Gray, Joe Brown and Don Lang]

23-07-79 – **'Oh Boy!' (UK): Bony Moronie / Move It** [with Joe Brown] *(Some sources state that this episode was postponed until a later date due to industrial action)*

30-07-79 – **'Oh Boy!' (UK): Good Golly Miss Molly / Deep Purple** [with Sharron Skelton] **/ Up The Lazy River**

06-08-79 – **'Oh Boy!' (UK): Rip It Up** [with Joe Brown] **/ Medley: Baby Blue – Be-Bop-A-Lula – Dance In The Street / A Wonderful Time Up There**

25-12-79 – **'Christmas Oh Boy!' (UK): Mary's Boy Child**

In 1981 Alvin Stardust returned to the UK charts with the No. 4 hit 'Pretend', and amassed five more hits up until 1985, including 'I Feel Like Buddy Holly' and 'I Won't Run Away'. He continued as a singer, actor and TV presenter up until his untimely death in 2014.

… Peter Checksfield

COZY POWELL

13-12-73 – 'Top Of The Pops' (UK): Dance With The Devil

03-01-74 – 'Top Of The Pops' (UK): Dance With The Devil

01-04-74 – 'Top Pop' (Holland): Dance With The Devil

03-05-74 – **'The Midnight Special' (USA): Dance With The Devil / Set Me Free**
(Promoted as the Glam-era equivalent of Sandy Nelson, a semi-reluctant Cozy Powell released a string of exciting singles. His 1st and biggest hit, 'Dance With The Devil' got to No. 3 in the UK charts and No. 49 in the US)

06-06-74 – **'Top Of The Pops' (UK): The Man In Black** *(Another instrumental, 'The Man In Black' was a No. 18 UK hit)*

15-08-74 – **'Top Of The Pops' (UK): Na Na Na** *(Finally releasing a vocal single instead of an instrumental, 'Na Na Na' is the equal to anything else on the charts in '74. Featuring vocalist Frank Aiello, the song reached No. 10 in the UK charts. This first of two surviving 'Top Of The Pops' performances features all band members wearing black)*

16-09-74 – 'Top Pop' (Holland): Na Na Na

20-09-74 – **'Top Of The Pops' (UK): Na Na Na** *(Another tremendous performance, this is distinguished from the earlier appearance by Frank Aiello's red shirt)*

21-11-74 – **'The Geordie Scene' (UK): Keep Your Distance / Little Woman / Hold On** *(A live studio performance, notable for not including any of the hits)*

25-01-75 – 'Rock On With 45' (UK)

Cozy Powell went on to tour with a number of high profile acts, including Rainbow, Whitesnake, Black Sabbath and Brian May, before sadly dying in a car crash in 1998.

LEO SAYER

09-10-73 – **'The Old Grey Whistle Test' (UK): The Show Must Go On / The Dancer** *(With his great songs, strong voice and memorable pierrot costume and makeup, Leo Sayer made a great impact at the height of '70s glam rock. 'The Show Must Go On' got to No. 2 in both the UK and Canada and No. 10 in Australia)*

00-11-73 – **Promo Video (UK): The Show Must Go On**

29-11-73 – 'Top Of The Pops' (UK): The Show Must Go On

13-12-73 – 'Top Of The Pops' (UK): The Show Must Go On

03-01-74 – 'Top Of The Pops' (UK): The Show Must Go On

11-01-74 – 'The Midnight Special' (USA): Tomorrow / Everything's Gonna Be Alright / The Show Must Go On

05-02-74 – **'In Concert' (UK): Tomorrow / One Man Band / Giving It All Away / Goodnight Old Friend / The Dancer / The Show Must Go On / Innocent Bystander / Slow Motion** *(This was repeated on 31-07-74. When issued as a single a few months later, 'One Man Band' was a UK No. 6, Australian No. 38 and a US No. 96 hit. Leo's composition 'Giving It All Away' was a hit for Roger Daltrey, who also cut 'One Man Band')*

20-02-74 – **'Musikladen' (Germany): The Show Must Go On**

25-02-74 – **'Top Pop' (Holland): The Show Must Go On**

10-05-74 – 'The Midnight Special' (USA): The Show Must Go On / Goodnight Old Friend

13-06-74 – 'Top Of The Pops' (UK): One Man Band

02-08-74 – **'ABC In Concert' (USA): The Show Must Go On / Innocent Bystander / The Dancer / One Man Band / Giving It All Away** *(This was taped in London for US TV broadcast)*

00-09-74 – **Promo Video (UK): Long Tall Glasses (I Can Dance) (I Can Dance)** *(Now dispensing with the costume and makeup, 'Long Tall Glasses (I Can Dance)' got to No. 4* in the UK and No. 7 in Australia, and was also Leo Sayer's first major US hit at No. 9)

20-09-74 – 'Top Of The Pops' (UK): Long Tall Glasses (I Can Dance)

27-09-74 – **'Top Of The Pops' (UK): Long Tall Glasses (I Can Dance)**

25-10-74 – **'Top Pop' (Holland): Long Tall Glasses (I Can Dance)**

01-11-74 – **'Russell Harty Plus' (UK): Another Time**

18-12-74 – **'Musikladen' (Germany): Long Tall Glasses (I Can Dance)**

31-12-74 – **'The Old Grey Whistle Test: Rock Till Two' (UK): In My Life / Drop Back / The Bells Of St Mary's / Another Time / Tomorrow / The Dancer** (Although largely an end of the year 'highlights' show, Leo Sayer performed again especially for this edition)

31-01-75 – 'Midem' (France) (This was also broadcast in Belgium on 02-08-75)

21-02-75 – **'Top Pop' (Holland): Train** (A non-UK single, 'Train' was issued as a 45 in Holland and some other European countries. This 'Top Pop' appearance features the show's usual highly imaginative sets and production)

07-03-75 – **'The Midnight Special' (USA): The Show Must Go On / Long Tall Glasses (I Can Dance) / It's Your Way / In My Life / The Dancer**

27-03-75 – 'GTK' (Australia)

18-04-75 – **'The Midnight Special' (USA): Long Tall Glasses (I Can Dance) / In My Life**

27-06-75 – **'The Midnight Special' (USA): One Man Band / Train**

00-08-75 – **Promo Video (UK): Moonlighting** ('Moonlighting' got to No. 2 in the UK and No. 13 in Australia)

21-08-75 – 'Top Of The Pops' (UK): Moonlighting

21-08-75 – **'45' (UK): The Last Gig Of Johnny B. Goode / Moonlighting**

04-09-75 – **'Top Of The Pops' (UK): Moonlighting**

19-09-75 – 'Top Pop' (Holland): Moonlighting

20-09-75 – 'Pop '75' (Germany)

29-09-75 – 'Music Aus Studio B' (Germany)

09-10-75 – **'Supersonic' (UK): Moonlighting**

14-10-75 – **'The Old Grey Whistle Test' (UK)**

20-11-75 – **'Supersonic' (UK): Let It Be** *(A fine version of The Beatles classic, 'Let It Be' unfortunately failed to chart)*

11-12-75 – **'Supersonic' (UK): Let It Be** *(This is a repeat of the 20-11-75 performance)*

20-12-75 – **'Saturday Scene' (UK): Moonlighting** *(This is a repeat of an earlier performance, broadcast date unknown)*

25-12-75 – **'Supersonic Christmas Special' (UK): Moonlighting** *(This is a repeat of the 09-10-75 performance)*

26-12-75 – **'The Midnight Special' (USA): Another Time**

28-02-76 – **'Disco' (Germany): Let It Be**

19-05-76 – 'Point Chaud' (France)

00-10-76 – **Promo Video (UK): You Make Me Feel Like Dancing** *('You Make Me Feel Like Dancing' got to No. 2 in the UK and Australia, and No. in the US and Canada)*

16-10-76 – **'Musikladen' (Germany): You Make Me Feel Like Dancing**

28-10-76 – **'Top Of The Pops' (UK): You Make Me Feel Like Dancing**

09-11-76 – **'Top Pop' (Holland): You Make Me Feel Like Dancing**

19-11-76 – **'The Midnight Special' (USA): You Make Me Feel Like Dancing / Reflections / Hold On To My Love**

00-01-77 – **Promo Video (UK): When I Need You** *(Leo Sayer's biggest worldwide hit, 'When I Need You' was a No. 1 in the UK, the US and Canada, and No. 8 in Australia. The video was filmed at a UK seaside resort)*

11-01-77 – **'The Musical Time Machine' (UK): When I Need You**

18-01-77 – **'Top Pop' (Holland): When I Need You**

20-01-77 – **'Top Of The Pops' (UK): When I Need You** *(The first of three surviving 'Top Of The Pops' performances for this song, here Leo wears a yellow jumper)*

21-01-77 – **'The Midnight Special' (USA): You Make Me Feel Like Dancing / When I Need You**

29-01-77 – **'Supersonic' (UK): You Make Me Feel Like Dancing / When I Need You**

29-01-77 – 'Ronnie Corbett's Saturday Special' (UK): When I Need You

29-01-77 – **'Saturday Night Live' (USA): When I Need You / You Make Me Feel Like Dancing**

03-02-77 – **'Top Of The Pops' (UK): When I Need You** *(This is a repeat of the 20-01-77 performance)*

14-02-77 – 'The Captain and Tennille' (USA): You Make Me Feel Like Dancing

17-02-77 – **'Top Of The Pops' (UK): When I Need You** *(This time Leo can be seen in a blue and yellow sports top)*

24-02-77 – **'Top Of The Pops' (UK): When I Need You** *(Leo wears a smart jacket with a red shirt this time)*

25-02-77 – **'The Midnight Special' (USA): You Make Me Feel Like Dancing / When I Need Love / Endless Flight**

26-02-77 – 'Multi-Coloured Swap Shop' (UK) *(Includes Swap Show Supergroup with Leo Sayer, Suzi Quatro, John Miles, John Christie, Kenney Jones)*

03-03-77 – 'Top Of The Pops' (UK): When I Need You

14-03-77 – **'The Captain and Tennille' (USA): You Make Me Feel Like Dancing / When I Need You**

19-03-77 – **'Supersonic' (UK): How Much Love** *('How Much Love' reached No. 10 in the UK, No. 8 in Canada, No. 17 in the US and No. 18 in Australia)*

26-03-77 – **'Supersonic' (UK): How Much Love** *(This is a repeat of the 19-03-77 performance)*

28-03-77 – **'Leo Sings' (UK): One Man Band / You Make Me Feel Like Dancing / Moonlighting / Hold On To My Love / How Much Love / When I Need You / Long Tall Glasses (I Can Dance) / The Show Must Go On** *(This was repeated on 18-10-77)*

03-04-77 – **'Countdown' (Australia): You Make Me Feel Like Dancing / When I Need You** (This was taped in London, UK, for Australian TV broadcast)

00-04-77 – **Promo Video (UK): How Much Love**

12-04-77 – 'Top Pop' (Holland): How Much Love

20-05-77 – **'The Midnight Special' (USA): When I Need You / You Make Me Feel Like Dancing**

29-05-77 – **'The Royal Windsor Big Top Show' (UK): You Make Me Feel Like Dancing / When I Need You / The Show Must Go On**

00-08-77 – **Promo Video (UK): Thunder In My Heart** ('Thunder In My Heart' was a No. 22 UK hit, also getting to No. 8 in Canada, No. 17 in the US and No. 18 in Australia)

03-10-77 – 'Marty Caine' (UK)

08-10-77 – **'Top Pop' (Holland): Thunder In My Heart**

00-11-77 – **Promo Video (UK): There Isn't Anything I Wouldn't Do** ('There Isn't Anything I Wouldn't Do' didn't chart)

04-11-77 – **'The Jack Jones Show' (UK): There's No Business Like Show Business / When I Need You**

24-11-77 – **'Top Of The Pops' (UK): There Isn't Anything I Wouldn't Do**

Late 1977 – 'Top Pop' (Holland): There Isn't Anything I Wouldn't Do

23-12-77 – **'Perry Como's Olde Englishe Christmas' (UK): You Make Me Feel Like Dancing / When I Need You** [with Perry Como] / **Christmas Carol Medley** [with Perry Como and entire cast]

24-12-77 – 'Swap Of The Pops' (UK) (This is a repeat of an earlier 'Multi-Coloured Swap Shop' performance, broadcast date unknown)

25-12-77 – **'Top Of The Pops' (UK): When I Need You** (This is a repeat of the 17-02-77 performance)

27-12-77 – **'The Littlest and Largest Show On Earth' (UK)**

06-02-78 – 'The Merv Griffin Show' (USA)

27-02-78 – 'Dinah!' (USA): Easy To Love / You Make Me Feel Like Dancing

26-03-78 – **'The Muppet Show' (UK): You Make Me Feel Like Dancing / The Show Must Go On / When I Need You** *(This was broadcast in the USA on 07-12-78)*

20-06-78 – **'Paul' (UK): Dancing The Night Away** *(This was repeated on 10-08-79. 'Dancing The Night Away' was another UK chart flop, though it did get as high as No. 15 in Australia)*

28-07-78 – **'The Midnight Special' (USA): How Much Love / Dancing The Night Away / Raining In My Heart / Something Fine (Looking Back Carefully) / The Show Must Go On / It's So Easy** [with Gary Busey and Wolfman Jack]

17-08-78 – 'The Merv Griffin Show' (USA)

07-09-78 – **'Top Of The Pops' (UK): I Can't Stop Loving You (Though I Try)** *(At No. 6, 'I Can't Stop Loving You (Though I Try)' returned Leo Sayer to the upper reaches of the UK chart, and also got to No. 37 in Australia. For this first of two 'Top Of The Pops' performances, Leo wears a short-sleeved Hawaiian shirt)*

18-09-78 – **'Des O'Connor Tonight' (UK): I Can't Stop Loving You (Though I Try)**

21-09-78 – **'Top Of The Pops' (UK): I Can't Stop Loving You (Though I Try)** *(Leo wears a grey jacket this time)*

05-10-78 – **'Top Of The Pops' (UK): I Can't Stop Loving You (Though I Try)** *(This is a repeat of the 07-09-78 performance)*

10-10-78 – 'Soundstage' (USA)

27-10-78 – **'Sounds Like Friday: Leo Sayer'' (UK): The Show Must Go On / Everything I've Got / Train / Dancing The Night Away / Frankie Lee / Giving It All Away** *(Tonight's guests are Frankie Miller and The Boomtown Rats. This was repeated on 04-05-79)*

03-11-78 – **'Sounds Like Friday: Leo Sayer' (UK): Thunder In My Heart / The Last Gig Of Johnny B.Goode / Johnny B. Goode / Why Is Everybody Going Home / Magdalena / Telepath / Moonlighting** *(Tonight's guests are Elkie Brooks and Robert Palmer. This was repeated on 22-05-79)*

10-11-78 – **'Sounds Like Friday: Leo Sayer' (UK): How Much Love / The Dancer / Fool**

For Your Love / **Bedsitterland** / **Long Tall Glasses (I Can Dance)** *(Tonight's guests are Stephen Bishop and The Dudley Moore Trio. This was repeated on 29-05-79)*

17-11-78 – **'Sounds Like Friday: Leo Sayer' (UK): La Booga Rooga** / **One Man Band** / **In My Life** / **I Hear The Laughter** / **You Make Me Feel Like Dancing** / **I Can't Stop Loving You (Though I Try)** *(Tonight's guests are Kate Bush and Randy Edelman. This was repeated on 10-07-79)*

24-11-78 – **'Sounds Like Friday: Leo Sayer' (UK): Endless Flight** / **Reflections** / **Don't Look Away** / **Raining In My Heart** / **Only Dreaming** / **There Isn't Anything** *(Tonight's guests are Marshall-Hain and The Four Tops. This was repeated on 17-07-79)*

30-11-78 – **'Top Of The Pops' (UK): Raining In My Heart** *(Leo's excellent update of Buddy Holly's 'Raining In My Heart' was a UK No. 21 hit, as well as getting to No. 47 in the US and No. 93 in Australia. The first of two 'Top Of The Pops' appearances for the song, on this one Leo wears a chunky cardigan with jeans)*

01-01-79 – **'The Didn't Quite Make It In Time For Christmas Video Show' (UK): Raining In My Heart**

11-01-79 – **'Top Of The Pops' (UK): Raining In My Heart** *(For this second 'Top Of The Pops' performance Leo wears a white jacket)*

15-02-79 – **'Leo Sayer' (UK)** *(Despite its new title, this is really the 6th and final episode of 'Sounds Like Friday: Leo Sayer'. Tonight's guests are Dave Edmunds' Rockpile and Barbara Dickson. This show was originally scheduled for broadcast on 22-12-78 but was postponed due to industrial action. It was repeated on 24-07-79)*

02-04-79 – 'The Tonight Show Starring Johnny Carson' (USA)

09-04-79 – **'Snowtime Special: Disco In The Snow' (UK): I Can't Stop Loving You (But I Try)** / **One Man Band**

07-11-79 – **'Live From Two' (UK): When The Money Runs Out** *(Although a minor Australian hit at No. 90, 'When The Money Runs Out' failed to chart in the UK)*

22-12-79 – **'Christmas Snowtime Special' (UK)** *(This features repeated footage from 'Snowtime Special: Disco In The Snow', 09-04-79)*

Leo Sayer had several further UK hits, including 1980's 'More Than I Can Say' (No. 2), and 2006's 'Thunder In My Heart Again' (a No. 1 collaboration with Meck). Despite financial difficulties, health issues and an ill-advised appearance in 2007's 'Celebrity Big Brother', he continues to record and tour.

Look Wot They Dun!

THE BAY CITY ROLLERS

30-09-71 – 'Top Of The Pops' (UK): Keep On Dancing *(The Bay City Rollers' 1st single, 'Keep On Dancing' got to No. 9 in the UK charts)*

14-10-71 – 'Top Of The Pops' (UK): Keep On Dancing *(This is a repeat of the 30-09-71 performance)*

03-05-72 – 'Lift Off With Ayshea' (UK): We Can Make Music *(The non-charting follow-up to their top 10 hit)*

08-11-72 – 'Lift Off With Ayshea' (UK): Manana *(A flop in the UK, 'Manana' did get to No. 25 in Germany. Reportedly, a performance of 'Manana' was also taped for 'Top Of The Pops', however, it remained un-broadcast due to the record's poor chart showing)*

09-01-74 – 'Lift Off With Ayshea' (UK): Remember (Sha-La-La) *(This was Nobby Clark's final TV appearance with the band. 'Remember (Sha-La-La)' was a UK No. 6 hit, also getting to No. 20 in Ireland, No. 37 in Germany and No. 67 in Australia)*

07-02-74 – **'Top Of The Pops' (UK): Remember (Sha-La-La)** *(Taped on 05-02-74, this was Les McKeown's TV debut with the band, though also still around was guitarist John Devine, miming on piano here. By the next single he'd be gone, to be replaced by Stuart 'Woody' Wood, completing the classic five-piece of Les, Alan, Eric, Woody and Derek)*

21-02-74 – 'Top Of The Pops' (UK): Remember (Sha-La-La) *(This is a repeat of the 07-02-74 performance)*

07-03-74 – 'Top Of The Pops' (UK): Remember (Sha-La-La)

04-04-74 – '45' (UK): Shang-A-Lang

18-04-74 – **'Top Of The Pops' (UK): Shang-A-Lang** *('Shang-A-Lang' got to No. 2 in the UK, No. 16 in Ireland, No. 28 in Australia and No. 41 in Germany. This is the first of two surviving 'Top Of The Pops' performances for this song)*

02-05-74 – **'Top Of The Pops' (UK): Shang-A-Lang**

16-05-74 – 'Top Of The Pops' (UK): Shang-A-Lang

25-05-74 – '45' (UK): Shang-A-Lang

15-07-74 – 'Top Pop' (Holland): Shang-A-Lang

29-07-74 – 'Lift Off With Ayshea' (UK): Shang-A-Lang / Summerlove Sensation

15-08-74 – **'Top Of The Pops' (UK): Summerlove Sensation** *('Summerlove Sensation' reached No. 3 in the UK, as well as No. 5 in Ireland and No. 53 in Australia)*

22-08-74 – 'Top Of The Pops' (UK): Summerlove Sensation

Late 1974 – **'Top Pop' (Holland): Summerlove Sensation**

05-10-74 – **'The Geordie Scene' (UK): Saturday Night / Shang-a-Lang / Be My Baby / Summerlove Sensation** *(Some sources also list 'All Of Me Loves All Of You')*

11-10-74 – 'Top Of The Pops' (UK): All Of Me Loves All Of You

15-10-74 – **'Lift Off With Ayshea' (UK): Raining In Your Heart / Freedom Road / Shang-A-Lang / All Of Me Loves All Of You** *('All Of Me Loves All Of You' was a No. 4 UK hit and No. 5 in Ireland)*

24-10-74 – 'Top Of The Pops' (UK): All Of Me Loves All Of You *(This is a repeat of the 11-10-74 performance)*

12-12-74 – **'45' (UK): Angel, Angel / Shang-A-Lang / Be My Baby**

25-12-74 – 'Rock On With 45' (UK)

01-03-75 – **'Supersonic' (UK): Bye Bye Baby** *(The Bay City Rollers' biggest hit outside the US and Canada, 'Bye Bye Baby' got to No. 1 in the UK, Ireland and Australia, No. 10 in Germany and No. 11 in Holland. By now all the band were in the tartan outfits that they're most remembered for)*

06-03-75 – **'Top Of The Pops' (UK): Bye Bye Baby** *(No less than four different 'Top Of The Pops' performances of 'Bye Bye Baby' still survive)*

13-03-75 – **'Top Of The Pops' (UK): Bye Bye Baby**

14-03-75 – **'Crackerjack' (UK): Bye Bye Baby**

20-03-75 – **'Top Of The Pops' (UK): Bye Bye Baby**

27-03-75 – 'Top Of The Pops' (UK): Bye Bye Baby

01-04-75 – **'Shang-A-Lang' (UK): Bye Bye Baby / It's For You / Summerlove Sensation** *(The 20-part 'Shang-A-Lang' series was taped on the following dates: 04-03-75, 05-03-75, 09-04-75, 10-04-75, 13-05-75 and 14-05-75. Tonight's guests include Lieutenant Pigeon and Big Jim Sullivan)*

03-04-75 – **'Top Of The Pops' (UK): Bye Bye Baby** *(This is a repeat of the 06-03-75 performance)*

08-04-75 – **'Shang-A-Lang' (UK): Keep On Dancing / Rock 'N' Roll Honeymoon / Once Upon A Star** *(Tonight's guests include Twynn and Big Jim Sullivan)*

10-04-75 – **'Top Of The Pops' (UK): Bye Bye Baby**

12-04-75 – **'Once Upon A Star' (UK): Bye Bye Baby / All Of Me Loves All Of You**

17-04-75 – 'Top Of The Pops' (UK): Bye Bye Baby *(This is a repeat of an earlier performance)*

22-04-75 – **'Shang-A-Lang' (UK): Disco Kid / La Belle Gene / All Of Me Loves All Of You** *(Tonight's guests include Mr Big and The Goodies)*

24-04-75 – 'Top Of The Pops' (UK): Bye Bye Baby *(This is a repeat of an earlier performance)*

25-04-75 – **'Top Pop' (Holland): Bye Bye Baby**

29-04-75 – **'Shang-A-Lang' (UK): Bye Bye Baby / My Teenage Heart / Will You Be Mine** *(Tonight's guests include The Rubettes and Big Jim Sullivan)*

30-04-75 – **'Musikladen' (Germany): Bye Bye Baby**

Spring 1975 – **'Musikladen' (Germany): It's For You** *(This is an outtake that wasn't shown at the time)*

06-05-75 – **'Shang-A-Lang' (UK): Angel Baby / Summerlove Sensation / Keep on Dancing** *(Tonight's guests include Cliff Richard and Big Jim Sullivan)*

13-05-75 – **'Shang-A-Lang' (UK): Let's Go / Hey Beautiful Dreamer / Angel, Angel** *(Tonight's guests include Bilbo Baggins, Cliff Richard and Big Jim Sullivan)*

20-05-75 – **'Shang-A-Lang' (UK): My Teenage Heart / Marlena / Shang-A- Lang** *(Tonight's guests include The Shadows [on video], Bruce Welch and Big Jim Sullivan)*

02-06-75 – **'Shang-A-Lang' (UK): Once Upon A Star / Angel Angel / La Belle Jeane / Give A Little Love** *(Tonight's guests include Mac and Katie Kissoon and Slade)*

09-06-75 – **'Shang-A-Lang' (UK): Angel Baby / Rock 'N' Roll Honeymoon / My Teenage Heart** *(Tonight's guests include Gary Glitter and Middle Of The Road)*

16-06-75 – **'Shang-A-Lang' (UK): Let's Go / When Will You Be Mine / Keep On Dancing** *(Tonight's guests include Showaddywaddy, Alan Price and Big Jim Sullivan)*

23-06-75 – **'Shang-A-Lang' (UK): Saturday Night / There Goes My Baby / Summer Love Sensation / Shout / Shang-A-Lang** *(Tonight's guests include The Goodies, Kristine and Gilbert O'Sullivan)*

30-06-75 – **'Shang-A-Lang' (UK): Bye Bye Baby / Shang-A- Lang / Ain't it Strange / Rock 'N' Roll Honeymoon** *(Tonight's guests include Bunny and Tony Orlando and Dawn)*

00-07-75 – **Promo Video (UK): Give A Little Love** *(The Bay City Rollers' 2nd UK No. 1, 'Give A Little Love' also reached No. 1 in Ireland, No. 2 in Australia and No. 11 in Germany)*

07-07-75 – **'Shang-A-Lang' (UK): Disco Kid / Give A Little Love / Remember / All Of Me Loves All Of You** *(Tonight's guests include Lynsey De Paul and Russell Harty)*

10-07-75 – 'Top Of The Pops' (UK): Give A Little Love

14-07-75 – **'Shang-A-Lang' (UK): Let's Go / Angel, Angel / Saturday Night** *(Tonight's guests include Johnny Nash)*

17-07-75 – 'Top Of The Pops' (UK): Give A Little Love *(This is a repeat of the 10-07-75 performance)*

21-07-75 – **'Shang-A-Lang' (UK): Shout / Give A Little Love / When Will You Be Mine / Keep On Dancing** *(Tonight's guests include David Cassidy and Son Of A Gun)*

28-07-75 – **'Shang-A-Lang' (UK): Once Upon A Star / Marlena / Give A Little Love / Disco Kid** *(Tonight's guests include Olivia Newton-John and Robin Nedwell)*

31-07-75 – 'Top Of The Pops' (UK): Give A Little Love *(This is a repeat of the 10-07-75*

performance)

02-08-75 – **'Disco' (Germany): Bye Bye Baby**

04-08-75 – **'Shang-A-Lang' (UK): Give A Little Love / My Teenage Heart / La Belle Jeane / Rock and Roll Honeymoon** *(Tonight's guests include Linda Lewis and Alvin Stardust)*

11-08-75 – **'Shang-A-Lang' (UK): Angel Baby / Hey Beautiful Dreamer / Give A Little Love** *(Tonight's guests include Sparks [on video] and T. Rex [on video])*

18-08-75 – **'Shang-A-Lang' (UK): I Only Wanna Be With You / Give It To Me / Saturday Night** *(Tonight's guests include The Glitter Band)*

19-08-75 – 'Iltatahti' (Finland)

20-08-75 – **'Musikladen' (Germany): Give A Little Love**

25-08-75 – **'Shang-A-Lang' (UK): Keep On Dancing / Just A Little Love / Shang-A-Lang / Boy Meets Girl** [with Lulu] *(Tonight's guests include Paul Curtis, The Drifters and Lulu)*

Summer 1975 – 'Top Pop' (Holland): Give A Little Love

18-09-75 – **'Supersonic' (UK): Rock 'N' Roll Honeymoon / Shout**

20-09-75 – **'Saturday Night Live With Howard Cosell' (USA)** *(See 29-11-75 entry!)*

27-09-75 – 'Saturday Night Live With Howard Cosell' (USA) *(See 29-11-75 entry!)*

04-10-75 – 'Saturday Night Live With Howard Cosell' (USA) *(Unlike the earlier performances on this show, this one was actually taped in the USA)*

16-10-75 – **'Supersonic' (UK): Rock 'N' Roll Honeymoon** *(This is a repeat of the 18-09-75 performance)*

04-11-75 – 'G.T.K.' (Australia)

08-11-75 – **'Disco' (Germany): Give A Little Love**

11-11-75 – **'The Musical Time Machine' (UK)**

13-11-75 – 'Supersonic' (UK): Money Honey *(This edition of 'Supersonic' is the only episode missing from the archives)*

17-11-75 – **'Musikladen' (Germany): Give A Little Love**

20-11-75 – 'Top Of The Pops' (UK): Money Honey

20-11-75 – **'Ann-Margret Smith' (USA): La Belle Jeane / Saturday Night** [with Ann-Margret] *('Saturday Night' was The Bay City Rollers' first and only US No. 1, also getting to No. 1 in Canada, No. 2 in Holland, No. 10 in Germany and No. 45 in Australia, though the song was actually a revamp of a flop UK single from 1973. The 'Ann-Margret Smith' TV special was broadcast in the UK on 24-07-76)*

22-11-75 – 'Saturday Scene: British Pop Awards (UK): Money Honey *(Also performed were 'Shout' and 'Bye Bye Baby'; however, these songs were not broadcast)*

29-11-75 – **'And Now….. The Bay City Rollers' (USA): Keep On Dancing / Shang-A-Lang / Remember (Sha-La-La) / Give A Little Love / All Of Me Loves All Of You / Let's Go / Disco Kid / Angel, Angel / My Teenage Heart / La Belle Jeane / Rock 'N' Roll Honeymoon / When Will You Be Mine / Shout / Be My Baby / Summerlove Sensation / Saturday Night** *(Taped in London, UK, for USA broadcast, on 20-09-75, parts of this performance were previously broadcast on 'Saturday Night Live With Howard Cosell' on 20-09-75 and 27-09-75. Note the lack of 'Bye Bye Baby'!)*

04-12-75 – 'Top Of The Pops' (UK): Money Honey *(This is a repeat of the 20-11-75 performance)*

11-12-75 – **'Supersonic' (UK): Money Honey** *('Money Honey' peaked at No. 3 in the UK and Australia, No. 1 in Canada, No. 4 in Ireland, No. 9 in the US and No. 16 in Germany)*

20-12-75 – 'Saturday Scene' (UK): Money Honey *(This is a repeat of the 22-11-75 performance)*

23-12-75 – **'Top Of The Pops' (UK): Give A Little Love** *(This 'performance' is a film of the band visiting children in hospital)*

25-12-75 – **'Top Of The Pops' (UK): Bye Bye Baby** *(This is a repeat of the 13-03-75 performance)*

25-12-75 – **'The Bay City Rollers with Gilbert O'Sullivan' (UK): Let's Go / Don't Stop The Music / Money Honey / Lovely To See You / Medley: The Christmas Song – My Sweet Lord** [with Gilbert O'Sullivan] *(Basically a 'Shang-A-Lang' Christmas special, guests include The Drifters, Elton John [on video], David Cassidy [on video] and*

Showaddywaddy)

25-12-75 – **'Supersonic' (UK): Money Honey** *(This is a repeat of an earlier performance)*

10-01-76 – 'Follies' (Belgium)

17-01-76 – 'Saturday Night Live With Howard Cosell' (USA): Saturday Night / Money Honey

02-02-76 – 'The Mike Douglas Show' (USA)

28-02-76 – **'Disco' (Germany): Money Honey**

05-03-76 – **'Top Pop' (Holland): Saturday Night**

00-04-76 – **Promo Video (UK): Love Me Like I Love You** *('Love Me Like I Love You' got to No. 4 in the UK, No. 7 in Australia, No. 8 in Ireland, No. 15 in Germany and No. 28 in Holland)*

16-04-76 – **'Russell Harty' (UK): Love Me Like I Love You**

23-04-76 – 'The Mike Douglas Show' (USA)

30-04-76 – **'The Midnight Special' (USA): Money Honey / Rock and Roll Love Letter** *(Not a single in the UK, 'Rock and Roll Love Letter' reached No. 6 in Canada, No. 9 in Australia, No. 13 in Germany and No. 28 in the US)*

05-05-76 – 'Young Music Show' (Japan) *(This was repeated on 31-07-76)*

17-05-76 – 'The Merv Griffin Show' (USA): Money Honey / Rock and Roll Love Letter

31-07-76 – **'Roller Coaster' (UK): Rock 'N' Roller / Don't Worry Baby / Money Honey / Dedication / Don't Stop The Music / Maybe I'm A Fool / Are You Cuckoo? / Shanghai'd In Love / Let's Pretend / Saturday Night / Rock and Roll Love Letter / Bye Bye Baby** *(This also includes special guest Twiggy, a replacement for the originally scheduled guest Rod Stewart)*

06-08-76 – **'Top Pop' (Holland): Rock and Roll Love Letter**

00-09-76 – **Promo Video (UK): I Only Wanna Be With You** *(The Bay City Rollers' version of Dusty Springfield's 'I Only Wanna Be With You' got to No. 4 in the UK, No. 2 in Ireland, No. 3 in Canada, No. 8 in Australia, No. 9 in Germany and Holland, and No. 12 in the US.*

By this time Alan Longmuir had quit the band, to be replaced by Ian Mitchell)

09-09-76 – **'Top Of The Pops' (UK):** I Only Wanna Be With You

21-09-76 – 'Dinah!' (USA): Rock 'N' Roller / I Only Wanna Be With You

27-09-76 – 'Dinah!' (USA): Dedication / Pub With No Beer [with entire cast]

05-10-76 – **'The Arrows' (UK):** I Only Wanna Be With You

17-10-76 – **'Cos' (USA):** I Only Wanna Be With You

29-10-76 – **'The Midnight Special' (USA):** I Only Wanna Be With You / Saturday Night / Rock 'N' Roller

12-11-76 – 'The Merv Griffin Show' (USA)

22-11-76 – **'Supersonic' (UK):** Rock and Roller / You're A Woman

22-11-76 – **'The Merv Griffin Show' (USA):** Rock 'N' Roller / Don't Worry Baby

03-12-76 – **'The Midnight Special' (USA):** Saturday Night

05-12-76 – **'Countdown' (Australia):** I Only Wanna Be With You

07-12-76 – **'Tony Orlando and Dawn' (USA):** I Only Wanna Be With You

00-12-76 – 'The Ernie Sigley Show' (Australia)

19-12-76 – **Tokyo (Japan):** Rock 'N' Roller / Rock and Roll Love Letter / Bye Bye Baby / Don't Worry Baby / Too Young To Rock and Roll / Don't Stop The Music / Maybe I'm A Fool To Love You / You're A Woman / Yesterday's Hero / Money Honey / I Only Wanna Be With You / Saturday Night *(By late 1976 Ian Mitchell was gone, to be briefly replaced by Pat McGlynn, who in turn quit. The band then spent much of 1977 and 1978 as a 4-piece)*

21-12-76 – **'The Arrows' (UK):** You're A Woman

08-01-77 – **'Young Music Show' (Japan):** It's A Game / Saturday Night / You're A Woman / Rock and Roll Love Letter / Rebel Rebel / Sweet Virginia / Lost Fever / Dance, Dance, Dance / Money Honey / Don't Let The Music Die

23-01-77 – **'Wonderama' (USA):** Saturday Night

Look Wot They Dun!

01-02-77 – 'The Mike Douglas Show' (USA): Dedication

Late 02-77 – **'The Mike Douglas Show' (USA): Saturday Night / Rock and Roll Love Letter / Let's Pretend / I Only Wanna Be With You / Dedication / Don't Worry Baby / Yesterday's Hero** + possibly other titles *(Taped on Miami Beach, Florida, this was broadcast over three days on 21-02-77, 22-02-77 and 23-02-77. Released as singles, 'Yesterday's Hero' got to No. 13 in Germany, No. 22 in Canada and No. 54 in the US, and 'Dedication' reached No. 60 in the US and No. 69 in Canada)*

05-03-77 – **'Disco' (Germany): Yesterday's Hero**

00-04-77 – **Promo Video (UK): It's A Game** *('It's A Game' got to No. 16 in the UK, No. 4 in Germany, No. 6 in Ireland and No. 9 in Australia)*

25-04-77 – **'Ein Kessel Buntes' (East Germany): Yesterday's Hero / It's A Game / Rock and Roll Love Letter**

30-04-77 – **'Disco' (Germany): It's A Game / Rock and Roll Love Letter**

05-05-77 – **'Top Of The Pops' (UK): It's A Game**

19-05-77 – **'Top Of The Pops' (UK): It's A Game** *(This is a repeat of the 05-05-77 performance)*

21-05-77 – 'Don Kirshner's Rock Concert' (USA)

00-07-77 – **Promo Video (UK): You Made Me Believe In Magic** *(A No. 34 UK hit, 'You Made Me Believe In Magic' also reached No. 5 in Canada, No. 10 in the US, No. 25 in Germany and No. 36 in Australia. Unfortunately it was The Bay City Roller's final UK hit)*

09-07-77 – **'American Bandstand' (USA): Saturday Night / You're A Woman / Dance, Dance, Dance / You Made Me Believe In Magic**

21-07-77 – **'Top Of The Pops' (UK): You Made Me Believe In Magic**

23-07-77 – 'Young Music Show' (Japan)

29-07-77 – **'The Midnight Special' (USA): Saturday Night**

12-08-77 – **'The Midnight Special' (USA): You Made Me Believe in Magic / Yesterday's Hero / It's A Game / Love Fever**

24-08-77 – 'Dinah!' (USA): You Made Me Believe In Magic

31-08-77 – **'Marc' (UK): You Made Me Believe In Magic**

14-09-77 – **'Top Pop' (Holland): Let's Pretend**

24-09-77 – **'Hit Kwiss' (Germany): You Made Me Believe In Magic**

12-11-77 – **'Disco' (Germany): Don't Stop The Music** *('Don't Stop The Music' failed to chart)*

17-11-77 – 'The Merv Griffin Show' (USA)

09-12-77 – **'Szene '77' (Germany): Yesterday's Hero / You Made Me Believe In Magic** *(This was taped on 25-02-77)*

27-12-77 – **'Get It Together' (UK): You Made Me Believe In Magic / Love Fever / It's A Game / La Belle Jeane**

06-01-78 – **'The Midnight Special' (USA): Money Honey / The Way I Feel Tonight / When I Say I Love You (The Pie) / Don't Let the Music Die / Wouldn't You Like It?** *(Another single, 'The Way I Feel Tonight' peaked at No. 23 in Canada, No. 24 in the US and No. 56 in Australia)*

07-02-78 – **'Dinah!' (USA): When I Say I Love You (The Pie) / Don't Stop The Music**

06-05-78 – **'Don Kirshner's Rock Concert' (USA): The Way I Feel Tonight / It's A Game / Rebel Rebel**

24-05-78 – 'Iltatahti' (Finland)

09-09-78 – **'The Krofft Superstar Hour' (USA): Let's Go / Rock and Roll Honeymoon / Too Young To Rock and Roll / Rock 'N Roll Love Letter**

16-09-78 – 'The Krofft Superstar Hour' (USA)

23-09-78 – 'The Krofft Superstar Hour' (USA)

30-09-78 – 'The Krofft Superstar Hour' (USA)

07-10-78 – 'The Krofft Superstar Hour' (USA)

14-10-78 – 'The Krofft Superstar Hour' (USA)

21-10-78 – 'The Krofft Superstar Hour' (USA)

28-10-78 – 'The Krofft Superstar Hour' (USA) *(After this episode, the show was shortened to 30 minutes, and renamed 'The Bay City Rollers Show'. This lasted another 5 episodes, which were broadcast throughout late 1978 and early 1979)*

Late 1978 – **'Live in Japan' (Japan): Rock 'N' Roller / Yesterday's Hero / Rock and Roll Love Letter / Rock and Roll Honeymoon / Bye Bye Baby / Love Brought Me Such A Magical Thing / You Made Me Believe In Magic / Love Fever / Saturday Night / Another Rainy Day In New York City / Back On The Street / Money Honey / I Only Wanna With You / Where Will I Be Now / Wouldn't You Like It / All The World Is Falling Love** *(Released as a single, 'Where Will I Be Now' was a No. 48 hit in Germany. Shortly after this performance Les McKeown quit the band, and they also fired long-time manager Tom Paton)*

10-01-79 – **'The Mike Douglas Show' (USA): Back On The Street / Love Brought Me Such A Magical Thing** *(Now with South African singer/guitarist Duncan Faure, the band continued under the name 'The Rollers', pursuing a more new-wave direction)*

00-05-79 – **Promo Video (UK): Turn On The Radio** *('Turn On The Radio' was not a hit)*

14-05-79 – **'Cheggers Plays Pop' (UK): Turn On The Radio**

17-05-79 – **'Musikladen' (Germany): Turn On The Radio**

18-09-79 – **'The Mike Douglas Show' (USA): Back On The Street / Elevator**

23-11-79 – **'The Merv Griffin Show' (USA): Elevator / Turn On The Radio**

The classic line-up of The Bay City Rollers reunited fully for Japanese tours in 1982 and 1983, and partially reunited several times since then. Alan died in 2018, and Derek has retired from the public eye, but Les, Woody and Eric all still record and perform with their own bands.

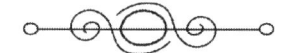

PAPER LACE

04-02-72 – 'Crackerjack' (UK): In The Morning (Morning Of My Life) *(A competent cover of a song originally recorded by The Bee Gees, this was not a hit)*

05-07-72 – 'Eddy Ready Go' (Holland): In The Morning (Morning Of My Life)

22-01-73 – 'Opportunity Knocks' (UK)

29-01-73 – 'Opportunity Knocks' (UK) *(Winners from the previous week's show)*

19-02-73 – 'Opportunity Knocks' (UK) *(This is a Winners show)*

00-01-74 – **Promo Video (UK): Billy Don't Be A Hero** *(Paper Lace's first hit single, 'Billy Don't Be A Hero' got to No. 1 in the UK, also scraping into the US hot 100 at No. 96. Dressed in American Civil War Yankee uniforms, this promo video features interesting negative effects)*

14-02-74 – **'Top Of The Pops' (UK): Billy Don't Be A Hero** *(Again in their Yankee uniforms, this is one of five surviving Paper Lace 'Top Of The Pops' performances from 1974, two of them for this song)*

28-02-74 – 'Top Of The Pops' (UK): Billy Don't Be A Hero

14-03-74 – 'Top Of The Pops' (UK): Billy Don't Be A Hero

17-03-74 – 'Sunday Night At The London Palladium' (UK): Billy Don't Be A Hero

21-03-74 – 'Top Of The Pops' (UK): Billy Don't Be A Hero

28-03-74 – 'Top Of The Pops' (UK): Billy Don't Be A Hero

00-00-74 – **Unknown TV show (Europe?): Billy Don't Be A Hero** *(A bit of a mystery this one: Dressed in normal '70s clothes and without an audience, the band play a terrific live version of the song. It was probably made for an unspecified European TV show)*

25-04-74 – 'Top Of The Pops' (UK): The Night Chicago Died

09-05-74 – **'Top Of The Pops' (UK): The Night Chicago Died** *(Now wearing '20s gangster outfits for their promotional TV appearances, 'The Night Chicago Died' was a No. 3 UK* hit, also getting all the way to No. 1 in the US)

09-05-74 – '45' (UK): The Night Chicago Died

23-05-74 – 'Top Of The Pops' (UK): The Night Chicago Died

30-05-74 – '45' (UK): The Night Chicago Died

17-06-74 – 'Top Pop' (Holland): The Night Chicago Died

05-08-74 – 'Top Pop' (Holland): The Night Chicago Died

12-08-74 – 'Lift Off With Ayshea' (UK): The Black-Eyed Boys

22-08-74 – 'Top Of The Pops' (UK): The Black-Eyed Boys

05-09-74 – **'Top Of The Pops' (UK): The Black-Eyed Boys** *(Seen here with motorbikes and wearing awful white outfits with large eyes on the fronts, 'The Black-Eyed Boys' was a UK No. 11 hit, as well as No. 41 in the US)*

20-09-74 – **'Top Of The Pops' (UK): The Black-Eyed Boys** *(This time the boys wear more straight-forward glam costumes, also dispensing with the motorbikes)*

04-10-74 – 'Top Pop' (Holland): The Black-Eyed Boys

24-11-74 – **'The Royal Variety Performance' (UK): Your Mother Should Know / Bye Bye Blues / Billy Don't Be A Hero** *(1974 really was their year, and a real high-point must've been this show. Taped on 18-11-74 and backed by The Jack Parnell Orchestra, they start with a brief version of The Beatles' 'Your Mother Should Know', continuing with the album track 'Bye Bye Blues' before finishing with their giant hit)*

25-12-74 – **'Top Of The Pops' (UK): Billy Don't Be A Hero** *(Complete with lots of atmospheric dry ice, this is a live version of the band's biggest UK hit)*

07-02-75 – **'Crackerjack' (UK): Hitchin' A Ride '75** *(An unappealing update of the old Vanity Fare hit, this made a poor follow-up to the three classic singles they released in 1974, and didn't chart)*

13-02-75 – 'Rock On With 45' (UK): Hitchin' A Ride '75

26-06-75 – 'Rock On With 45' (UK): So What If I Am

20-08-75 – **'Musikladen' (Germany): So What If I Am / The Night Chicago Died / The**

Black-Eyed Boys *(Performed live here, the stomping 'So What If I Am' was perhaps a little too different from their earlier hits to be a big success, and failed to chart. The versions of the two earlier hits performed here are outtakes that weren't broadcast at the time, and are further proof of how good the band were live)*

Following a 1978 hit single with Nottingham Forest F.C., the band split in 1980, though within a few years a version of Paper Lace was touring again. Today, there are two bands, both featuring ex-members of the classic 1974 line-up; 'Paper Lace' includes guitarists Carlo Paul Santanna and, occasionally, Chris Morris, while 'Phil Wright's Original 1970's Paper Lace' feature singer/drummer Phil Wright and bassist Cliff Fish.

MICK RONSON

00-01-74 – **Promo Video (UK): Only After Dark** *(Released as the far superior B-side to Mick's rather overwrought version of Elvis Presley's 'Love Me Tender', the single failed to chart, as did two more 1974 singles, 'Slaughter On Tenth Avenue' and 'Billy Porter')*

11-04-75 – **'The Old Grey Whistle Test' (UK): Play Don't Worry / Angel No. 9** *(A fine live studio performance, showing off both his vocal and guitar talents)*

More comfortable as a sideman than a star in his own right, Mick Ronson briefly joined Mott The Hoople, then went on to spend several years in Ian Hunter's band, also working with John Mellencamp, Midge Ure, and The Wildhearts, amongst others. He reunited with both Ian Hunter and David Bowie at the 1991 'Freddie Mercury Memorial Concert', and contributed to the latter's 'Black Tie White Noise' album in 1993, the same year he died from liver cancer.

QUEEN

24-07-73 – **'The Old Grey Whistle Test' (UK): Keep Yourself Alive** (This 'video' consisted of dubbed vintage silent movie footage, with NO on-screen appearance by Queen. The band's 1st single, 'Keep Yourself Alive' was not a hit)

00-08-73 – **Promo Video #1 (UK): Keep Yourself Alive** (Taped in London on 09-08-73, this and the similar first video for 'Liar' were rejected by the band in favour of the remakes. These first versions can easily be identified by Freddie's all-white outfit)

00-08-73 – **Promo Video #1 (UK): Liar** (Taped in London on 09-08-73, again this features Freddie in white)

00-10-73 – **Promo Video #2 (UK): Keep Yourself Alive** (For this 2nd video, Freddie wears black trousers and a black and white jacket. This was taped in London on 01-10-73)

00-10-73 – **Promo Video #2 (UK): Liar** (Taped in London on 01-10-73, Freddie wears the same clothes as in the 2nd 'Keep Yourself Alive' video)

21-02-74 – **'Top Of The Pops' (UK): Seven Seas Of Rhye** (Queen's 1st UK hit, 'Seven Seas Of Rhye' peaked at No. 10. For this first of three 'Top Of The Pops' performances, Freddie wears a black shirt and black trousers with a silver belt)

14-03-74 – **'Top Of The Pops' (UK): Seven Seas Of Rhye** (This time Freddie wears a black V-neck shirt and a gauntlet on the right hand)

28-03-74 – **'Top Of The Pops' (UK): Seven Seas Of Rhye** (For the 3rd and final performance of this song on the show, Freddie wears a two-tone shirt and trousers with the gauntlet on the right hand)

31-03-74 – **Rainbow Theatre, London (UK): Son and Daughter / Modern Times Rock 'N' Roll** (The earliest known live Queen footage, unfortunately, these are the only surviving songs from this concert. Taped on the 'Queen II' tour, the most notable thing is that 'Modern Times Rock 'N' Roll' is sung by Freddie, whereas on the record Roger sings it)

11-10-74 – **'Top Of The Pops' (UK): Killer Queen** (The band's 1st worldwide hit, 'Killer Queen' got to No. 2 in the UK and Ireland, No. 3 in Holland, No. 12 in the US and

Germany, No. 15 in Canada and No. 24 in Australia. For this first 'Top Of The Pops' performance, Freddie wears a white shirt and a black sparkled jacket. Unfortunately only part of this still survives)*

24-10-74 – **'Top Of The Pops' (UK): Killer Queen** *(Freddie wears a fur coat on this 2nd 'Killer Queen' performance)*

07-11-74 – **'Top Of The Pops' (UK): Killer Queen** *(This is a repeat of the 11-10-74 performance)*

21-11-74 – 'Top Of The Pops' (UK): Killer Queen *(Unlike with 'Seven Seas Of Rhye', not all performances of 'Killer Queen' survive, with this particular one lost)*

00-11-74 – **Rainbow Theatre, London (UK): Procession / Now I'm Here / Ogre Battle / Father To Son / White Queen (As It Began) / Flick Of The Wrist / In The Lap Of The Gods / Medley: Killer Queen - The March Of The Black Queen - Bring Back That Leroy Brown / Son And Daughter / Keep Yourself Alive / Seven Seas Of Rhye / Stone Cold Crazy / Liar / In The Lap Of The Gods...Revisited / Big Spender / Modern Times Rock 'n' Roll / Jailhouse Rock / God Save The Queen** *(Compiled from two shows taped on 19-11-74 and 20-11-74, this stunning film from the 'Sheer Heart Attack' tour is the earliest full-length Queen performance footage)*

06-12-74 – **'Top Pop' (Holland): Killer Queen** *(Queen's only appearance on this important Dutch TV show)*

25-12-74 – **'45' (UK): Now I'm Here** *(The band's only appearance on '45', this no longer exists)*

27-12-74 – **'Top Of The Pops' (UK): Killer Queen** *(This is a repeat of the 24-10-74 performance)*

16-01-75 – 'Top Of The Pops' (UK): Now I'm Here *(Only one of Queen's two 'Top Of The Pops' performances of 'Now I'm Here' are known to survive)*

30-01-75 – **'Top Of The Pops' (UK): Now I'm Here** *('Now I'm Here' reached No. 11 in the UK, No. 14 in Ireland, No. 25 in Germany and No. 29 in Holland)*

13-02-75 – 'Top Of The Pops' (UK): Now I'm Here *(This is a repeat of an earlier performance)*

01-05-75 – **Nippon Budokan, Tokyo (Japan): Now I'm Here / Killer Queen / In The Lap Of The Gods...Revisited** *(Often almost drowned out by Beatlemania-type screams, this footage from Queen's first Japanese tour shows just how popular they were even in the spring of '75)*

00-11-75 – **Promo Video (UK): Bohemian Rhapsody** *(Although there were plenty of promo videos long before this, notably by The Beatles and The Rolling Stones, it was 'Bohemian Rhapsody' that changed everything. Soon, it would be an essential practice for bands to make promo videos for single releases. With the video taped in London on 10-11-75, 'Bohemian Rhapsody' was a No. 1 in the UK, Australia, Canada, Ireland and Holland, as well as No. 7 in Germany and No. 9 in the US)*

24-12-75 – **'The Old Grey Whistle Test' (UK): Now I'm Here / Ogre Battle / White Queen (As It Began) / Medley: Bohemian Rhapsody - Killer Queen - The March Of The Black Queen - Bohemian Rhapsody** (reprise) **/ Bring Back That Leroy Brown / Brighton Rock / Son And Daughter / Keep Yourself Alive / Liar / In The Lap Of The Gods...Revisited / Medley: Big Spender -Jailhouse Rock** *(The closing date of Queen's UK 'A Night At The Opera' tour, this was broadcast, live, from The Hammersmith Odeon, London)*

00-06-76 – **Promo Video (UK): You're My Best Friend** *(Despite the influence of the ground-breaking 'Bohemian Rhapsody' video, rarely before the '80s did Queen make videos that were more than simple mimed performances. A lesser hit than the previous single, John Deacon's 'You're My Best Friend' still reached No. 7 in the UK, No. 2 in Canada, No. No. 3 in Ireland, No. 6 in Holland, No. 16 in the US and No. 40 in Australia)*

18-09-76 – **Hyde Park, London (UK): A Day At The Races overture / Bohemian Rhapsody** (ending) **/ Ogre Battle / Sweet Lady / White Queen (As It Began) / Flick Of The Wrist / You're My Best Friend / Medley: Bohemian Rhapsody - Killer Queen - The March Of The Black Queen - Bohemian Rhapsody (reprise) / Bring Back That Leroy Brown / Brighton Rock / Son And Daughter / '39 / You Take My Breath Away / The Prophet's Song / Stone Cold Crazy / Keep Yourself Alive / Liar / In The Lap Of The Gods...Revisited** *(The culmination of a short 4-date summer tour, this was right in the middle of recording the 'A Day At The Races' album, from which they previewed 'You Take My Breath Away'. Unfortunately, owing to time constraints, they had to drop a few* scheduled songs from their set-list, including another new song 'Tie Your Mother Down'. Incidentally, this was the last time Freddie sported very long hair, getting it severely trimmed in time for the 'Somebody To Love' video shoot the following month)

00-11-76 – **Promo Video (UK): Somebody To Love** (This was taped in a London studio in October 1976, with additional scenes from Hyde Park, 18-09-76. 'Somebody To Love' was a UK No. 2, also getting to No. 1 in Holland, No. 6 in Ireland, No. 13 in the US, No. 15 in Australia and No. 21 in Germany)

00-03-77 – **Promo Video (USA): Tie Your Mother Down** (With a promo video taped in Miami on 19-02-77, 'Tie Your Mother Down' peaked at No. 31 in the UK, No. 10 in Holland, No. 47 in Australia and No. 49 in the US)

06-06-77 – **Earl's Court, London (UK): Procession / A Day At The Races overture / Tie Your Mother Down / Ogre Battle / White Queen (As It Began) / Somebody To Love / Medley: Killer Queen - Good Old-Fashioned Lover Boy - The Millionaire Waltz - You're My Best Friend - Bring Back That Leroy Brown - Death On Two Legs / Doing All Right / Brighton Rock / '39 / You Take My Breath Away / White Man / The Prophet's Song / Bohemian Rhapsody / Keep Yourself Alive / Stone Cold Crazy / In The Lap Of The Gods...Revisited / Now I'm Here / Liar / Lucille / Jailhouse Rock / Saturday Night's Alright For Fighting / God Save The Queen** (Filmed on the penultimate date of Queen's 'A Day At The Races' UK tour, this is a strong candidate for the greatest ever filmed Queen concert, capturing the group when they were still willing to include such early fare as 'Doing All Right', as well as their most recent material)

16-06-77 – **'Top Of The Pops' (UK): Good Old-Fashioned Lover Boy** (As the band had no video ready for this song, they agreed to appear on TV for the first time in 30 months. Released as the key track on a UK-only EP, 'Good Old-Fashioned Lover Boy' got to No. 17)

30-06-77 – **'Top Of The Pops' (UK): Good Old-Fashioned Lover Boy** (This is a repeat of the 16-06-77 performance)

21-07-77 – **'Top Of The Pops' (UK): Good Old-Fashioned Lover Boy** (This is a repeat of the 16-06-77 performance)

14-09-77 – **Promo Video (UK): I Wanna Testify** (Roger Taylor wasn't the first Queen member to release a single – that distinction goes to Freddie Mercury, who released the one-off 'I Can Hear Music' b/w 'Goin' Back' under the alias Larry Lurex in 1973. However, Roger was the first to have a Promo Video. This was broadcast on 'Marc' on 14-09-77) – **ROGER TAYLOR**

00-10-77 – **Promo Video #1 (UK): We Are The Champions** *(A double A-side, 'We Are The Champions' b/w 'We Will Rock You' was a big worldwide hit, reaching No. 2 in the UK and Holland, No. 3 in Canada and Ireland, No. 4 in the US, No. 8 in Australia and No. 13 in Germany. Taped in London on 07-10-77, this first video, which starts with close-ups of Freddie, was shown several times on 'Top Of The Pops' in 1977)*

00-10-77 – **Promo Video #2 (UK): We Are The Champions** *(Also taped in London on 07-10-77, this inferior alternate video wasn't shown until the 1981 'Greatest Flix' official video collection)*

12-12-77 – **The Summit, Houston (USA): We Will Rock You** (slow/fast) / **Brighton Rock / Somebody To Love / Death On Two Legs / Medley: Killer Queen - Good Old-Fashioned Lover Boy - I'm In Love With My Car - Get Down Make Love - The Millionaire Waltz - You're My Best Friend / Liar / Love Of My Life / '39 / My Melancholy Blues / White Man / The Prophet's Song / Guitar Solo / Now I'm Here / Stone Cold Crazy / Bohemian Rhapsody / Keep Yourself Alive / Tie Your Mother Down / We Will Rock You / We Are The Champions / Sheer Heart Attack / Jailhouse Rock / God Save The Queen** *(Taped towards the end of their US 'News Of The World' tour, this show captures Queen very much at a transitional phase: early favourites like 'Liar' and 'Stone Cold Crazy' are still present and correct, but new anthems 'Tie Your Mother Down', 'We Will Rock You' and 'We Are The Champions' are taking pride of place in their set)*

00-01-78 – **Promo Video (UK): We Will Rock You** *(The other A-side to their recent double-sided single, this video was taped outdoors in the snow in Surrey in January 1978)*

00-02-78 – **Promo Video (UK): Spread Your Wings** *(With a video also taped in the Surrey snow, 'Spread Your Wings' was only a moderate hit, getting to No. 34 in the UK, No. 26 in Holland and No. 29 in Germany)*

03-05-78 – **Olympiahalle, Munich (Germany): Keep Yourself Alive / We Are The Champions** *(Pro footage from 1978 is almost non-existent, so these songs filmed during* the European 'News Of The World' tour are very welcome)

00-10-78 – **Promo Video #1 (UK): Bicycle Race** (Due to the fact that this video featured dozens of naked women riding bikes – and why not – this 1st edit wasn't issued until the 2002 'Greatest Video Hits 1' official DVD. Another double A-side, 'Bicycle Race' b/w 'Fat Bottomed Girls' peaked at No. 11 in the UK, No. 5 in Holland, No. 10 in Ireland, No. 17 in Canada, No. 24 in the US, No. 25 in Australia and No. 27 in Germany)

00-10-78 – **Promo Video #2 (UK/USA): Bicycle Race** (With the bike race scenes cleverly censored, and with additional performance scenes taped in Dallas on 28-10-78, this is the video that was seen by the public in 1978)

00-11-78 – **Promo Video (USA): Fat Bottomed Girls** (Also taped in Dallas on 28-10-78, this is a straight performance video)

00-01-79 – **Promo Video (Belgium): Don't Stop Me Now** (Taped in Brussels in January 1979, this is another straight mimed performance video. 'Don't Stop Me Now' was a UK No. 9 hit, No. 10 in Ireland, No. 16 in Holland, No. 35 in Germany, No. 85 in Australia and No. 86 in the US)

26-01-79 – **Forest National, Brussels (Belgium): Now I'm Here / We Will Rock You** (fast) **/ Fat Bottomed Girls / Brighton Rock / Tie Your Mother Down / Bohemian Rhapsody / Dreamers Ball / Spread Your Wings / We Are The Champions** (In complete contrast to 1978, there is quite a lot of good footage from the 1979 European 'Jazz' tour, though in the case of this show most songs are incomplete)

04-02-79 – **Hallenstadion, Zurich (Switzerland): We Will Rock You / We Are The Champions**

11-02-79 – **Rudi-Sedlmayer-Halle, Munich (Germany): Let Me Entertain You / Now I'm Here / Bohemian Rhapsody** (incomplete) **/ Sheer Heart Attack / We Will Rock You / We Are The Champions / God Save The Queen**

23-02-79 - **Pabellon de Deportes, Madrid (Spain): We Will Rock You** (fast) **/ Let Me Entertain You / Somebody To Love / Sheer Heart Attack / We Will Rock You / We Are The Champions**

28-02-79 – **Pavillon, Paris (France): We Will Rock You** (fast) **/ Let Me Entertain You /**

Somebody To Love / If You Can't Beat Them / Get Down Make Love / Now I'm Here / Bohemian Rhapsody / Tie Your Mother Down / Sheer Heart Attack / We Will Rock You

(Due to a combination of too much work and too much partying, Freddie's voice wasn't always on top form during this period, but the Paris concerts are among the better ones)

01-03-79 – **Pavillon, Paris (France): We Will Rock You** (fast) / **Let Me Entertain You / Fat Bottomed Girls / You're My Best Friend / Now I'm Here / Don't Stop Me Now / If You Can't Beat Them / Spread Your Wings / Dreamer's Ball / Bohemian Rhapsody / Tie Your Mother Down / Sheer Heart Attack / We Are The Champions / God Save The Queen**

25-04-79 – **Nippon Budokan, Tokyo (Japan): We Will Rock You** (fast) / **Let Me Entertain You / Medley: Killer Queen - Bicycle Race - I'm In Love With My Car / Teo Torriatte (Let Us Cling Together) / Keep Yourself Alive / Don't Stop Me Now / Bohemian Rhapsody** (incomplete) / **We Will Rock You / We Are The Champions** *(Wearing an outfit camp enough to make The Village People blush, Freddie is, unfortunately, struggling vocally here, with 'Don't Stop Me Now' sounding particularly ropey. 'Teo Torriatte (Let Us Cling Together)' was performed live for the first time on this tour)*

00-06-79 – **Promo Video (Japan): Love Of My Life** *(This live video was taped in Tokyo on 25-04-79, though the audio soundtrack was taped in Frankfurt, Germany, on 02-02-79. Released as a UK single, the live 1979 version of 'Love Of My Life' got to No. 63)*

00-10-79 – **Promo Video (UK): Crazy Little Thing Called Love** *(Taped in London, on 22-09-79, this features a now short-haired Freddie in leather with a cast of dancing extras, a sign of things to come. 'Crazy Little Thing Called Love' was No. 2 in the UK and Ireland, No. 1 in Australia, Canada, the US and Holland, and No. 13 in Germany)*

26-12-79 – **Hammersmith Odeon, London (UK): Jailhouse Rock** (incomplete) / **We Will Rock You** (fast) / **Let Me Entertain You / Somebody To Love / Death On Two Legs / Medley: Killer Queen - I'm In Love With My Car - Get Down Make Love - You're My Best Friend / Save Me / Now I'm Here / Don't Stop Me Now / Love Of My Life / '39 / Crazy Little Thing Called Love / Bohemian Rhapsody** (incomplete) / **Tie Your Mother Down / Sheer Heart Attack / We Will Rock You / We Are The Champions / God Save The Queen** *(Part of the 'Concerts For The People Of Kampuchea' shows that also featured Paul McCartney and The Who among others, this show captures Queen on top* *form)*

00-01-80 – **Promo Video (UK): Save Me** *(A performance video that was taped in London on 22-12-79, hence its inclusion here, 'Save Me' peaked at No. 11 in the UK, No. 6 in Holland, No. 8 in Ireland, No. 42 in Germany and No. 76 in Australia)*

Queen went on to become an even bigger band during the '80s, particularly after their show-stealing performance at 1985's 'Live Aid' concert, while Freddie Mercury concurrently had a successful solo career. Freddie died in 1991, and John Deacon retired from the public eye by the late '90s, but Brian and Roger have carried on the band name, firstly as 'Queen + Paul Rodgers' from 2004 to 2009, then as 'Queen + Adam Lambert' since 2011.

Peter Checksfield

THE GLITTER BAND

04-04-74 – **'Top Of The Pops' (UK): Angel Face** *(After 18 months being just Gary Glitter's backing band, The Glitter Band emerged as recording artists in their own right, having a string of hits the equal to their leader's. Their first single, 'Angel Face' got to No. 4 in the UK charts. This 1st 'Top Of The Pops' performance features them in all their multi-coloured glittering glory, with many close-up shots)*

11-04-74 – **'Top Of The Pops' (UK): Angel Face** *(This 2nd performance features the band superimposed on scenes of the crowd dancing during the show's closing credits, with no close-ups of band members' faces)*

18-04-74 – **'Top Of The Pops' (UK): Angel Face** *(This is repeat of the 11-04-74 performance minus the titles)*

08-08-74 – **'Top Of The Pops' (UK): Just For You** *('Just for You' was a No. 10 UK hit, and is seen here in a performance that features lots of vivid background effects)*

12-08-74 – 'Lift Off With Ayshea' (UK): Just For You

15-08-74 – **'Top Of The Pops' (UK): Just For You** *(This 2nd performance has no background effects)*

19-09-74 – '45' (UK): Just For You

21-09-74 – 'Kaleidos-Pop' (Switzerland)

24-10-74 – 'Top Of The Pops' (UK): Let's Get Together Again

07-11-74 – **'Top Of The Pops' (UK): Let's Get Together Again** *('Let's Get Together Again' reached No. 8 in the UK charts)*

Late 1974 – **'Hits A Go Go' (Switzerland): Let's Get Together Again / All I Have To Do Is Dream / Rock On**

09-01-75 – **'The Geordie Scene' (UK): Let's Get Together Again / Angel Face / Rock On / Goodbye My Love / Sealed With A Kiss / Gimme Some Lovin'**

16-01-75 – 'Top Of The Pops' (UK): Goodbye My Love

Look Wot They Dun!

30-01-75 – **'Top Of The Pops' (UK): Goodbye My Love** *(The Glitter Band's biggest hit, 'Goodbye My Love' just missed the top spot at No. 2 in the UK charts)*

30-01-75 – 'Rock On With 45' (UK): Goodbye My Love

31-01-75 – **'Crackerjack' (UK): Goodbye My Love**

00-00-75 – **'Never Too Young To Rock' movie (UK): Angel Face / Shout It Out / Let's Get Together Again / Just For You / Never Too Old To Rock** [with Mud and The Rubettes]

03-04-75 – **'Top Of The Pops' (UK): The Tears I Cried** *('The Tears I Cried' got to No. 8 in the UK charts)*

17-04-75 – 'Top Of The Pops' (UK): The Tears I Cried

01-05-75 – 'Top Of The Pops' (UK): The Tears I Cried

15-05-75 – 'Rock On With 45' (UK): The Tears I Cried

07-08-75 – 'Top Of The Pops' (UK): Love In The Sun

18-08-75 – **'Shang-A-Lang' (UK): Love In The Sun** *(The Beach Boys-styled 'Love In The Sun' was a No. 15 UK hit)*

21-08-75 – 'Top Of The Pops' (UK): Love In The Sun

04-09-75 – **'Top Of The Pops' (UK): Love In The Sun**

13-12-75 – **'Supersonic' (UK): Goodbye My Love / Alone Again**

19-02-76 – 'Top Of The Pops' (UK): People Like You and People Like Me

23-02-76 – **'Plattenkuche' (Germany): Painted Lady**

04-03-76 – 'Top Of The Pops' (UK): People Like You and People Like Me

20-03-76 – **'Supersonic' (UK): People Like You and People Like Me** *(The band's final UK hit, 'People Like You and People Like Me' got to No. 5)*

25-03-76 – 'Top Of The Pops' (UK): People Like You and People Like Me

02-04-76 – 'Top Pop' (Holland): People Like You and People Like Me

10-04-76 – **'Goodbye Gary Glitter' (UK): Angel Face / People Like You and People Like Me / Goodbye My Love** *(This was taped at The New London Victoria Theatre, London,* *on 14-03-76, and the whole show is essential viewing throughout)*

03-06-76 – **'Top Of The Pops' (UK): Don't Make Promises (You Can't Keep)**

22-06-76 – **'The Arrows' (UK): Don't Make Promises (You Can't Keep)**

21-08-76 – 'The New Seekers' (UK)

15-11-76 – **'Supersonic' (UK): Goodbye My Love / Lay Your Love On Me / People Like You and People Like Me**

16-11-76 – **'The Arrows' (UK): Lay Your Love On Me**

27-11-76 – **'The Basil Brush Show' (UK): Lay Your Love On Me**

25-12-76 – **'Supersonic' Christmas Special (UK): People Like You and People Like Me** *(This was taped on 19-12-76)*

12-03-77 – **'Supersonic' (UK): Look What You've Been Missing**

13-04-77 – **'Get It Together' (UK): Look What You've Been Missing**

The Glitter Band split in 1977, but there have been several partial reunions since 1987. Gerry Shepherd died in 2003 and Harvey Ellison died in 2017, but today John Springate, Pete Phipps and friends tour as The Glitter Band, while John Rossall tours with his own band, which also included the late Harvey Ellison.

SPARKS

29-07-72 – 'American Bandstand' (USA): Wonder Girl / (No More) Mr Nice Guys *(Fresh from changing their name from Halfnelson to Sparks, this was the group's TV debut. At the time the group was all American – brothers Ron and Russell Mael would recruit UK musicians later – and they both sported long hair, though Ron's trademark 'Hitler' moustache was already intact)*

21-11-72 – **'The Old Grey Whistle Test' (UK): (No More) Mr Nice Guys / Girl From Germany** *(Sparks' UK TV debut, it would be another 18 months before they had a hit)*

07-12-72 – **'Hits A Go Go' (Switzerland): Wonder Girl / Do-Re-Mi** *(Not quite breaking the US hot 100 and failing elsewhere, 'Wonder Girl' was Sparks' 1*st *single)*

12-02-73 – 'Top Pop' (Holland): Wonder Girl

00-04-74 – **Promo Video (UK): This Town Ain't Big Enough For Both Of Us** *(Never making much chart impact in their native USA, the immortal 'This Town Ain't Big Enough For Both Of Us' was Sparks' biggest hit at No. 2 in the UK, No. 4 in Holland, No. 12 in Germany and No. 15 in France. Ahead of their time both musically and visually, this interesting video includes scenes of Russell running on a beach and of both of them together in a lounge. Sparks were scheduled to appear on 'Top Of The Pops' on 25-04-74, but there was a problem with their work permits, so The Rubettes replaced them, making THEIR 'Top Of The Pops' debut, which resulted in a No. 1 hit for the band)*

09-05-74 – 'Top Of The Pops' (UK): This Town Ain't Big Enough For Both Of Us

23-05-74 – 'Top Of The Pops' (UK): This Town Ain't Big Enough For Both Of Us *(This is a repeat of the 09-05-74 performance)*

27-05-74 – 'Top Pop' (Holland): This Town Ain't Big Enough For Both Of Us

02-06-74 – **'Sports En Fete' (France): This Town Ain't Big Enough For Both Of Us**

06-06-74 – **'Top Of The Pops' (UK): This Town Ain't Big Enough For Both Of Us**

20-06-74 – 'Arnaud Leys Melody' (France): This Town Ain't Big Enough For Both Of Us / **Thank God It's Not Christmas**

05-08-74 – 'Top Pop' (Holland): Amateur Hour *('Amateur Hour' was a UK No. 7 hit, also reaching No. 6 in Holland, No. 12 in Germany and No. 19 in Ireland)*

28-09-74 – **'Disco' (Germany): This Town Ain't Big Enough For Both Of Us**

30-09-74 – **'Follies' (Belgium): Thanks But No Thanks**

10-10-74 – **'45' (UK): At Home, At Work, At Play / Thanks But No Thanks / Never Turn Your Back On Mother Earth**

19-10-74 – **'Top A' (France?): This Town Ain't Big Enough For Both Of Us**

24-10-74 – **'Top Of The Pops' (UK): Never Turn Your Back On Mother Earth**

07-11-74 – **'Top Of The Pops' (UK): Never Turn Your Back On Mother Earth** *('Never Turn Your Back On Mother Earth' got to No. 13 in the UK and No. 40 in Germany)*

08-11-74 – **'Top Pop' (Holland): Never Turn Your Back On Mother Earth**

08-11-74 – **'ABC In Concert' (USA): Something For The Girl With Everything / Talent Is An Asset / B.C. / Amateur Hour** *(This was taped in London for US TV broadcast. 'Something For The Girl With Everything' was a No. 17 hit in the UK)*

22-11-74 – **'The Midnight Special' (USA): Talent Is An Asset / This Town Ain't Big Enough For Both Of Us / Amateur Hour / Here In Heaven**

27-12-74 – **'Top Of The Pops' (UK): This Town Ain't Big Enough For Both Of Us** *(This is a repeat of the 06-06-74 performance)*

09-01-75 – 'Top Of The Pops' (UK): Something For The Girl With Everything

23-01-75 – 'Top Of The Pops' (UK): Something For The Girl With Everything *(This is a repeat of the 09-01-75 performance)*

00-02-75 – **'Musikladen Extra' (Germany): This Town Ain't Big Enough For Both Of Us / Amateur Hour / B.C. / Never Turn Your Back On Mother Earth / Something For The Girl With Everything**

05-02-75 – **'Musikladen' (Germany): Something For The Girl With Everything** *(This is the same performance as featured in 'Musikladen Extra')*

08-02-75 – **'Don Kirshner's Rock Concert' (USA): Something For The Girl With**

Everything / Talent Is An Asset / Hasta Mañana Monseuir / Thank God It's Not Christmas / B.C. / Here In Heaven

21-02-75 – **'Top Pop' (Holland): Something For The Girl With Everything**

21-03-75 – 'Popmatine' (Sweden)

12-04-76 – 'Pop Scene' (Switzerland)

00-07-75 – **Promo Video (UK): Get In The Swing** *(Despite several major TV appearances to promote it, 'Get In The Swing' stalled at No. 27 in the UK charts)*

12-07-75 – 'American Bandstand' (USA): This Town Ain't Big Enough For Both Of Us

24-07-75 – **'Top Of The Pops' (UK): Get In The Swing**

31-07-75 – **'Top Of The Pops' (UK): Get In The Swing** *(This is a repeat of the 24-07-75 performance)*

07-08-75 – 'Rock On With 45' (UK): Get In The Swing

12-08-75 – **'Shang-A- Lang' (UK): Get In The Swing** (on film)

11-09-75 – **'Fairfield Halls' Croydon (UK): Get In The Swing / Achoo / Talent Is An Asset / Hospitality On Parade / Looks, Looks, Looks / Amateur Hour**

25-09-75 – 'Top Of The Pops' (UK): Looks, Looks, Looks

25-09-75 – **'Supersonic' (UK): Looks, Looks, Looks** *('Looks, Looks, Looks' got to No. 26 in the UK charts. They wouldn't have another hit until 1979)*

00-10-75 – **'Szene '75' (Germany): Girl From Germany**

09-10-75 – 'Top Of The Pops' (UK): Looks, Looks, Looks

21-10-75 – **'Iltatahti' (Finland): Get In The Swing**

Late 1975 – 'Top Pop' (Holland): Looks, Looks, Looks

23-01-76 – **'Don Kirshner's Rock Concert ' (USA): This Town Ain't Big Enough For The Both Of Us / Without Using Hands / Hospitality On Parade / How Are You Getting Home / In The Future / Looks, Looks, Looks**

27-11-76 – **The Capitol Theatre, Largo (USA): Nothing To Do / I Want To Be Like**

Everybody Else / Something For The Girl With Everything / White Woman / Talent Is An Asset / I Bought The Mississippi River / Everybody's Stupid / B.C. / Equator / This Town Isn't Big Enough For The Both Of Us / Amateur Hour / I Like Girls / Big Boy / Fill 'Er Up

Mid 1977 – **'Rollercoaster' Movie (USA): Fill 'Er Up / Big Boy** *(A cameo in a corny movie, this remains Sparks' most widely seen footage)*

02-10-77 – **'Ces Messieurs Nous Disent' (France): A Big Surprise**

16-10-77 – **'Musique and Music' (France): A Big Surprise**

25-10-77 – **'Plattenkuche' (Germany): A Big Surprise**

Late 1977 – 'Top Pop' (Holland): A Big Surprise

00-03-79 – **Promo Video (UK): The Number One Song In Heaven** *(Returning to the charts with an updated sound courtesy of Giorgio Moroder, 'The Number One Song In Heaven' got to No. 14 in the UK charts)*

10-05-79 – **'Top Of The Pops' (UK): The Number One Song In Heaven** *(The first of two 'Top Of The Pops' performances, this one features Russell in a black and white striped jumper, while Ron had never looked scarier)*

00-05-79 – **Promo Video (UK): La Dolce Vita**

11-05-79 – **'Szene '79' (Germany): La Dolce Vita**

Spring 1979 – 'Top Pop' (Holland): La Dolce Vita

31-05-79 – **'Top Of The Pops' (UK): The Number One Song In Heaven** *(This time Russell wears a white jacket)*

03-06-79 – **'Top Club' (France): La Dolce Vita**

13-06-79 – **'Les Visiteurs Du Mercredi' (France): La Dolce Vita**

00-07-79 – **Promo Video (UK): Beat The Clock** *(Sparks' biggest hit since 1974, 'Beat The Clock' reached No. 10 in the UK charts, with this very modern looking video undoubtedly helping)*

19-07-79 – **'Top Of The Pops' (UK): Beat The Clock** *(For this first 'Top Of The Pops'* *performance Russell wears a grey jacket and red trousers)*

02-08-79 – **'Top Of The Pops' (UK): Beat The Clock** *(Now featuring Russell in a green jacket and yellow trousers, this performance is also notable for lots of special effects incorporating clocks)*

00-10-79 – **Promo Video (UK): Tryouts For The Human Race** *(Their 3rd hit of the year, 'Tryouts For The Human Race' peaked at No. 45 in the UK charts)*

06-10-79 – 'Follies' (Belgium)

01-11-79 – **'Top Of The Pops' (UK): Tryouts For The Human Race**

Sparks have continued recording and touring throughout the subsequent decades, but perhaps their most extraordinary series of events was in London in 2008, when they performed each of their past 20 albums in full over twenty nights, and then premiered their 21st and latest album 'Exotic Creatures of the Deep' on the 21st night.

THE RUBETTES

13-09-70 – **'Hits A Go Go' (Switzerland): I Never See The Sun** *(Baskin and Copperfield were actually Alan Williams and John Richardson, later the lead singer and drummer respectively for The Rubettes)* – **BASKIN and COPPERFIELD**

15-10-70 – **'Top Of The Pops' (UK): I Never See The Sun** *(Despite appearing on the UK's most influential music TV shows, 'I Never See The Rain' did not chart, and neither did their other three singles)* – **BASKIN and COPPERFIELD**

04-11-70 – 'Lift Off' (UK): I Never See The Sun – **BASKIN and COPPERFIELD**

00-01-74 – **Promo Video (UK): Sugar Baby Love** *(The Rubettes' first and biggest hit, 'Sugar Baby Love' was a UK No. 1, as well as a US No. 37)*

25-04-74 – 'Top Of The Pops' (UK): Sugar Baby Love *(The Rubettes were booked as a last minute replacement for the work permit-less Sparks, and this was a major factor in the group's initial success)*

09-05-74 – 'Top Of The Pops' (UK): Sugar Baby Love

16-05-74 – 'Top Of The Pops' (UK): Sugar Baby Love

23-05-74 – 'Top Of The Pops' (UK): Sugar Baby Love *(This is a repeat of an earlier performance)*

30-05-74 – 'Top Of The Pops' (UK): Sugar Baby Love *(This is a repeat of an earlier performance)*

06-06-74 – 'Top Of The Pops' (UK): Sugar Baby Love

01-07-74 – **'Top Pop' (Holland): Sugar Baby Love**

00-07-74 – **Promo Video (UK): Tonight** *('Tonight' got to No. 12 in the UK)*

03-08-74 – **'Disco' (Germany): Sugar Baby Love**

08-08-74 – **'Top Of The Pops' (UK): Tonight**

22-08-74 – 'GTK' (Australia)

Late 1974 – **'Ring Parade' (France): Sugar Baby Love**

Late 1974 – **Unknown TV show (France): Sugar Baby Love**

00-11-74 – **Promo Video (UK): Jukebox Jive** *('Jukebox Jive' was a No. 3 UK hit)*

07-11-74 – **'Top Of The Pops' (UK): Jukebox Jive** *(Only surviving in incomplete form, this first 'Top Of The Pops' performance features the band in pink shirts and black suits)*

21-11-74 – 'Top Of The Pops' (UK): Jukebox Jive

23-11-74 – **'Disco' (Germany): Tonight**

29-11-74 – **'Top Pop' (Holland): Jukebox Jive**

05-12-74 – **'Top Of The Pops' (UK): Jukebox Jive** *(This 2nd performance shows the band wearing their red shirts and white suits)*

27-12-74 – **'Top Of The Pops' (UK): Sugar Baby Love**

31-12-74 – **'Sylvester Tanzparty' (Germany): Sugar Baby Love / Tonight**

03-01-75 – **'Crackerjack' (UK): Juke Box Jive**

00-00-75 – **'Never Too Young To Rock' movie (UK): Tonight / Sugar Baby Love / Juke Box Jive / Never Too Young To Rock** [with Mud and The Glitter Band]

00-02-75 – **Promo Video (UK): I Can Do It** *(Their most exciting single, 'I Can Do It' peaked at No. 7 in the UK charts)*

27-02-75 – 'Top Of The Pops' (UK): I Can Do It

01-03-75 – **'Disco' (Germany): Jukebox Jive**

09-03-75 – **'Spotlight' (Austria): Way Back In The Fifties / Tonight / Jukebox Jive / Sugar Baby Love**

13-03-75 – **'Top Of The Pops' (UK): I Can Do It**

20-03-75 – 'Rock On With 45' (UK): I Can Do It

21-03-75 – **'Crackerjack' (UK): I Can Do It**

27-03-75 – 'Top Of The Pops' (UK): I Can Do It

29-04-75 – **'Shang-A-Lang' (UK)**: I Can Do It

04-05-75 – **'Ring Parade' (France)**: Jukebox Jive

24-05-75 – **'Disco' (Germany)**: I Can Do It

00-00-75 – **'Side By Side' movie (UK)**: I Can Do It

Mid 1975 – **'Rund' (Germany)**: I Can Do It / Sugar Baby Love / Saturday Night

00-06-75 – **Promo Video (UK)**: Foe-Dee-O-Dee *(One of the band's lesser songs, 'Foe-Dee-O-Dee' was a No. 15 UK hit)*

26-06-75 – **'Top Of The Pops' (UK)**: Foe-Dee-O-Dee

10-07-75 – 'Top Of The Pops' (UK): Foe-Dee-O-Dee

11-07-75 – 'Top Pop' (Holland): Foe-Dee-O-Dee

19-08-75 – 'Iltatahti' (Finland)

20-08-75 – **'Musikladen' (Germany)**: Foe-Dee-O-Dee

13-09-75 – **'Disco' (Germany)**: Foe-Dee-O-Dee

14-09-75 – **'Ring Parade' (France)**: Tonight

Late 1975 – **'Ein Kessel Buntes' (Germany)**: I Can Do It / Tonight / Foe-Dee-O-Dee

00-10-75 – **Promo Video (UK)**: Little Darling *(Their UK popularity in decline, 'Little Darling' stalled at No. 30)*

06-11-75 – 'Top Of The Pops' (UK): Little Darling

19-11-75 – 'Top Pop' (Holland): Little Darling

23-11-75 – **'Ring Parade' (France)**: Foe-Dee-O-Dee

25-11-75 – **'Look Alive' (UK)**: Little Darling

30-11-75 – **'Pop '75' (Germany)**: Little Darling

31-12-75 – **'Sylvester Tanzparty' (Germany)**: Jukebox Jive / I Can Do It / Foe-Dee-O-Dee

02-01-76 – **'Crackerjack' (UK)**: Little Darling

03-01-76 – **'Supersonic' (UK)**: Little Darling

28-02-76 – **'Disco' (Germany): Little Darling**

13-03-76 – **'Supersonic' (UK): Little Darling** (This is a repeat of the 03-01-76 performance)

00-04-76 – **Promo Video (UK): You're The Reason Why** (At No. 28 in the UK charts, 'You're The Reason Why' did marginally better than their previous single)

21-04-76 – 'Point Chaud' (France)

22-04-76 – **'Top Of The Pops' (UK): You're The Reason Why**

23-04-76 – 'Top Pop' (Holland): You're The Reason Why

13-07-76 – **'Disco' (Germany): You're The Reason Why**

00-00-76 – **'Chambres D' Agriculture' (France): Sugar Baby Love / Julia**

00-00-76 – **Unknown TV show (France): I Can Do It / Julia**

15-09-76 – 'Point Chaud' (France)

24-09-76 – 'Top Pop' (Holland): Under One Roof

31-10-76 – **'Pop '76' (Germany): Under One Roof** ('Under One Roof' peaked at No. 40 in the UK charts)

08-11-76 – **'Supersonic' (UK): I Can Do It / Under One Roof**

13-12-76 – **'Supersonic' (UK): Miss Goodie Two Shoes / Baby I Know** (When released as a single the following month, the country ballad 'Baby I Know' got to No. 10 in the UK charts. It was The Rubettes' final UK hit)

00-01-77 – **Promo Video (UK): Baby I Know**

03-02-77 – **'Top Of The Pops' (UK): Baby I Know** (With lead vocals by guitarist Tony Thorpe, The Rubettes performed this song three times on 'Top Of The Pops'. For this first performance Tony wears a black shirt and white waistcoat)

17-02-77 – **'Top Of The Pops' (UK): Baby I Know** (This time Tony wears a black shirt with a black waistcoat)

10-03-77 – **'Top Of The Pops' (UK): Baby I Know** (For this third and final performance

Tony is wearing a white shirt with a black waistcoat)

Early 1977 – 'Top Pop' (Holland): Baby I Know

00-03-77 – **Promo Video, 1977 (UK): Ooh La La**

Early 1977 – 'Top Pop' (Holland): Ooh La La

23-07-77 – 'Pop At The Mill' (UK)

17-09-77 – **'Disco' (Germany): Ooh La La**

00-10-77 – **Promo Video (UK): Come On Over**

00-10-77 – **Promo Video (UK): Cherie Amour**

00-01-78 – **'Pop '78' (Germany): Cherie Amour**

00-02-78 – **Promo Video (UK): Sometime In Oldchurch**

05-02-78 – **'Blue Jean' (France): Cherie Amour**

11-03-78 – **'Hit Kwiss' (Germany): Ooh La La**

22-04-78 – **'Hit Kwiss' (Germany): Cherie Amour**

14-05-78 – **'Blue Jean' (France): Little 69**

00-06-78 – **Promo Video (UK): Great Be The Nation**

09-09-78 – 'Top Pop' (Holland): Little 69

Early 1979 – **'Pop '79' (Germany): Stay With Me** *(By this time, guitarist Tony Thorpe had left the band, to be replaced by former The Tremeloes guitarist Bob Benham)*

The Rubettes split in 1980, but most of them reconvened from 1982 to 1999. Since 2000 there have been two, rival, groups, 'The Rubettes featuring Alan Williams' and 'The Rubettes featuring Bill Hurd'.

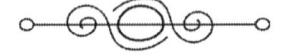

PAUL DA VINCI

22-07-74 – 'Lift Off With Ayshea' (UK): Your Baby Ain't Your Baby Anymore

29-07-74 – **'Top Pop' (Holland): Your Baby Ain't Your Baby Anymore** *(Although it was Paul Da Vinci who sang lead on The Rubettes' debut single 'Sugar Baby Love', he chose not to be in the group that was put together for TV and future recording purposes. Choosing a solo career instead, the UK No. 20 'Your Baby Ain't Your Baby Anymore' was his only hit)*

08-08-74 – **'Top Of The Pops' (UK): Your Baby Ain't Your Baby Anymore** *(Owing to prolonged industrial action, the 08-08-74 edition of 'Top Of The Pops' was the first since 13-06-74, and it was on this episode that Paul Da Vinci made his only solo appearance. Performing live, the song is nothing special, but just listen to that closing high note for proof of what a singer Paul was)*

26-08-74 – 'Top Pop' (Holland): Your Baby Ain't Your Baby Anymore

In 1981, Paul Da Vinci sang most of the voices for the Tight Fit hit 'Back to the Sixties, Part 2', performing on 'Top of The Pops' with the group. Since then he has performed mostly in musicals, though he did, finally, become a member of a version of The Rubettes, singing for Bill Hurd's group from 2000 to 2006.

STEVE HARLEY and COCKNEY REBEL

26-11-73 – 'Top Pop' (Holland): Sebastian *(Billed as just 'Cockney Rebel', 'Sebastian' didn't chart in the UK, though it did get to No. 2 in both Holland and Belgium, as well as No. 30 in Germany)*

10-02-74 – **'The Old Grey Whistle Test' (UK): Hideaway / My Only Vice**

00-03-74 – **Promo Video (UK): Judy Teen** *('Judy Teen' was a No. 5 UK hit, as well as No. 23 in Belgium and No. 26 in Holland)*

01-04-74 – 'Top Pop' (Holland): Judy Teen

06-04-74 – 'Artiesten Helpen UNICEF' (Holland)

23-05-74 – **'Top Of The Pops' (UK): Judy Teen**

30-05-74 – **'Top Of The Pops' (UK): Judy Teen** *(This is a repeat of the 23-05-74 performance)*

03-06-74 – **'Pink Pop Festival' (Holland): Sebastian** *(This live footage is dubbed with the studio recording)*

10-07-74 – **'Top Pop' (Holland): Mr Soft** *('Mr Soft' got to No. 8 in the UK and No. 16 in Ireland)*

15-08-74 – **'Top Of The Pops' (UK): Mr Soft**

22-08-74 – 'Top Of The Pops' (UK): Mr Soft

24-10-74 – **'45' (UK): Bed In The Corner / Big, Big Deal**

00-01-75 – **Promo Video (UK): Make Me Smile (Come Up And See Me)** *(Now with a new line-up and billed as 'Steve Harley and Cockney Rebel', 'Make Me Smile (Come Up and See Me)' got to No. 1 in the UK and Ireland, No. 5 in Holland, No. 7 in Belgium, No. 20 in Germany and No. 96 in the US)*

30-01-75 – 'Top Of The Pops' (UK): Make Me Smile (Come Up And See Me)

13-02-75 – 'Top Of The Pops' (UK): Make Me Smile (Come Up And See Me) *(This is a* repeat of the 30-01-75 performance)

20-02-75 – 'Top Of The Pops' (UK): Make Me Smile (Come Up And See Me) *(This is a repeat of the 30-01-75 performance)*

27-02-75 – **'Top Of The Pops' (UK): Make Me Smile (Come Up And See Me)**

07-03-75 – **'Russell Harty' (UK): Make Me Smile (Come Up And See Me)**

07-03-75 – **'Top Pop' (Holland): Make Me Smile (Come Up And See Me)** *(With Steve's long red coat and matching bowler hat, this is the most visual of the various TV performances of his biggest hit)*

14-04-75 – **Hammersmith Odeon, London (UK): Mad Mad Moonlight / Panorama / Bed In The Corner / Sling It / Mr Raffles (Man, It Was Mean) / Back To The Farm / Sebastian / Judy Teen / Best Years Of Our Lives / Make Me Smile (Come Up and See Me) / Tumbling Down / Mr Soft** *(An edited version of this impassioned performance was issued as 'Between The Lines' and shown as a support feature at various cinemas. 'Mr Raffles (Man, It Was Mean)' was issued as a single, becoming a No. 13 UK hit)*

24-04-75 – 'Rock On With 45' (UK): Make Me Smile (Come Up And See Me)

05-06-75 – 'Top Of The Pops' (UK): Mr Raffles (Man, It Was Mean)

19-06-75 – 'Top Of The Pops' (UK): Mr Raffles (Man, It Was Mean)

12-07-75 – 'Un Jour Futur' (France)

00-11-75 – **Promo Video (UK): Black Or White** *('Black Or White' was a UK No. 52 hit)*

13-11-75 – 'Supersonic' (UK) *(This edition of 'Supersonic' is the only episode missing from the archives)*

23-12-75 – **'Top Of The Pops' (UK): Make Me Smile (Come Up And See Me)** *(This is a repeat of the 27-02-75 performance)*

10-01-76 – 'Follies' (Belgium)

16-01-76 – **'Top Pop' (Holland): Black Or White** *(As usual with 'Top Pop', this is a mimed performance on a great looking set)*

07-02-76 – **'Supersonic' (UK): White White Dove** *('White White Dove' got to No. 56 in* *the UK charts)*

19-03-76 – 'Iltatahti' (Finland)

17-04-76 – 'Spotlight' (Sweden)

17-04-76 – 'Kaleidos-Pop' (Switzerland)

00-07-76 – **Promo Video (UK): Here Comes The Sun** *(A none-too subtle cover of The Beatles' classic, 'Here Comes The Sun' got to No. 10 in the UK and No. 7 in Ireland)*

16-07-76 – 'Szene '76' (Germany)

22-07-76 – **'Top Of The Pops' (UK): Here Comes The Sun**

16-10-76 – **'Musikladen' (Germany): Here Comes The Sun**

21-10-76 – **'Top Of The Pops' (UK): (I Believe) Love's A Prima Donna** *('(I Believe) Love's a Prima Donna' stalled at No. 41 in the UK charts)*

08-11-76 – **'Supersonic' (UK): (I Believe) Love's A Prima Donna**

Late 1976 – **'Musikladen Extra' (Germany): Mad Mad Moonlight / Make Me Smile (Come Up And See Me) / Red Is A Mean Mean Colour / Here Comes The Sun / Sweet Dreams / Psychomodo / Sling It / Sebastian**

11-05-77 – 'Juke Box' (France)

03-11-79 – 'Tiswas' (UK): Freedom's Prisoner *('Freedom's Prisoner' got to No. 58 in the UK charts)* – **STEVE HARLEY**

Cockney Rebel disbanded in 1977, with Steve Harley pursuing a solo career and Jim Cregan joining Rod Stewart's band. Steve reformed the band in 1998, albeit with drummer Stuart Elliott as the only other member from the '70s line-ups. Original 1972 – 1974 bassist Paul Jeffreys died in 1988, with his 1975 – 1977 successor George Ford dying in 2007.

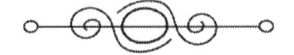

SHOWADDYWADDY

17-11-73 – 'New Faces' (UK): Rock 'N' Roll Medley *(Showaddywaddy's TV debut, this no longer survives)*

29-12-73 – **'New Faces' (All Winners Final) (UK): Medley: Let There Be Drums – Shazam! – Three Stars – Rave On – Bony Moronie** *(This is the earliest surviving footage of the band)*

00-04-74 – **Promo Video (UK): Hey Rock and Roll** *(A near-perfect combination of '50s rock 'n' roll and '70s glam, and featuring Showaddywaddy's other lead singer Bill 'Buddy' Gask, 'Hey Rock and Roll' got to No. 2 in the UK charts and was No. 5 in Ireland)*

23-05-74 – 'Top Of The Pops' (UK): Hey Rock and Roll

25-05-74 – '45' (UK): Hey Rock and Roll

30-05-74 – 'Top Of The Pops' (UK): Hey Rock and Roll *(This is a repeat of the 23-05-74 performance)*

13-06-74 – 'Top Of The Pops' (UK): Hey Rock and Roll

01-07-74 – 'Top Pop' (Holland): Hey Rock and Roll

06-07-74 – **'New Faces All Winners Show' (UK)**

22-08-74 – 'Top Of The Pops' (UK): Rock 'N' Roll Lady

29-08-74 – 'Top Of The Pops' (UK): Rock 'N' Roll Lady *(This is a repeat of the 22-08-74 performance)*

10-09-74 – 'Lift Off With Ayshea' (UK): Rock 'N' Roll Lady

26-09-74 – **'45' (UK): Medley: Three Stars - Rave On / Bony Moronie / Rock 'N' Roll Lady** *(Performed here live, 'Rock 'N' Roll Lady' peaked at No. 15 in the UK)*

28-09-74 – **'The Geordie Scene (UK): Hey Rock and Roll / The Party / Rock 'N' Roll Lady**

22-11-74 – **'Hits A Go Go' (Switzerland): Hey Rock and Roll**

12-12-74 – 'Top Of The Pops' (UK): Hey Mr Christmas

17-12-74 – **'Lift Off With Ayshea' (UK): Hey Mr Christmas** *(Performed here on the final edition of Ayshea Brough's long-running TV show, 'Hey Mr Christmas' got to No. 13 in the UK and No. 15 in Ireland)*

25-12-74 – **'A Stocking Full Of Stars' (UK): Hey Mr Christmas**

06-02-75 – **'Top Of The Pops' (UK): Sweet Music** *('Sweet Music' reached No. 15 in the UK and No. 12 in Ireland)*

21-02-75 – **'Crackerjack' (UK): Sweet Music** *(This was taped on 18-02-75)*

27-02-75 – 'Top Of The Pops' (UK): Sweet Music

06-03-75 – 'Top Of The Pops' (UK): Sweet Music

00-05-75 – **'Three For All' Movie (UK): The Party** *(Showaddywaddy's cameo for this movie was taped at The Suite, Brighton, sometime in 1974)*

15-05-75 – 'Top Of The Pops' (UK): Three Steps To Heaven

29-05-75 – 'Top Of The Pops' (UK): Three Steps To Heaven

05-06-75 – **'45' (UK): Three Steps To Heaven** *(Despite often being labelled as a covers act, of the first 9 singles, 7 of them were self-composed. Their first single to be a revival of an old song, Showaddywaddy's superior version of Buddy Holly's 'Three Steps To Heaven', got to No. 2 in the UK and No. 1 in Ireland)*

16-06-75 – **'Shang-A-Lang' (UK): Three Steps To Heaven**

21-08-75 – 'Rock On With 45' (UK); Heartbeat

28-08-75 – **'Rock On With 45' (UK): Heartbeat** *(Another excellent revival, this time with a Buddy Holly song, 'Heartbeat' reached No. 7 in the UK and No. 5 in Ireland)*

04-09-75 – **'Top Of The Pops' (UK): Heartbeat** *(There were two 'Top Of The Pops' performances for this song, with this one featuring the band in yellow suits)*

13-09-75 – **'Supersonic' (UK): Heartbeat / King Of The Jive** *(An early stage favourite, 'King Of The Jive' was a showcase for the 'Mind Games'-era John Lennon look-a-like band member Malcolm 'The Duke' Allured. Showaddywaddy's 'Supersonic' performance isn't included on some edits of this particular episode.)*

25-09-75 – **'Top Of The Pops' (UK): Heartbeat** *(The group are all in blue here)*

15-10-75 – **'Musikladen' (Germany): Rock and Roll Music / Three Steps To Heaven**

00-10-75 – **'Musikladen' (Germany): Rock and Roll Music / Sweet Music / Rock 'N' Roll Lady / Johnny Remember Me / King Of The Jive / Medley: Three Stars - Rave On / Three Steps To Heaven / Heartbeat / Hey Rock and Roll** *(This is the complete uncut and, at the time, unseen 'Musikladen' show, from which just three songs were originally broadcast: 'Rock and Roll Music' and 'Three Steps To Heaven' on 15-10-75, and 'Heartbeat' on 22-12-75. The full show was eventually issued as an official DVD)*

27-11-75 – **'Supersonic' (UK): Heavenly** *(Back to a self-composed single, 'Heavenly' stalled at No. 34 in the UK charts)*

16-12-75 – **'Look Alive' (UK): Heavenly**

Late 1975 – 'Top Pop' (Holland): Heartbeat

22-12-75 – **'Musikladen' (Germany): Heartbeat**

25-12-75 – **'Shang-A-Lang' Christmas Special (UK): Heavenly**

31-01-76 – **'Disco' (Germany): Heartbeat**

06-03-76 – 'Pop' (Germany): Heavenly

Spring 1976 – **'Multi-Coloured Swap Shop' (UK): Hey Rock and Roll / King Of The Jive**

04-05-76 – **'The Arrows' (UK): Trocadero** *(Another great self-written single, 'Trocadero' was a UK No. 32. The poorly-promoted follow-up, 'Take Me In Your Arms', didn't chart at all)*

20-05-76 – **'Top Of The Pops' (UK): Trocadero**

19-06-76 – **'Seaside Special' (UK): Trocadero** *(This was taped in Blackpool on 13-06-76)*

19-06-76 – **'Showaddywaddy' (Denmark): Rock 'N' Roll Lady / Johnny Remember Me / King Of The Jive / Heavenly / Three Steps To Heaven / Heartbeat / Hey Rock and Roll** *(This was probably taped in late 1975 or early 1976)*

31-07-76 – **'Superpop' (UK): King Of The Jive / Rock and Roll Music / Sweet Music / Rave On / Trocadero / Hey Rock and Roll** *(This was taped on 07-07-76)*

18-09-76 – **'Musikladen' (Germany):** Trocadero

20-09-76 – **'Plattenkuche' (Germany): Rock 'N' Roll Lady**

19-10-76 – **'The Arrows' (UK): Under The Moon Of Love** *(After poor chart positions for three self-written singles in a row, Showaddywaddy stuck to covers for A-sides from now on. 'Under The Moon Of Love' got to No. 1 in the UK and No. 6 in Ireland)*

30-10-76 – 'Multi-Coloured Swap Shop' (UK): Under The Moon Of Love

01-11-76 – **'Supersonic' (UK): Under The Moon Of Love**

04-11-76 – **'Top Of The Pops' (UK): Under The Moon Of Love** *(No less than five 'Top Of The Pops' performances for this song survive, with this one featuring the band in their white suits with red shirts, cleverly intercut with footage of them wearing black suits)*

15-11-76 – **'Blue Peter' (UK): Under The Moon Of Love**

18-11-76 – **'Top Of The Pops' (UK): Under The Moon Of Love** *(The band wear red suits for this performance)*

28-11-76 – **'Hits A Go Go' (Switzerland): Under The Moon Of Love**

30-11-76 – **'Top Pop' (Holland): Under The Moon Of Love**

02-12-76 – **'Top Of The Pops' (UK): Under The Moon Of Love** *(This is a repeat of an earlier performance from either 04-11-76 or 18-11-76)*

09-12-76 – **'Top Of The Pops' (UK): Under The Moon Of Love** *(This is a repeat of the 04-11-76 performance)*

16-12-76 – **'Top Of The Pops' (UK): Under The Moon Of Love** *(The band all wear different coloured suits from each other this time)*

26-12-76 – **'Top Of The Pops' (UK): Under The Moon Of Love** *(This time the band wear white suits with black shirts, but again the footage is, briefly, intercut with them wearing other outfits)*

27-12-76 – 'Swap Of The Pops' (UK): Under The Moon Of Love *(This is a repeat of the 30-10-76 'Multi-Coloured Swap Shop' performance)*

22-01-77 – **'Jim'll Fix It' (UK): Under The Moon Of Love**

04-02-77 – **'Disco' (Germany):** Under The Moon Of Love

Early 1977 – **'Szene' (Germany):** Under The Moon Of Love

22-02-77 – **'Top Pop' (Holland): When** *('When' was a UK No. 3 hit, also getting to No. 7 in Ireland)*

03-03-77 – **'Top Of The Pops' (UK): When** *(The first of three 'Top Of The Pops' performances, for this one Dave wears a blue suit)*

04-03-77 – **'Crackerjack' (UK):** When

17-03-77 – **'Top Of The Pops' (UK): When** *(Dave is in orange this time)*

03-04-77 – **'Countdown' (Australia):** When

06-04-77 – **'Get It Together' (UK):** When

07-04-77 – **'Top Of The Pops' (UK): When** *(For this one Dave wears pink)*

16-07-77 – **'Seaside Special' (UK):** You Got What It Takes *(This was taped in Bournemouth on 13-07-77. 'You Got What It Takes' reached No. 2 in the UK and No. 12 in Ireland)*

26-07-77 – 'Top Pop' (Holland): You Got What It Takes

28-07-77 – **'Top Of The Pops' (UK): You Got What It Takes** *(The first of three 'Top Of The Pops' performances, Dave wears a yellow suit)*

11-08-77 – **'Top Of The Pops' (UK): You Got What It Takes** *(Dave is in a red suit this time)*

13-08-77 – **'Musikladen' (Germany):** You Got What It Takes

24-08-77 – **'Marc' (UK):** You Got What It Takes

27-08-77 – **'Pop At The Mill' (UK):** Hey Rock And Roll / Under The Moon Of Love / King Of The Jive / You Got What It Takes *(This was taped on 03-08-77)*

20-10-77 – **'Top Of The Pops' (UK): Dancin' Party** *('Dancin' Party' reached No. 4 in the UK and No. 6 in Ireland)*

23-10-77 – **'Popscope' (Austria): You Got What It Takes** *(This is partly the same performance as was used for 'Marc' on 24-08-77)*

03-11-77 – **'Top Of The Pops' (UK): Dancin' Party** *(This is a repeat of the 20-10-77 performance)*

05-11-77 – **'Multi-Coloured Swap Shop' (UK): Dancin' Party**

17-11-77 – **'Top Of The Pops' (UK): Dancin' Party** *(This is a repeat of the 20-10-77 performance)*

Late 1977 – 'Top Pop' (Holland): Dancin' Party

03-12-77 – **'Musikladen' (Germany): Dancin' Party**

24-12-77 – 'Swap Of The Pops' (UK) *(This is a repeat of an earlier 'Multi-Coloured Swap Shop' performance, broadcast date unknown)*

25-12-77 – **'Top Of The Pops' (UK): You Got What It Takes** *(Dave wears a pink satin suit for this performance)*

26-12-77 – **'Top Of The Pops' (UK): Under The Moon Of Love** *(Reprising their big hit from a year earlier, the band wear white suits with black shirts, though unlike previously this is without intercut costume changes)*

23-01-78 – **'Disco' (Germany): Dancin' Party**

00-03-78 – **Promo Video (UK): I Wonder Why** *('I Wonder Why' reached No. 2 in the UK and No. 10 in Ireland)*

11-03-78 – **'Jim'll Fix It' (UK): I Wonder Why**

23-03-78 – **'Top Of The Pops' (UK): I Wonder Why** *(The first of three 'Top Of The Pops' appearances, this one features Bill in a yellow suit)*

25-03-78 – **'Multi-Coloured Swap Shop' (UK): Somethin' Else / I Wonder Why**

06-04-78 – **'Top Of The Pops' (UK): I Wonder Why** *(Bill wears a white suit for this)*

17-04-78 – **'Cheggers Plays Pop' (UK): I Wonder Why** *(This was taped on 16-04-78)*

20-05-78 – **'Top Pop' (Holland): I Wonder Why**

29-05-78 – **'Multi-Coloured Swap Shop Rock Garden Party' (UK): Say Mama / I Wonder Why / A Little Bit Of Soap** *(This was repeated on 24-11-79)*

01-06-78 – **'Musikladen' (Germany): I Wonder Why**

00-06-78 – **Promo Video (UK): A Little Bit Of Soap** *('A Little Bit Of Soap' got to No. 5 in the UK and No. 2 in Ireland)*

22-06-78 – **'Top Of The Pops' (UK): A Little Bit Of Soap** *(The first of two 'Top Of The Pops' performances, this features the entire band in black)*

06-07-78 – **'Top Of The Pops' (UK): A Little Bit Of Soap** *(This time the band all wear different colour suits)*

08-07-78 – **'Seaside Special' (UK): A Little Bit Of Soap** *(This was taped in Torbay, Devon)*

00-10-78 – **Promo Video (UK): Pretty Little Angel Eyes** *('Pretty Little Angel Eyes' again reached No. 5 in the UK and No. 2 in Ireland, though it was to be Showaddywaddy's last UK top 10 hit)*

14-10-78 – **'Ein Kessel Buntes' (East Germany): Under The Moon Of Love / Hey Rock and Roll / Pretty Little Angel Eyes**

19-10-78 – **'Top Of The Pops' (UK): Pretty Little Angel Eyes** *(The first of two 'Top Of The Pops' performances, for this one The Duke wears a purple suit)*

21-10-78 – **'The Little and Large Show' (UK): Under The Moon Of Love**

28-10-78 – **'Multi-Coloured Swapshop' (UK): Dancin' Party / Pretty Little Angel Eyes**

31-10-78 – **'Get It Together' (UK): Hits Medley**

02-11-78 – **'Top Of The Pops' (UK): Pretty Little Angel Eyes** *(The Duke is in pink for this)*

13-11-78 – **'The Royal Variety Show' (UK): Pretty Little Angel Eyes** *(Unlike many Royal Variety Shows, this was broadcast on the day of taping)*

16-11-78 – **'Top Of The Pops' (UK): Pretty Little Angel Eyes** *(This is a repeat of the 02-11-78 performance)*

28-11-78 – **'Get It Together' (UK): Pretty Little Angel Eyes**

25-12-78 – **'Top Of The Pops' (UK): I Wonder Why** *(This time Bill is in a green suit)*

26-12-78 – **'Get It Together Christmas Special' (UK): Pretty Little Angel Eyes** *(Some sources list this as a repeat of the 28-11-78 performance)*

00-03-79 – **Promo Video (UK): Remember Then** *('Remember Then' peaked at No. 17 in the UK, though got as high as No. 7 in Ireland)*

24-03-79 – **'Multi-Coloured Swapshop' (UK): Remember Then**

29-03-79 – **'Top Of The Pops' (UK): Remember Then**

12-04-79 – **'Top Of The Pops' (UK): Remember Then** *(This is a repeat of the 29-03-79 performance)*

17-04-79 – **'Seaside Special' (UK): Remember Then**

01-05-79 – **'Get It Together' (UK): Remember Then**

07-05-79 – **'Cheggers Plays Pop' (UK): Remember Then** *(This was taped on 02-05-79)*

00-06-79 – **Promo Video (UK): Sweet Little Rock 'N' Roller** *('Sweet Little Rock 'N' Roller' got to No. 15 in the UK and No. 9 in Ireland)*

14-07-79 – **'Seaside Special' (UK): Dancin' Party / Sweet Little Rock 'N' Roller** *(This was taped in Blackpool on 05-07-79)*

26-07-79 – **'Top Of The Pops' (UK): Sweet Little Rock 'N' Roller** *(The first of two performances, for this one the band all wear different colour suits)*

09-08-79 – **'Top Of The Pops' (UK): Sweet Little Rock 'N' Roller** *(All of the band are in pale blue suits this time)*

23-08-79 – **'Top Of The Pops' (UK): Sweet Little Rock 'N' Roller** *(This is a repeat of the 26-07-79 performance)*

00-10-79 – **Promo Video (UK): A Night At Daddy Gee's** *('A Night At Daddy Gee's' reached just No. 39 in the UK, as well as No. 26 in Ireland)*

15-11-79 – **'Top Of The Pops' (UK): A Night At Daddy Gee's**

07-12-79 – **'Crackerjack' (UK): A Night At Daddy Gee's**

13-12-79 – **'Musikladen' (Germany): A Night At Daddy Gee's** *(Showaddywaddy's final TV appearance of the '70s, this is also one of the most mysterious, as it features an* *unknown drummer! The best explanation band members could later come up with is that he was a fan who they'd met in a club the night before)*

The original 8-piece line-up remained together for over 10 years. In 1984 Malcolm 'The Duke' Allured left the group, with Russ Field following in 1985, and Bill 'Buddy' Gask leaving in 1987. After a couple of decades of relative stability, Al James and Trevor Oakes left in 2008, Dave Bartram quit 3 years later in 2011, and Rod Deas announced his retirement in January 2019. Bill died in 2011, and Al died in 2018, but the band continues with a line-up that includes just one original member, the exotically-named drummer Romeo Challenger.

THE ARROWS

16-05-74 – 'Top Of The Pops' (UK): Touch Too Much *(The Arrows' debut single, 'Touch Too Much' was a UK No. 8 hit, while the follow-up, 'Toughen Up', got to No. 51)*

30-05-74 – 'Top Of The Pops' (UK): Touch Too Much *(This is a repeat of the 16-05-74 performance)*

13-06-74 – 'Top Of The Pops' (UK): Touch Too Much

08-07-74 – 'Top Pop' (Holland): Touch Too Much

23-01-75 – **'Top Of The Pops' (UK): My Last Night With You** *(The Arrows 3rd and final UK hit, the ballad 'My Last Night With You' peaked at No. 25)*

08-02-75 – 'Don Kirshner's Rock Concert' (USA): Touch Too Much / Tough Enough *(both songs are on film)*

13-02-75 – 'Top Of The Pops' (UK): My Last Night With You

27-02-75 – **'Top Of The Pops' (UK): My Last Night With You** *(This is a repeat of an earlier performance)*

11-11-75 – **'Look Alive' (UK): Hard Hearted** *(A flop single for the group)*

02-03-76 – 'The Arrows' (UK): The Boogiest Band In Town / Once Upon A Time / Gotta Be Near You *(Tonight's guests are Peter Noone, Glyder and Jesse Green. Incredibly, throughout the whole run of their two 1976 TV series, The Arrows never released any records. This was due to a dispute between their manager Ian Wright and their producer Mickie Most)*

09-03-76 – **'The Arrows' (UK): I Love Rock 'n' Roll / Once Upon A Time / A Touch Too Much** *(Tonight's guests are Bilbo Baggins, Slade and Him and Us Plus One. Originally the B-side of The Arrows' flop single 'Broken Down Heart', 'I Love Rock 'n' Roll' was not a hit for the group. However, in 1982 Joan Jett and The Blackhearts had huge success with the song, getting to No. 3 in the US charts)*

23-03-76 – **'The Arrows' (UK): The Boogiest Band In Town / Thanks / First Hit** *(Tonight's* guests are Dana, Paul Nicholas and Him and Us Plus One. This was postponed from 16-03-76)

30-03-76 – **'The Arrows' (UK): Don't Worry 'Bout Love / Hard Hearted / Love Is Easy** (Tonight's guests are Hello, Scottie and Him and Us Plus One. This was postponed from 23-03-76)

13-04-76 – **'The Arrows' (UK): Once Upon A Time / The Boogiest Band In Town / Gotta Be Near You** (Tonight's guests are The Drifters, Randy Edelman and Him and Us Plus One)

20-04-76 – **'The Arrows' (UK): Don't Worry 'Bout Love / I Love Rock 'n' Roll / My Last Night With You / Once Upon A Time** (Tonight's guests are Butterflies and The Frank Jennings Syndicate)

27-04-76 – **'The Arrows' (UK): Once Upon A Time / Gotta Be Near You / Thanks / What Comes Between Us** (Tonight's guests are Louisa Jane White, Sheer Elegance, Flintlock and Him and Us Plus One)

04-05-76 – **'The Arrows' (UK): Gotta Be Near You / First Hit / Feeling This Way** (Tonight's guests are Gilbert O'Sullivan, Showaddywaddy, Simon May and Him and Us Plus One)

11-05-76 – **'The Arrows' (UK): The Boogiest Band In Town / What's Come Between Us / Don't Worry 'Bout Love / Love Is Easy** (Tonight's guests are Bilbo Baggins, Smokie and Him and Us Plus One)

18-05-76 – **'The Arrows' (UK): Thanks / Once Upon A Time / Feeling This Way** (Tonight's guests are Lynsey De Paul, Alvin Stardust and Him and Us Plus One)

25-05-76 – **'The Arrows' (UK): Moving Next Door To You / Once Upon A Time / Gotta Be Near You** (Tonight's guests are Kathy Jones, Stevenson's Rocket and Him and Us Plus One)

01-06-76 – **'The Arrows' (UK): My World is Turning On You / My Last Night With You / Let Me Love You** (Tonight's guests are Slik, Geraldine and Him and Us Plus One)

08-06-76 – **'The Arrows' (UK): Hard Hearted / The Boogiest Band In Town / Don't Worry 'Bout Love / First Hit / What's Come Between Us** (Tonight's guests are

Lieutenant Pigeon, Buster and Him and Us Plus One)

15-06-76 – **'The Arrows' (UK): I Love Rock 'n' Roll / Love Is Easy / Feeling This Way / A Touch Too Much** *(Tonight's guests are The Real Thing, Marmalade and Him and Us Plus One)*

22-06-76 – **'The Arrows' (UK): Gotta Be Near You / Moving Next Door To You / My World Is Turning On You** *(Tonight's guests are The Wurzels, The Glitter Band and Him and Us Plus One)*

28-09-76 – **'The Arrows' (UK): The Boogiest Band In Town / Bring Back The Fire / Don't Worry 'Bout Love / Gotta Be Near You** *(Tonight's guests are Paul Nicholas, The Real Thing and Him and Us Plus One)*

05-10-76 – **'The Arrows' (UK): Moving Next Door To You / Faith In You / I Love Rock 'n' Roll** *(Tonight's guests are The Bay City Rollers, Dana and Him and Us Plus One)*

12-10-76 – **'The Arrows' (UK): Bring Back The Fire / Don't Worry 'Bout Love / First Hit / Feeling This Way** *(Tonight's guests are The Drifters, Pilot and Him and Us Plus One)*

19-10-76 – **'The Arrows' (UK): Love Is Easy / Love Rider / My World Is Turning On Love / A Touch Too Much** *(Tonight's guests are Showaddywaddy, J. Vincent Edwards and Him and Us Plus One)*

26-10-76 – **'The Arrows' (UK): The Boogiest Band In Town / Faith In You / First Hit** *(Tonight's guests are Child, Gilbert O'Sullivan, The Wurzels and Him and Us Plus One)*

02-11-76 – **'The Arrows' (UK): Bring Back The Fire / Once Upon A Time / Moving Next Door To You** *(Tonight's guests are Sunshine, T-Rex and Him and Us Plus One)*

09-11-76 – **'The Arrows' (UK): I Love Rock 'n' Roll / Dare You Not To Dance / Feeling This Way** *(Tonight's guests are Keeley Ford, Billy Ocean, Arbré and Him and Us Plus One)*

16-11-76 – **'The Arrows' (UK): Love Rider / Faith In You / Dare You Not To Dance / Bring Back The Fire** *(Tonight's guests are The Glitter Band, Red Hurley, Chris Neal and Him and Us Plus One)*

23-11-76 – **'The Arrows' (UK): Gotta Be Near You / My World Is Turning On You / Love Is Easy** *(Tonight's guests are Kettle, Billy J. Kramer, Paul Nicholas and Him and Us Plus One)*

30-11-76 – **'The Arrows' (UK): I Love Rock 'n' Roll / Once Upon A Time / Dare You Not To Dance / A Touch Too Much** *(Tonight's guests are The Dodgers, Jonathan King and Him and Us Plus One)*

07-12-76 – **'The Arrows' (UK): First Hit / Goodbyes Don't Bother Me / Don't Worry 'Bout Love** *(Tonight's guests are Glyder, Gene Pitney and Him and Us Plus One)*

14-12-76 – **'The Arrows' (UK): The Boogiest Band In Town / Bring Back The Fire / My World Is Turning On Love** *(Tonight's guests are Robin Sarstedt, The Wurzels, John Christie and Him and Us Plus One)*

21-12-76 – **'The Arrows' (UK): Faith In You / Hard Hearted Love / Love Rider** *(Tonight's guests are The Bay City Rollers, Slik and Him and Us Plus One)*

Following The Arrows' 1977 demise, vocalist/bassist Alan Merrill's subsequent career included several years recording and touring with US musician Rick Derringer. Drummer Paul Varley died in 2008 and guitarist Jake Hooker died in 2014.

Peter Checksfield

THE HEAVY METAL KIDS

25-06-74 – **'The Old Grey Whistle Test' (UK): Hangin' On / It's The Same** *(This live studio performance, featuring Gary Holton in his trade-mark top-hat, is the earliest known footage of the band)*

18-11-74 – **'Panorama: Younger Every Day' (UK): The Cops Are Coming** *(An appearance in this prime-time documentary gave the band some major publicity)*

12-07-75 – **'Jukebox' (France): The Turk / Crisis / The Cops Are Coming / It's The Same** *(This French TV performance fully captures the group's anarchic live performances)*

27-05-76 – **'Top Of The Pops' (UK): She's No Angel** *(Now with shorter hair and what looks like a dead animal around his neck, Gary Holton gives it his all here. Not that it helped sales, as 'She's No Angel' was another non-hit, just like all other singles)*

10-09-77 – **'Rock-Pop In Concert' (Germany): Jackie The Lad / She's No Angel** *(Taped on 26-08-77, this mimed performance includes 'Jackie The Lad', a song that could almost be 'Ogden's Nut Gone Flake' era The Small Faces)*

15-10-77 – **'Disco' (Germany): Delirious** *(One of The Heavy Metal Kids' most frantic/punk-like songs, this fit in perfectly with the spirit of '77)*

21-10-77 – **'Szene '77' (Germany): She's No Angel** *(Performed almost 18 months after their 'Top Of The Pops' performance, it somehow fits in better on a show that also includes Eddie and The Hot Rods)*

Following the band's 1978 split, Gary Holton formed the duo Holton/Steel with Norwegian musician Casino Steel, though he later concentrated more on acting, resulting in his memorable role as Wayne in 'Auf Wiedersehen, Pet'. Gary died in 1985 and original guitarist Mickey Waller died in 2013.

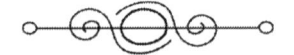

PILOT

04-10-74 – **'Top Of The Pops' (UK): Magic** *(Never the most visually entertaining of bands, instead they concentrated on good, classy, pop-rock, with at least two true classics. 'Magic', their first and best hit, got to No. 11 in the UK, as well as No. 5 in the US, No. 1 in Canada and No. 12 in Australia)*

07-11-74 – **'Top Of The Pops' (UK): Magic** *(Pilot are luckier than most mid-'70s bands when it comes to surviving 'Top Of The Pops' appearances; of the 12 times they appeared on the show, 9, possibly 10, still survive)*

17-11-74 – 'The Basil Brush Show' (UK): Magic

28-11-74 – 'Top Of The Pops' (UK): Magic *(One of Pilot's few missing 'Top Of The Pops' appearances)*

00-01-75 – **Promo Video (UK): January** *('January' got to No. 1 in the UK, as well as in Australia, where it topped the charts for an incredible 8 weeks. It also got to No. 21 in Germany and No. 87 in the US)*

02-01-75 – **'Top Of The Pops' (UK): January**

16-01-75 – 'Top Of The Pops' (UK): January *(This is rumoured to survive, but unconfirmed at present)*

23-01-75 – 'Rock On With 45' (UK): January

24-01-75 – **'Crackerjack' (UK): January**

30-01-75 – **'Top Of The Pops' (UK): January**

31-01-75 – **'Top Pop' (Holland): Magic**

06-02-75 – **'Top Of The Pops' (UK): January**

07-02-75 – **'Top Pop' (Holland): Magic** *(This is a repeat of the 31-01-75 performance)*

13-02-75 – 'Top Of The Pops' (UK): January *(Another missing performance)*

21-03-75 – **'Top Pop' (Holland): January** *(This was taped in London)*

03-04-75 – **'Top Of The Pops' (UK): Call Me Round** *('Call Me Round' reached No. 34 in the UK charts, though didn't do much elsewhere)*

30-04-75 – 'Iltatahti' (Finland)

00-09-75 – **Promo Video (UK): Just A Smile** *(Pilot's last hit, 'Just A Smile' got to No. 31 in the UK, No. 49 in Australia and No. 90 in the US)*

11-09-75 – **'Top Of The Pops' (UK): Just a Smile**

18-09-75 – **'Supersonic' (UK): Just a Smile**

25-10-75 – **'The Basil Brush Show' (UK): Just A Smile**

21-12-75 – **'Pop '75' (Germany): Just A Smile**

25-12-75 – **'Top Of The Pops' (UK): January**

24-01-76 – **'Supersonic' (UK): January / High Into The Sky**

00-06-76 – Promo Video (UK): Canada

24-06-76 – **'Top Of The Pops' (UK): Canada**

28-08-76 – **'Superpop '76' (UK): Magic / Penny In My Pocket / Hold On / Never Give Up / Canada / Lovely Lady Smile / January** *(Taped on 17-07-76, this is an excellent live performance, with raw but competent versions of the big hits)*

12-10-76 – **'The Arrows' (UK): Penny In My Pocket**

Following the band's split in 1977, David Paton, Ian Bairnson and Stuart Tosh all joined The Alan Parsons Project, with David then going on to work with Kate Bush, Elton John and Rick Wakeman. Billy died in 1989, but David and Ian reunited Pilot in 2002, with all three surviving members reuniting in 2014.

HELLO

21-06-72 – 'Lift Off With Ayshea' (UK): You Move Me *(Their first single, 'You Move Me' was not a hit)*

05-07-72 – 'Eddy Ready Go' (Holland): You Move Me

08-10-74 – 'Lift Off With Ayshea' (UK): Tell Him

31-10-74 – 'Top Of The Pops' (UK): Tell Him

21-11-74 – **'Top Of The Pops' (UK): Tell Him** *(Copying The Glitter Band's arrangement of The Exciters' 'Tell Him', this was Hello's biggest UK hit at No. 6. This is the first of two surviving 'Top Of The Pops' performances of the song, and features lead singer Rob Bradbury in a white top)*

05-12-74 – **'Top Of The Pops' (UK): Tell Him** *(A second surviving appearance on the show, for this performance Rob wears a black top)*

20-02-75 – 'Top Of The Pops' (UK): Game's Up

Early 1975 – **'Side By Side' Movie (UK): Bend Me Shape Me / Side By Side** [with Mud] *(This movie cameo did nothing to boost the sales of 'Bend Me Shape Me' when it was released as a single)*

03-03-75 – **'The Geordie Scene' (UK): Let's Spend The Night Together / Another School Day / And Then She Kissed Me / Carol / Shakin' All Over / Games Up / Time Out / Tell Him** *(Playing live in the studio, this includes their most recent single 'Game's Up')*

20-03-75 – 'Rock On With 45' (UK): Game's Up

22-05-75 – **'Rock On With 45' (UK): Bend Me Shape Me / Then She Kissed Me / Let's Spend The Night Together** *(The band performed three cover versions for this show, including their latest single 'Bend Me Shape Me')*

25-09-75 – **'Supersonic' (UK): New York Groove** *('New York Groove' reached No. 9 in the UK charts and was their 2nd and final hit. When Ace Frehley of Kiss cut his first solo album four years later, it was 'New York Groove' that was one of the key songs on it)*

09-10-75 – 'Top Of The Pops' (UK): New York Groove

30-10-75 – 'Top Of The Pops' (UK): New York Groove *(This is a repeat of the 09-10-75 performance)*

13-11-75 – 'Top Of The Pops' (UK): New York Groove

18-11-75 – **'Look Alive' (UK): New York Groove** *(More 'New York Groove' plugging, on this short-lived TV series)*

06-12-75 – **'Disco' (Germany): New York Groove** *(Singing live, their voices are unfortunately far too low in the mix)*

Late 1975 – 'Top Pop' (Holland): New York Groove

14-02-76 – **'Supersonic' (UK): Star-Studded Sham** *(A disappointing follow-up, neither this performance or the subsequent one on 'The Arrows' were enough to get it in the charts)*

23-03-76 – **'The Arrows' (UK): Star-Studded Sham**

28-03-76 – **'Spotlight' (Austria): New York Groove / Game's Up / Tell Him** *(Performing three of their best singles for Austrian TV)*

01-07-76 – **'Top Of The Pops' (UK): Love Stealer** *(Another mediocre single, and time for Hello to say goodbye to 'Top Of The Pops')*

09-10-76 – **'Disco' (Germany): Love Stealer**

The original line-up of Hello split in 1979, though singer Rob Bradbury has fronted a new line-up of the band since 2002.

KENNY

28-11-74 – 'Top Of The Pops' (UK): The Bump

19-12-74 – 'Top Of The Pops' (UK): The Bump

02-01-75 – **'Top Of The Pops' (UK): The Bump** *(Originally a The Bay City Rollers B-side, 'The Bump' was Kenny's first and biggest hit, getting to No. 3 in the UK charts. The earliest surviving footage of the band, Kenny's late-era glam image here featured red flares, leather jackets and T-shirts with the letter "K" on them)*

09-01-75 – 'Top Of The Pops' (UK): The Bump

Early 1975 – **'Side By Side' Movie (UK): Fancy Pants** *(An appearance in one of the less essential music movies of the '70s, 'Fancy Pants' was another big UK hit at No. 4)*

28-02-75 – **'Crackerjack' (UK): Fancy Pants**

06-03-75 – 'Top Of The Pops' (UK): Fancy Pants

20-03-75 – **'Top Of The Pops' (UK): Fancy Pants** *(Kenny are now wearing white "K" shirts and truly dreadful multi-coloured high-waisted trousers)*

03-04-75 – 'Top Of The Pops' (UK): Fancy Pants

29-05-75 – 'Top Of The Pops' (UK): Baby I Love You, OK!

12-06-75 – 'Top Of The Pops' (UK): Baby I Love You, OK!

26-06-75 – **'Top Of The Pops' (UK): Baby I Love You, OK!** *('Baby I Love You, OK!', got to No. 12 in the UK charts)*

05-07-75 – **'Disco' (Germany): Fancy Pants**

31-07-75 – 'Top Of The Pops' (UK): Julie-Ann

28-08-75 – **'Top Of The Pops' (UK): Julie-Ann** *(Kenny's final UK hit at No. 10, 'Julie-Ann' also got to No. 4 in Australia)*

11-09-75 – 'Top Of The Pops' (UK): Julie-Ann

06-12-75 – **'The Basil Brush Show' (UK): Nice To Have You Home** *(One of their better singles, 'Nice To Have You Home' wasn't a hit for Kenny, but under the title 'It's So Nice (To Have You Home)', it was a UK No. 44 hit for The New Seekers)*

03-01-76 – **'Disco' (Germany): Julie Anne**

10-01-76 – **'Supersonic' (UK): Nice To Have You Home**

00-03-76 – **Promo Video (UK): Hot Lips** *('Hot Lips' was a No. 20 hit in Germany, while the follow-up 'Red Headed Lady' got to No. 49 in the same country)*

20-03-76 – **'Supersonic' (UK): Hot Lips** *(By now Kenny are wearing white flares and red satin jackets. Not that it helped this mediocre record)*

19-06-76 – **'Disco' (Germany): Hot Lips**

Kenny went their separate ways in 1979. They have never reformed.

FOX

00-01-75 – **Promo Video (UK): Only You Can** (Fox's biggest UK hit, 'Only You Can' got to No. 3, as well as No. 2 in Germany, No. 16 in Australia and No. 53 in the US. This video sees the band miming in what looks like a sunny lounge and conservatory)

13-02-75 – **'Top Of The Pops' (UK): Only You Can** (The first of two 'Top Of The Pops' performances for 'Only You Can', on this one Noosha Fox wears a flowery chiffon dress while the drummer wears a black hat with a red feather)

27-02-75 – **'Top Of The Pops' (UK): Only You Can** (This is a repeat of the 13-02-75 performance)

13-03-75 – **'Top Of The Pops' (UK): Only You Can** (A 2nd 'Top Of The Pops' performance, this time Noosha is in white, and the drummer is hat-less)

29-03-75 – **'Top Pop' (Holland): Only You Can** (This is effectively a Noosha Fox solo appearance, as she is the only band member seen – twice, as the whole thing is broadcast in a split-screen format. Outtake footage survives from this performance)

20-04-75 – **'Pop '75' (Germany): Only You Can** (The first of two German TV performances in the space of a week)

26-04-75 – **'Disco' (Germany): Only You Can** (On German TV again, 'Disco' was one of the most popular music TV shows in the country)

15-05-75 – 'Top Of The Pops' (UK): Imagine Me, Imagine You (Fox's one performance on this show of 'Imagine Me, Imagine You' is lost)

29-05-75 – 'Top Of The Pops' (UK): Imagine Me, Imagine You (This is a repeat of the 15-05-75 performance)

Mid 1975 – **'Side By Side' movie (UK): Imagine Me, Imagine You** ('Imagine Me, Imagine You' was a No. 15 hit in the UK, also getting to No. 7 in Germany and No. 53 in the US. 'Side By Side' is a far from a great movie, but Fox's cameo helps make it a little more watchable)

10-07-75 – **'Rock On With 45' (UK): Red Letter Day / The Juggler / Imagine Me, Imagine

You *(Along with their current single, Fox perform two songs from their first album)*

17-11-75 – **'Musikladen' (Germany): He's Got Magic** *(Also covered by Pan's People during their all-too-brief recording career, 'He's Got Magic' lacked the chart magic of its predecessors and wasn't a hit)*

Late 1975 – **'Musikladen' (Germany): Strange Ships** *(Not broadcast at the time and only surfacing recently, this performance sees Noosha in a strange metallic mini-dress and hat. The song is nothing special though, and was a chart flop everywhere – which is probably why this TV appearance wasn't shown)*

00-01-76 – **Promo Video (UK): S-S-S-Single Bed** *('S-S-S-Single Bed' got to No. 4 in the UK, No. 10 in Holland, and all the way to No. 1 in Australia. The very good video features Noosha in black hot pants, white top and white cape, with purple laser effects in the background)*

01-04-76 - **'Top Of The Pops' (UK): S-S-S-Single Bed** *(For this first 'Top Of The Pops' performance for their current single, Noosha wears the same outfit as seen in the promo video)*

15-04-76 – **'Top Of The Pops' (UK): S-S-S-Single Bed** *(This time Noosha is dressed in black)*

06-05-76 – **'Top Of The Pops' (UK): S-S-S-Single Bed** *(This is a repeat of the 01-04-76 performance)*

04-06-76 – **'Top Pop' (Holland): S-S-S-Single Bed** *(For this performance Noosha is seen wearing a white dress and wearing a headband over her tied-back hair)*

17-11-77 – **'Top Of The Pops' (UK): Georgina Bailey** *(Noosha Fox's debut solo single, 'Georgina Bailey' got to No. 31 in the UK charts. A change of image, gone are the '20s outfits and in their place is a school uniform)* – **NOOSHA FOX**

03-12-77 – **'Musikladen' (Germany): Georgina Bailey** *(For this performance, Noosha wears a beautiful white outfit with a straw summer hat)* – **NOOSHA FOX**

00-06-79 – **Promo Video (UK): The Heat Is On** *(Later a hit for ABBA's Agnetha Fältskog, 'The Heat Is On' was not a hit for Noosha Fox – despite this great looking soft-focus video featuring her in red)* – **NOOSHA FOX**

10-08-79 – **'Szene '79' (Germany): The Heat Is On** *(Wearing little more than strips of red chiffon and with both voice and dance moves similar to Kat Bush, Noosha should've been one of the biggest stars of the era, but sadly it was not to be)* – **NOOSHA FOX**

Fox briefly reunited in 1980 to record the single 'Electro People', the theme tune to Kenny Everett's BBC TV series. Noosha Fox retired from the music business soon afterwards, and allthough several comebacks have been rumoured they have never materialised.

Peter Checksfield

THE SENSATIONAL ALEX HARVEY BAND

00-01-73 – **'New Musical Express – The Giants Of Tomorrow'**, **The Marquee, London (UK): Framed / There's No Lights On The Christmas Tree Mother, They're Burning Big Louie Tonight / St. Anthony** *(The earliest known footage of The Sensational Alex Harvey Band – or S.A.H.B. for short – the showmanship and Alex's trade-mark striped T-shirt are already in place, though guitarist Zal Cleminson has yet to start wearing his white mime make-up. The snappily-titled 'There's No Lights On The Christmas Tree Mother, They're Burning Big Louie Tonight' was The Sensational Alex Harvey Band's debut single)*

07-10-73 – **'Hits A Go Go' (Switzerland): Giddy Up A Ding Dong / Midnight Moses** *(A fun, mimed, performance, though Alex is looking a bit dishevelled. 'Giddy Up A Ding Dong' was issued as a single, though it failed to chart)*

18-12-73 – **'The Old Grey Whistle Test' (UK): Next... / The Faith Healer** *(Forget Scott Walker and David Bowie, 'Next...' was THE most significant Jacque Brel interpretation of the rock era! 'The Faith Healer' was another single, and another flop)*

16-06-74 – **'Ragnarock Festival', Oslo (Norway): Midnight Moses / Framed** *(Stunning live footage, complete with Alex wearing a stocking over his head during 'Framed' – a stocking that emerges from his mouth)*

05-07-74 – **'ABC In Concert' (USA): The Hot City Symphony (Part 1: Vambo) / Sergeant Fury / Framed / Dance To The Music** *(This was taped in the UK for US TV broadcast)*

20-10-74 – **'Spotlight' (Austria): Giddy Up A Ding Dong / Sergeant Fury** *(Possibly the most chart-friendly thing they ever did, 'Sergeant Fury' was issued as a single. It didn't chart)*

Late 1974 – **Syracuse, New York (USA): The Faith Healer / Midnight Moses / Next... / Sergeant Fury / The Hot City Symphony (Part 1: Vambo) / School's Out / The Impossible Dream / Framed / I Just Want To Make Love To You / Anthem** *(Although only available in black and white, this footage is notable for being the only available full-length S.A.H.B. concert)*

31-12-74 – **'Spotlight' (Austria): Sergeant Fury** *(A repeat of the 20-10-74 performance)*

07-02-75 – **'The Old Grey Whistle Test'** (on film)

22-02-75 – 'Un Jour Futur' (France)

30-05-75 – **'The Old Grey Whistle Test' (UK): Give My Compliments To The Chef / Delilah** (The band's 2nd appearance on the show, and just as memorable as their first. A cover of the Tom Jones classic, 'Delilah' was the band's biggest hit single at No. 7 in the UK charts, and check out the little dance routine during the solo. You never got that from Roxy Music or Be-Bop Deluxe!)

17-07-75 – 'Top Of The Pops' (UK): Delilah

31-07-75 – 'Top Of The Pops' (UK): Delilah *(This is a repeat of the 17-07-75 performance)*

14-08-75 – 'Top Of The Pops' (UK): Delilah *(This is a repeat of the 17-07-75 performance)*

27-11-75 – 'Top Of The Pops' (UK): Gamblin' Bar Room Blues

04-12-75 – **'Supersonic' (UK): Delilah / Gamblin' Bar Room Blues** *(As well as a reprise of their top ten hit from earlier in the year, performed here is their current single 'Gamblin' Bar Room Blues', an old country-blues song from the '30s. The brilliant performance here features the band dressing up and acting out the song's storyline, but despite this being one of the most memorable TV appearances of the era, 'Gamblin' Bar Room Blues' stalled at No. 38 in the UK charts)*

24-01-76 – **'Don Kirshner's Rock Concert' (USA): Delilah / The Hot City Symphony (Part 1: Vambo) / The Hot City Symphony (Part 2: Man In The Jar)** *(One of The Sensational Alex Harvey Band's all-too-rare appearances on US TV)*

13-03-76 – **'Supersonic' (UK): Runaway** *(With Alex looking surprisingly clean-cut and sober here, this cover of the Del Shannon classic didn't chart)*

10-06-76 – **'Top Of The Pops' (UK): Boston Tea Party** *(The band's final hit, 'Boston Tea Party' reached No. 13 in the UK charts. This is the first of two 'Top Of The Pops' performances of the song, and features Alex in his usual striped T-shirt and jeans)*

24-06-76 – **'Top Of The Pops' (UK): Boston Tea Party** *(This is a repeat of the 10-06-76 performance)*

08-07-76 – **'Top Of The Pops' (UK): Boston Tea Party** *(For this second performance, Alex* looks like he'd been sleeping rough since the previous appearance. Dishevelled and tired-looking, he is seated throughout the performance while wearing a hat)

22-07-76 – **'Top Of The Pops' (UK): Boston Tea Party** *(This is a repeat of the 10-06-76 performance)*

00-08-76 – **Promo Video (UK): Amos Moses** *(The band's last single prior to Alex Harvey temporarily leaving the band, 'Amos Moses' wasn't a hit)*

22-08-76 – 'Iltatahti' (Finland)

00-01-77 – **'The Old Grey Whistle Test' (UK): Pick It Up And Kick It** *(Promo Film compiled from archive dance routine footage – audio features SAHB without Alex Harvey)*

The Sensational Alex Harvey Band were scheduled to appear on 'Sight and Sound In Concert' on 29-10-77, but Alex walked out of rehearsals, so the band were forced to cancel. They were replaced by AC/DC.

After rejoining the band in mid-1977, Alex Harvey left again in 1978, this time permanently. He pursued an unsuccessful solo career but died in 1982. All four surviving members reunited as SAHB from 1993 to 2008.

CHRIS SPEDDING

00-07-75 – **Promo Video (UK): Motor Bikin'** *(Chris Spedding's only hit, the memorable 'Motor Bikin'' got to No. 14 in the UK charts)*

28-08-75 – **'Top Of The Pops' (UK): Motor Bikin'** *(Intercut with footage of someone on a motorbike, this is an excellent live version of Chris' hit)*

11-09-75 – 'Top Of The Pops' (UK): Motor Bikin'

11-09-75 – **'Supersonic' (UK): Motor Bikin'** *(The first of several appearances on this show)*

31-01-76 – **'Supersonic' (UK): Jump In My Car** *(More laid-back and slower than the previous single, 'Jump In My Car' was the first of several non-hits)*

15-02-76 – **'Pop '76' (Germany): Jump In My Car** *(German TV promotion)*

13-12-76 – **'Supersonic' (UK): Motor Bikin' / Pogo Dancing** *(Backed on both songs by The Vibrators, these are fast 'n' furious versions. 'Pogo Dancing' was Chris Spedding's latest, flop, single)*

26-03-77 – **'Musikladen' (Germany): Pogo Dancing** *(More German TV promotion)*

01-04-78 – **'Rock-Pop' (Germany): Get Outta My Pagoda** *(Punk/New Wave in all but name, this didn't chart)*

21-04-78 – **'Szene '78' (Germany): Silver Bullet** *(A jangly mid-paced flop single)*

Chris Spedding has remained a much in demand guitarist, recording or touring with Paul McCartney, Bryan Ferry, Elton John and Roger Daltrey, amongst many others.

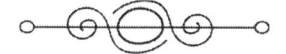

SAILOR

00-08-74 – **Promo Video (UK): Traffic Jam** *(This video features Sailor all in matching sailor outfits, and with their trademark nickelodeon, a bizarre-looking contraption featuring two pianos facing each other and with a bass drum attached to the front. Sailor's debut single, 'Traffic Jam' got to No. 47 in Australia)*

04-09-74 – **'In Concert' (UK): Let's Go To Town / Josephine Baker / Blame It On The Soft Spot / Blue Desert / The Street / Sailor's Night On The Town / Traffic Jam / Harbour** *(Sailor were fortunate enough to make their UK TV debut with this 30 minute performance on BBC's 'In Concert')*

27-10-74 – **'The Basil Brush Show' (UK): Traffic Jam**

01-11-74 – **'Top Pop' (Holland): Traffic Jam**

07-02-75 – **'Top Pop' (Holland): Sailor**

13-02-75 – 'Rock On With 45' (UK): Blue Desert *(Sailor's 2nd UK flop single)*

23-05-75 – 'Top Pop' (Holland): Let's Go To Town

11-06-75 – **'Musikladen' (Germany): Sailor** *(A German TV performance of Sailor's 3rd UK single, but just like the other two, it didn't chart)*

20-09-75 – **'Pop '75' (Germany)**

00-11-75 – **Promo Video (UK): A Glass Of Champagne** *(The greatest song Roxy Music never recorded, 'A Glass Of Champagne' was Sailor's big breakthrough and biggest hit, getting to No. 2 in the UK, No. 1 in Ireland and No. 4 in Australia)*

13-11-75 – 'Supersonic' (UK): A Glass Of Champagne *(This edition of 'Supersonic' is the only episode that is thought not to survive)*

27-11-75 – **'Supersonic' (UK): A Glass Of Champagne** *(Although this performance survives, at time of writing it isn't available for review)*

04-12-75 – 'Top Of The Pops' (UK): A Glass Of Champagne

11-12-75 – 'Top Of The Pops' (UK): A Glass Of Champagne

18-12-75 – **'Supersonic' (UK): Traffic Jam / A Glass Of Champagne** *(This one features Georg wearing a red and white striped top, and on stage with the rest of the band. 'A Glass Of Champagne' is possibly a repeat from 13-11-75 and/or 27-11-75)*

19-12-75 – **'Top Pop' (Holland): Girls, Girls, Girls** *(Performed on a great set with four well-dressed women, 'Girls, Girls, Girls' was a No. 7 hit in the UK, also getting to No. 21 in Australia)*

06-01-76 – **'Look Alive' (UK): A Glass Of Champagne**

08-01-76 – **'Top Of The Pops' (UK): A Glass Of Champagne** *(For this first surviving 'Top Of The Pops' performance, the drummer is more or less behind Georg)*

22-01-76 – **'Top Of The Pops' (UK): A Glass Of Champagne** *(Wearing the same clothes as the 22-01-76 performance, this time the drummer is on the far side of the stage from Georg)*

31-01-76 – **'Supersonic' (UK): A Glass Of Champagne / Girls, Girls, Girls** *(For this performance Georg again wears a red a white striped top, but is on a raised platform above the rest of the band)*

00-03-76 – **Promo Video (UK): Girls, Girls, Girls**

06-03-76 – **'Musikladen' (Germany): A Glass Of Champagne / Girls, Girls, Girls**

Early 1976 – **'Musikladen' (Germany): Panama / The Old Nickelodeon Sound** *(These are outtakes that weren't broadcast at the time)*

27-03-76 – **'Supersonic' (UK): Girls, Girls, Girls** *(This is a repeat of the 31-01-76 performance)*

27-03-76 – **'Disco' (Germany): A Glass Of Champagne**

01-04-76 – **'Top Of The Pops' (UK): Girls, Girls, Girls** *(The first of two 'Top Of The Pops' performances for this song)*

15-04-76 – **'Top Of The Pops' (UK): Girls, Girls, Girls** *(A 2nd performance, similar to the first, though the main difference is that the song starts with a close-up of a sailor doll)*

01-05-76 – **'Sailor with Sutherland Brothers and Quiver' (UK): Blame It On The Soft Spot / The Street / Let's Go To Town / The Old Nickelodeon Sound / Vera From Veracruz / Blue Desert / Jacaranda / Girls, Girls, Girls / Panama / Traffic Jam / A Glass Of Champagne** *(Taped live in Southend-on-Sea, this captures the band at their commercial peak)*

15-05-76 – **'Starparade' (Germany): A Glass Of Champagne / Girls, Girls, Girls / The Old Nickelodeon**

18-09-76 – **'Musikladen' (Germany): Cool Breeze / Stiletto Heels**

04-10-76 – **'Supersonic' (UK): Girls, Girls, Girls / Stiletto Heels** *(A performance that features Georg in a white jacket, 'Stiletto Heels' was the weak non-charting UK follow-up to 'Girls, Girls, Girls')*

03-11-76 – **'Sailor Spezial' (Switzerland): Sailor / Panama / The Old Nickelodeon Sound / Josephine Baker / The Street / Trouble In Hong Kong / My Kind Of Girl / Blue Desert / A Glass Of Champagne / Girls, Girls, Girls / Jacaranda** *(Taped without an audience in Zurich, this mimed performance also includes interviews and scenes of the band in the recording studio)*

04-12-76 – **'Disco' (Germany): Stiletto Heels**

26-12-76 – **'Top Of The Pops' (UK): A Glass Of Champagne** *(A reprise of their biggest and best hit, with all the band smartly dressed in black tuxedos and bow ties)*

10-02-77 – **'Top Of The Pops' (UK): One Drink Too Many** *(Sailor's final hit, 'One Drink Too Many' peaked at No. 35 in the UK charts)*

19-02-77 – **'Supersonic' (UK): Girls, Girls, Girls / One Drink Too Many** *(For this performance the band wear tuxedos and bow ties, the same as they did on the Boxing Day edition of 'Top Of The Pops' a couple of months earlier)*

05-03-77 – **'Supersonic' (UK): One Drink Too Many**

05-03-77 – **'Disco' (Germany): One Drink Too Many**

25-03-77 – **'MOT' (France): One Drink Too Many**

Early 1977 – **'Top Pop' (Holland): One Drink Too Many**

Summer 1977 – **'Pop '77' (Germany): Down By The Docks**

15-05-78 – **'Cheggers Plays Pop' (UK): All I Need Is A Girl**

01-06-78 – **'Musikladen' (Germany): All I Need Is A Girl**

19-06-78 – **'Cheggers Plays Pop' (UK): The Runaway**

10-07-78 – **'Disco' (Germany): All I Need Is A Girl**

10-11-78 – **'Crackerjack' (UK): Stay The Night** *(The producers felt that the lyrics of 'Stay The Night' weren't suitable for a children's TV show, so instead the band changed it to 'Stay A While')*

Late 1978 – **'Drehscheibe' (Germany): Give Me Shakespeare** *(After several mediocre sound-a-like singles, 'Give Me Shakespeare' was a real departure, featuring tough-sounding guitars and not a keyboard in sight. It didn't chart)*

22-12-78 – **'Szene '78' (Germany): Give Me Shakespeare**

Lead singer Georg Kajanus left Sailor in 1979, with the rest of the band splitting the following year. The hit-making '70s line-up reunited from 1990 to 1995, and various incarnations of the band have continued to date. Henry Marsh became the luckiest man in pop when he married Pan's People legend Dee Dee Wilde.

BE-BOP DELUXE

00-06-75 – **Promo Video (UK): Maid In Heaven** *(Fronted by be-suited and over-serious vocalist/guitarist Bill Nelson, 'Maid In Heaven' comes across sounding like a Queen mid-'70s album track)*

19-07-75 – **'The Old Grey Whistle Test' (UK): Maid In Heaven / Sister Seagull** *(The first of three appearances on this influential late-night music TV show)*

00-01-76 – **Promo Video (UK): Ships In The Night** *(Be-Bop Deluxe's only hit, 'Ships In The Night' got to No. 23 in the UK charts)*

13-01-76 – **'The Old Grey Whistle Test' (UK): Ships In The Night / Fair Exchange** *(The 2nd appearance on this show)*

24-01-76 – **'Supersonic' (UK): Ships In The Night** *(More promotion for the band's minor hit)*

05-02-76 – 'Top Of The Pops' (UK): Ships In The Night *(Be-Bop Deluxe's only 'Top Of The Pops' performance, this is unfortunately lost)*

20-02-76 – 'Iltatahti' (Finland)

18-03-76 – 'Top Of The Pops' (UK): Ships In The Night *(This is a repeat of the 05-02-76 performance)*

07-08-76 – **'Saturday Scene: Superpop '76' (UK): Sister Seagull** *(The first of two TV performances on the same day for this slower song)*

07-08-76 – **'So It Goes' (UK): Sister Seagull** *('Sister Seagull' – again)*

13-09-76 – **'Supersonic' (UK): Kiss Of Light** *(Performed here, 'Kiss Of Light' was the non-hit follow-up to 'Ships In The Night')*

16-11-76 – **'The Old Grey Whistle Test' (UK): Forbidden Lovers / Down On Terminal Street** *(Their 3rd appearance on the show in the space of 16 months)*

14-04-77 – 'Star Rider' (UK)

02-08-77 – 'Concert Special' (UK)

04-02-78 – **'Sight and Sound In Concert' (UK): New Precision / Superenigmatix / Possession / Dangerous Stranger / Islands Of The Dead / Lovers Are Mortal / Panic In The World** *(Promoting their final album, the new wave-inspired 'Drastic Plastic', here the band perform only songs from that album, ignoring the "oldies" altogether. Taped in Oxford, this show was later rebroadcast as 'Rock Goes To College' on 03-02-79)*

05-05-78 – **'The Midnight Special' (USA): Panic In The World / New Precision**
(Performing live, this was Be-Bop Deluxe's only US TV appearance)

Bill Nelson dissolved Be-Bop Deluxe in 1978; since then he has prolifically released many recordings, both as a solo artist and in a variety of collaborations. Early Be-Bop Deluxe members Nicholas Chatterton-Dew and Ian Rankin both died in 1995.

BILBO BAGGINS

29-07-74 – 'Lift Off With Ayshea' (UK): Saturday Night *(Not to be confused with The Bay City Rollers' song of the same name, Bilbo Baggins' debut single is both faster and tougher. Unfortunately it wasn't a hit, and neither was the follow-up 'The Sha Na Na Na Song')*

01-05-75 – 'Rock On With 45' (UK): Hold Me

13-05-75 – **'Shang-A-Lang' (UK): Hold Me** *(A worthy revival of the P.J. Proby hit, but another flop)*

30-12-75 – **'Look Alive' (UK): Back Home** *(With Colin Chisholm's strong vocals and good looks, a memorable image incorporating long denim coats and one of the catchiest songs of the mid-'70s, the band couldn't miss, could they? They did)*

00-01-76 – **Promo Video (UK): Back Home**

03-01-76 – **'Supersonic' (UK): Back Home** *(The first of two performances of 'Back Home' on 'Supersonic', this first one features lots of coloured streams of paper blowing about, and the 2nd appearance doesn't)*

24-01-76 – **'Supersonic' (UK): Back Home**

09-03-76 – **'The Arrows' (UK): Back Home**

11-05-76 – **'The Arrows' (UK): It's A Shame** *(A weaker follow-up, this failed once again)*

28-11-76 – **'Second City Firsts: Glitter' (UK): Dream Maker** [with Toyah Wilcox] *(A TV drama featuring a youthful, chubby and dark-haired Toyah Wilcox in one of her first acting roles, in this, she bizarrely dreams of appearing on 'Top Of The Pops' while backed by Bilbo Baggins)*

20-04-78 – **'In Concert' (UK): Sign On The Dotted Line / Shout If You're Mental / I Fooled Around and Fell In Love / Dole Q Blues / You're A Liar / Let's Spend The Night Together / My Generation / You're Not Sorry** *(Taped at The Gateway Theatre in Edinburgh, by now the band had changed their image to smart jackets and skinny ties – like a cross between The Jam and Tom Robinson – and largely changed their musical* direction too, to a more new wave-influenced sound. Oddly, this tremendous live performance doesn't include their current single at the time, 'I Can Feel Mad', though they did feature the B-side, 'Dole Q Blues')

00-08-78 – **Promo Video (UK): She's Gonna Win** *(Never charting under their original name, as the newly-christened 'Bilbo' the band finally had a hit with the new wave pop-rock of 'She's Gonna Win', which peaked at No. 42 in the UK charts)* – **BILBO**

24-08-78 – **'Top Of The Pops' (UK): She's Gonna Win** *(A fine live vocal performance of their hit)* – **BILBO**

Late 1978 – **'The Entertainers' (UK)** – **BILBO**

28-05-79 – **'Cheggers Plays Pop' (UK): America** *(Another change of sound, this time to synthesized pop, but it didn't help matters as it never charted. This was Bilbo Baggins / Bilbo's last single)* – **BILBO**

Splitting in 1979, the band attempted a reunion in 2014 but, plagued by bad luck till the end, they were thwarted when the USA owner of the rights to J.R.R. Tolkien's work objected to the use of the 'Bilbo Baggins' name. The year previous to this, Colin Chisholm auditioned for a place on 'The Voice UK' TV show.

SLIK

00-10-74 – **Promo Video (UK): The Boogiest Band In Town** *(First issued in late 1974 and then re-promoted in March 1975, Slik's first single, 'The Boogiest Band In The World', was not a hit. Midge Ure has long hair over his shoulders in this video, but it's bassist Jim McGinlay who catches the eye with his cropped hair and Clark Gable moustache – exactly the same look Midge would later adopt in Ultravox!)*

Early 1975 – **'Never Too Young To Rock' Movie (UK): The Boogiest Band In Town** *(A cameo in this movie didn't help the single)*

01-01-76 – **'Top Of The Pops' (UK): Forever and Ever** *(By now changing their image to American baseball outfits, 'Forever and Ever' was Slik's biggest and best-known hit, and a UK No. 1)*

10-01-76 – **'Supersonic' (UK): Forever and Ever** *(The first of two performances of this song on 'Supersonic', for this one the band wear monks' habits)*

22-01-76 – **'Top Of The Pops' (UK): Forever and Ever** *(This 'Top Of The Pops' appearance features some red special effects on the keyboard player's hands)*

31-01-76 – **'Supersonic' (UK): Forever and Ever** *(Back to the baseball outfits for this performance)*

05-02-76 – 'Top Of The Pops' (UK): Forever and Ever *(This particular 'Top Of The Pops' appearance is lost)*

12-02-76 – **'Top Of The Pops' (UK): Forever and Ever** *(This is a repeat of the 22-01-76 performance)*

27-02-76 – **'Top Pop' (Holland): Forever and Ever** *(A rather futuristic looking set for this Dutch TV appearance)*

29-04-76 – **'Top Of The Pops' (UK): Requiem** *(The band's 2nd and last hit, 'Requiem' got to No. 24 in the UK charts. This performance features Midge in red)*

13-05-76 – **'Top Of The Pops' (UK): Requiem** *(Midge is wearing green for this appearance)*

22-05-76 – **'Disco' (Germany): Forever and Ever**

28-05-76 – **'Top Pop' (Holland): Requiem** *(Another fabulous looking set on 'Top Pop')*

01-06-76 – **'The Arrows' (UK): Requiem**

10-06-76 – **'Top Of The Pops' (UK): Requiem** *(This is a repeat of the 13-05-76 performance)*

05-08-76 – **'Top Of The Pops' (UK): The Kid's A Punk**

14-08-76 – **'Saturday Scene: Superpop '76' (UK): The Kid's A Punk** *('The Kid's A Punk' was the first of several flop singles, none of them as memorable as the two hits)*

04-09-76 – **'Top Pop' (Holland): The Kid's A Punk** *(Where did 'Top Pop' get these great sets? This really was one of the most visual music TV shows of the '70s and early '80s)*

11-10-76 – **'Supersonic' (UK): Forever and Ever / When Will I Be Loved** *('When Will I Be Loved' is a revival of The Everly Brothers' classic)*

08-11-76 – **'Supersonic' (UK): When Will I Be Loved**

06-12-76 – **'Plattenkuche' (Germany): Don't Take Your Love Away**

21-12-76 – **'The Arrows' (UK): Don't Take Your Love Away**

25-12-76 – **'Top Of The Pops' (UK): Forever and Ever** *(Midge wears a red jacket for this reprise of their No. 1 hit)*

22-01-77 – **'Supersonic' (UK): Don't Take Your Love Away**

17-04-77 – **'Hits A Go Go' (Switzerland): Dancerama**

Following a change of name to PVC2 for their final single, Midge Ure left the band in late 1977. While the remaining members formed the short-lived Zones, Midge Ure went on to a glittering career that includes Rich Kids, Visage, Thin Lizzy, Ultravox and Band Aid.

Peter Checksfield

PAN'S PEOPLE

'Top Of The Pops'

00-05-68 - Young Girl [Gary Puckett and The Union Gap] *(Several other dates have been suggested as the TOTP debut by Pan's People – including an 18-04-68 routine to 'Cry Like A Baby' by The Box Tops – but these were probably by The Go-Jo's or other pre-Pan's People groups. The real debut is most likely to this song, probably on either 16-05-68 or 23-05-68. The line-up by this time had settled on Andi Rutherford, Babs Lord, Dee Dee Wilde, Flick Colby, Louise Clarke and Ruth Pearson, a line-up that would remain unchanged until the spring of 1972)*

30-05-68 – U.S. Male [Elvis Presley]

08-08-68 – Mony Mony [Tommy James & The Shondells]

15-08-68 – Mony Mony [Tommy James & The Shondells] *(This is probably a repeat of the 08-08-68 performance)*

05-09-68 – I Say A Little Prayer [Aretha Franklin]

24-10-68 – The Good, The Band and The Ugly [Hugh Montenegro]

31-10-68 – This Old Heart Of Mine [The Isley Brothers]

07-11-68 – Breakin' Down The Walls Of Heartache [The Bandwagon]

14-11-68 – All Along The Watchtower [The Jimi Hendrix Experience]

21-11-68 – This Old Heart Of Mine [The Isley Brothers]

28-11-68 – The Good, The Band and The Ugly [Hugh Montenegro]

26-12-68 – The Good, The Band and The Ugly [Hugh Montenegro]

27-03-69 – Gentle On My Mind [Dean Martin]

01-05-69 – Get Back [The Beatles with Billy Preston]

29-05-69 – Get Back [The Beatles with Billy Preston]

Look Wot They Dun!

19-06-69 – The Ballad Of John and Yoko [The Beatles]

03-07-69 – Gimme Gimme Good Lovin' [Crazy Elephant]

11-09-69 – Marrakesh Express [Crosby, Stills & Nash]

02-10-69 – Bad Moon Rising [Creedence Clearwater Revival]

23-10-69 – The Return Of Django [The Upsetters]

01-01-70 – **Green River [Creedence Clearwater Revival]** *(The earliest surviving Pan's People TOTP performance, or sort of, as the circulating video is actually a rehearsal)*

08-01-70 – Tracy [The Cuff Links]

22-01-70 – **Wedding Bell Blues [The 5th Dimension]**

29-01-70 – **I'm A Man [Chicago]**

05-02-70 – **Both Sides Now [Judy Collins]**

12-02-70 – **I Want You Back [The Jackson 5]**

19-02-70 – Na Na Hey Hey (Kiss Him Goodbye) [Steam]

26-02-70 – **Temma Harbour [Mary Hopkin]**

05-03-70 – Bridge Over Troubled Water [Simon and Garfunkel]

12-03-70 – Something's Burning [Kenny Rogers and The First Edition]

19-03-70 – Govinda [Rhada Krishna Temple] *(Pan's People dance while Rhada Krishna Temple perform in the studio)*

19-03-70 – Rag Mama Rag [The Band]

26-03-70 – Who Do You Love [Juicy Lucy]

02-04-70 – Spirit In The Sky [Norman Greenbaum]

09-04-70 – Farewell Is A Lonely Sound [Jimmy Ruffin]

16-04-70 – Never Had A Dream Come True [Stevie Wonder]

23-04-70 – House Of The Rising Sun [Frijid Pink]

23-04-70 – Who Do You Love [Juicy Lucy]

30-04-70 – If You Gotta Make A Fool Of Somebody [Bobbie Gentry] *(Pan's People dance while Bobbie Gentry performs in the studio. This wasn't the first time they had worked with Bobbie Gentry, as they were the resident dancers on her TV show)*

30-04-70 – Do The Funky Chicken [Rufus Thomas]

07-05-70 – Travellin' Band [Creedence Clearwater Revival]

14-05-70 – **Do The Funky Chicken [Rufus Thomas]**

14-05-70 – Daughter Of Darkness [Tom Jones]

21-05-70 – Up The Ladder To The Roof   [The Supremes]

28-05-70 – ABC [The Jackson 5]

04-06-70 – Cottonfields [The Beach Boys]

11-06-70 – Abraham, Martin and John [Marvin Gaye]

18-06-70 – The Green Manalishi (With The Two Prong Crown) [Fleetwood Mac]

18-06-70 – **Bet Yer Life I Do [Herman's Hermits]**

There were no shows on 25-06-70 and 02-07-70 due to TV coverage of the tennis at Wimbledon and the 1970 World Cup.

09-07-70 – It's All In The Game [The Four Tops]

16-07-70 – Love Like A Man [Ten Years After]

23-07-70 – Something [Shirley Bassey]

30-07-70 – Big Yellow Taxi [Joni Mitchell]

06-08-70 – **Signed, Sealed, Delivered (I'm Yours) [Stevie Wonder]**

13-08-70 – **The Love You Save [The Jackson 5]**

20-08-70 – The Tears Of A Clown [Smokey Robinson and The Miracles]

27-08-70 – **The Weaver's Answer [Family]** *(This features Flick only)*

27-08-70 – It's So Easy [Andy Williams] *(This featured Andi only)*

27-08-70 – **Give Me Just A Little More Time [Chairmen Of The Board]** *(Only* *approximately 12 seconds of this performance survives. Andi is missing from this dance)*

03-09-70 – **Make It With You [Bread]** *(Andi is missing from this dance)*

10-09-70 – **Jimmy Mack [Martha and The Vandellas]** *(Flick is missing from all surviving dances from this date until 26-12-70)*

17-09-70 – **Montego Bay [Bobby Bloom]**

24-09-70 – Don't Play That Song [Aretha Franklin]

01-10-70 – Ball Of Confusion [The Temptations]

15-10-70 – **(They Long To Be) Close To You [The Carpenters]**

29-10-70 – War [Edwin Starr]

05-11-70 – Whole Lotta Love [C.C.S.]

12-11-70 – Voodoo Chile [The Jimi Hendrix Experience]

19-11-70 – Cracklin' Rosie [Neil Diamond]

26-11-70 – You've Got Me Dangling On A String [Chairmen Of The Board]

10-12-70 – I'll Be There [The Jackson 5]

10-12-70 – Cannikin Clink [Lance Le Gault] *(Pan's People danced while Lance De Gault performed in the studio)*

There were no shows on 17-12-70 and 24-12-70.

25-12-70 – The Tears Of A Clown [Smokey Robinson and The Miracles]

26-12-70 – **Spirit In The Sky [Norman Greenbaum]**

31-12-70 – Everybody Get Together [Lulu] *(Pan's People danced while Lulu performed in the studio)*

07-01-71 – You're Ready Now [Frankie Valli]

07-01-71 – Grandad [Clive Dunn] *(Pan's People danced while Clive Dunn performed in the studio. With Pan's People dressed as school girls, it's a wonder grandad didn't have a heart attack!)*

14-01-71 – **We've Only Just Begun [The Carpenters]**

14-01-71 – **Amazing Grace [Judy Collins]** *(This features Flick only)*

21-01-71 – **My Sweet Lord [George Harrison]**

28-01-71 – Stoned Love [The Supremes]

28-01-71 – **My Sweet Lord [George Harrison]** *(This is a repeat of the 21-01-71 performance)*

04-02-71 – Resurrection Shuffle [Ashton, Gardner and Dyke]

25-02-71 – **Everything's Tuesday [Chairmen Of The Board]**

04-03-71 – **Allemande / Wedding March [Early Music Consort]**

11-03-71 – Another Day [Paul McCartney]

11-03-71 – **Hot Love [T. Rex]** *(Pan's People dance while T. Rex perform in the studio. The first of two 'Hot Love' performances, this time the girls dance while part of the audience)*

18-03-71 – **Walking [C.C.S.]** *(Flick is missing from this dance)*

25-03-71 – **Hot Love [T. Rex]** *(Pan's People dance while T. Rex perform in the studio, by themselves away from the audience while wearing hot pants and bikinis. Some sources list this as 18-03-71)*

25-03-71 – Bridget The Midget [Ray Stevens]

01-04-71 – Walking [C.C.S.]

15-04-71 – Remember Me [Diana Ross]

29-04-71 – **Mama's Pearl [The Jackson 5]**

29-04-71 – **Everybody Clap [Lulu]** *(Pan's People dance while Lulu performs in the studio. This was also broadcast on 'Disco', German TV, on 03-07-71)*

06-05-71 – Heaven Must Have Sent You [The Elgins]

27-05-71 – Rain [Bruce Ruffin]

17-06-71 – **Joy To The World [Three Dog Night]**

Look Wot They Dun!

01-07-71 – **River Deep - Mountain High [The Supremes and The Four Tops]** *(Andi is missing from this dance)*

12-08-71 – Move On Up [Curtis Mayfield]

19-08-71 – Hey Girl, Don't Bother Me [The Tams]

26-08-71 – Nathan Jones [The Supremes]

09-09-71 – Maggie May [Rod Stewart]

16-09-71 – **Tap Turns On The Water [C.C.S.]**

30-09-71 – **Tweedle Dee, Tweedle Dum [Middle Of The Road]** *(Only approximately 15 seconds of this performance survives)*

14-10-71 – The Witch Queen Of New Orleans [Redbone]

21-10-71 – Sultana [Titanic]

04-11-71 – Run, Baby, Run (Back Into My Arms) [The Newbeats]

11-11-71 – Surrender [Diana Ross]

18-11-71 – **Let's See Action [The Who]**

02-12-71 – **Fireball [Deep Purple]**

09-12-71 – Theme From Shaft [Isaac Hayes]

25-12-71 – **Tap Turns On The Water [C.C.S.]** *(This is a repeat of the 16-09-71 performance)*

27-12-71 – **My Sweet Lord [George Harrison]** *(This is a repeat of the 21-01-71 performance)*

30-12-71 – **Stoney End [Barbra Streisand]**

30-12-71 – **Jeepster [T. Rex]**

13-01-72 – Stay With Me [The Faces]

20-01-72 – **Theme From The Persuaders [John Barry]**

There was no show on 10-02-72 due to TV coverage of the Winter Olympics.

24-02-72 – Mother and Child Reunion [Paul Simon]

16-03-72 – Floy Joy [The Supremes]

30-03-72 – Without You [Nilsson]

13-04-72 – Sweet Talking Guy [The Chiffons] *(Flick Colby stopped dancing with Pan's People sometime in April 1972, exact date and performance unknown, though she continued choreographing the group afterwards)*

27-04-72 – **Runnin' Away [Sly & The Family Stone]** *(The line-up is now Andi Rutherford, Babs Lord, Dee Dee Wilde, Louise Clarke and Ruth Pearson. This would remain unchanged until October)*

04-05-72 – Wade In The Water [Ramsey Lewis]

11-05-72 – Saturday Night At The Movies [The Drifters]

18-05-72 – Me and Julio Down By The Schoolyard [Paul Simon]

15-06-72 – Rockin' Robin [Michael Jackson]

22-06-72 – **A Little Bit Of Love [Free]**

06-07-72 – I've Been Lonely For So Long [Frederick Knight]

13-07-72 – Betcha By Golly, Wow [The Stylistics]

20-07-72 – My Guy [Mary Wells]

27-07-72 – Popcorn [Hot Butter]

03-08-72 – Working On A Building Of Love [Chairmen Of The Board]

17-08-72 – I Get The Sweetest Feeling [Jackie Wilson]

24-08-72 – Too Busy Thinking 'bout My Baby [Mardi Gras]

07-09-72 – Come On Over To My Place [The Drifters]

14-09-72 – **Ain't No Sunshine [Michael Jackson]**

21-09-72 – Walk In The Night [Junior Walker and The All Stars]

28-09-72 – **Back Stabbers [The O'Jays]** *(Only rehearsal footage survives for this)*

28-09-72 – **John I'm Only Dancing [David Bowie]** *(This features Ruth only)*

05-10-72 – The Guitar Man [Bread] *(Andi Rutherford quit Pan's People around October 1972, exact date and performance unknown. She was replaced by Cherry Gillespie, though she didn't join the group for a dance routine until 28-12-72. In the meantime, Babs, Dee Dee, Louise and Ruth carried on as a four-piece)*

12-10-72 – In A Broken Dream [Python Lee Jackson]

26-10-72 – Here I Go Again [Archie Bell and The Drells]

02-11-72 – **Let's Dance [Chris Montez]**

23-11-72 – Crocodile Rock [Elton John]

30-11-72 – My Ding-A-Ling [Chuck Berry]

07-12-72 – Crazy Horses [The Osmonds]

21-12-72 – The Jean Genie [David Bowie]

25-12-72 – Popcorn [Hot Butter]

28-12-72 – **Without You [Nilsson]** *(A quintet again, the line-up is now Babs Lord, Cherry Gillespie, Dee Dee Wilde, Louise Clarke and Ruth Pearson. This would remain unchanged for 18 months)*

04-01-73 – **You're So Vain [Carly Simon]**

11-01-73 – I'm On My Way To A Better Place [Chairmen Of The Board]

18-01-73 – Wishing Well [Free]

25-01-73 – **Papa Was A Rollin' Stone [The Temptations]**

01-02-73 – **You're So Vain [Carly Simon]** *(This is a repeat of the 04-01-73 performance)*

08-02-73 – Superstition [Stevie Wonder]

15-02-73 – Hocus Pocus [Focus]

22-02-73 – Doctor My Eyes [The Jackson 5]

01-03-73 – Killing Me Softly With His Song [Roberta Flack]

08-03-73 – Feel The Need In Me [The Detroit Emeralds]

15-03-73 – Love Train [The O'Jays]

22-03-73 – **Tie A Yellow Ribbon Round The Ole Oak Tree [Dawn Featuring Tony Orlando]**

29-03-73 – Why Can't We Live Together [Timmy Thomas]

05-04-73 – Tweedlee Dee [Little Jimmy Osmond]

There were no shows on 12-04-73 and 19-04-73 due to a BBC strike.

27-04-73 – The Right Thing To Do [Carly Simon]

27-04-73 – Wam Bam [The Handley Family]

04-05-73 – Could It Be I'm Falling In Love [The Detroit Spinners]

11-05-73 – **Also Sprach Zarathustra (2001) [Eumir Deodato]**

18-05-73 – You Want It You Got It [The Detroit Emeralds]

25-05-73 – Walk On The Wild Side [Lou Reed]

01-06-73 – **Walking In The Rain [The Partridge Family]**

08-06-73 – Frankenstein [The Edgar Winter Group]

15-06-73 – Hallelujah Day [The Jackson 5]

22-06-73 – **Take Me To The Mardi Gras [Paul Simon]**

06-07-73 – **Finders Keepers [Chairmen Of The Board]**

20-07-73 – **Spanish Eyes [Al Martino]**

27-07-73 – All Right Now [Free]

03-08-73 – **You Can Do Magic [Limmie & Family Cookin']**

10-08-73 – **Smarty Pants [First Choice]**

17-08-73 – **I'm Doin' Fine Now [New York City]**

Look Wot They Dun!

24-08-73 – Fool [Elvis Presley]

31-08-73 – **I Think Of You [The Detroit Emeralds]**

There was no show on 06-09-73.

13-09-73 – **Monster Mash [Bobby Boris Pickett and The Crypt-Kickers]**

20-09-73 – **Nutbush City Limits [Ike and Tina Turner]** *(Dee Dee is missing from this dance)*

27-09-73 – **Monster Mash [Bobby Boris Pickett and The Crypt-Kickers]**

04-10-73 – That Lady [The Isley Brothers]

11-10-73 – **Ghetto Child [The Detroit Spinners]**

01-11-73 – Daydreamer [David Cassidy]

15-11-73 – **Do You Wanna Dance [Barry Blue]**

22-11-73 – **Keep On Truckin' [Eddie Kendricks]**

29-11-73 – Lamplight [David Essex]

06-12-73 – **Truck On (Tyke) [T. Rex]**

13-12-73 – **Dance With The Devil [Cozy Powell]**

13-12-73 – Gaudete [Steeleye Span] *(Pan's People danced while Steeleye Span performed in the studio)*

20-12-73 – **Love On A Mountain Top [Robert Knight]**

25-12-73 – **Get Down [Gilbert O'Sullivan]**

27-12-73 – **Spirit In The Sky [Norman Greenbaum]**

03-01-74 – **Love On A Mountain Top [Robert Knight]** *(This is a repeat of the 20-12-73 performance)*

10-01-74 – **All Of My Life [Diana Ross]**

17-01-74 – **Dance With The Devil [Cozy Powell]**

24-01-74 – Rockin' Roll Baby [The Stylistics]

31-01-74 – **The Love I Lost [Harold Melvin and The Blue Notes]**

07-02-74 – **All Of My Life [Diana Ross]** *(This is a repeat of the 10-01-74 performance. A routine for 'Highways Of My Life' [The Isley Brothers] was rehearsed for this date, but wasn't used as the record went down in the charts)*

14-02-74 – **Love's Theme [Love Unlimited Orchestra]**

21-02-74 – Highways Of My Life [The Isley Brothers]

28-02-74 – The Most Beautiful Girl [Charlie Rich]

07-03-74 – **Rebel Rebel [David Bowie]**

14-03-74 – **Until You Come Back To Me [Aretha Franklin]** *(Dee Dee is missing from this dance)*

21-03-74 – You Are Everything [Diana Ross and Marvin Gaye]

28-03-74 – **Seasons In The Sun [Terry Jacks]**

04-04-74 – Seasons In The Sun [Terry Jacks]

11-04-74 – Homely Girl [The Chi-Lites]

18-04-74 – **The Entertainer [Marvin Hamlisch]**

25-04-74 – I Know What I Like (In Your Wardrobe) [Genesis] *(A Screen-shot image survives from this, prompting rumours that the whole video may still exist)*

02-05-74 – **I Can't Stop [The Osmonds]** *(Dee Dee is missing from this dance)*

09-05-74 – TSOP (The Sound Of Philadelphia) [MFSB Featuring The Three Degrees]

16-05-74 – There's A Ghost In My House [R. Dean Taylor] *(This was the last performance to feature Louise Clark. Her replacement was Sue Menhenick, who made her debut on the show 3 weeks later. Dee Dee is missing from this dance)*

23-05-74 – **I Can't Stop [The Osmonds]** *(Dee Dee is missing from this dance. This is a repeat of the 02-05-74 performance)*

There was no Pan's People performance on 30-05-74, possibly to give them more time to rehearse with new member Sue.

06-06-74 – **Summer Breeze [The Isley Brothers]** *(Sue's TOTP debut, the line-up is now Babs Lord, Cherry Gillespie, Dee Dee Wilde, Ruth Pearson and Sue Menhenick. The next change would be 15 months later)*

13-06-74 – **Don't Let The Sun Go Down On Me [Elton John]**

There were no shows on 20-06-74, 27-06-74, 04-07-74, 11-07-74, 18-07-74, 25-07-74 and 01-08-74 due to a BBC strike. A routine for 'I Won't Last A Day Without You' [The Carpenters] was rehearsed for 20-06-74, but obviously wasn't used as the show was cancelled.

08-08-74 – **When Will I See You Again [The Three Degrees]**

15-08-74 – **You Make Me Feel Brand New [The Stylistics]**

15-08-74 – **Having A Party [The Osmonds]** *(Pan's People dance while The Osmonds perform in the studio)*

22-08-74 – What Becomes Of The Brokenhearted [Jimmy Ruffin]

29-08-74 – Annie's Song [John Denver]

05-09-74 – Baby Love [Diana Ross and The Supremes]

13-09-74 – **Another Saturday Night [Cat Stevens]**

13-09-74 – **The Tango's Over [Mick Robertson]** *(Pan's People dance while Mick Robertson performs in the studio)*

13-09-74 – **Leave It [Mike McGear]** *(This features Babs only)*

20-09-74 – **Machine Gun [The Commodores]**

27-09-74 – **It's Better To Have (And Don't Need) [Don Covay]**

04-10-74 – **You Little Trustmaker [The Tymes]**

11-10-74 – **I Get A Kick Out Of You [Gary Shearston]**

17-10-74 – Samba Pa Ti [Santana]

24-10-74 – Let's Put It All Together [The Stylistics]

31-10-74 – Da Doo Ron Ron [The Crystals]

07-11-74 – **Then Came You [Dionne Warwick and The Spinners]**

14-11-74 – You're The First, The Last, My Everything [Barry White]

21-11-74 – **You Ain't Seen Nothing Yet [Bachman-Turner Overdrive]**

28-11-74 – Sha-La-La (Make Me Happy) [Al Green]

05-12-74 – **You're The First, The Last, My Everything [Barry White]** *(A routine for 'Lucy In The Sky With Diamonds' [Elton John] was rehearsed for this date, but was replaced at the request of the show's producer, Robin Nash)*

A routine for 'Zing Went The Strings Of My Heart' [The Trammps] was rehearsed for 12-12-74, but wasn't used as the record went down in the charts. There was no replacement.

19-12-74 – **Never Can Say Goodbye [Gloria Gaynor]**

25-12-74 – **You Won't Find Another Fool Like Me [The New Seekers]**

25-12-74 – **You're The First, The Last, My Everything [Barry White]**

02-01-75 – **Help Me Make It Through The Night [John Holt]** *(Dee Dee is missing from this dance)*

09-01-75 – Ms. Grace [The Tymes] *(Dee Dee was missing from this dance)*

16-01-75 – **Down Down [Status Quo]** *(Dee Dee is missing from this dance)*

16-01-75 – Help Me Make It Through The Night [John Holt] *(Dee Dee was missing from this dance)*

23-01-75 – **Boogie On Reggae Woman [Stevie Wonder]** *(Dee Dee is missing from this dance)*

30-01-75 – **Promised Land [Elvis Presley]** *(Dee Dee is missing from this dance)*

06-02-75 – **Star On A TV Show [The Stylistics]**

13-02-75 – Please Mr Postman [The Carpenters]

Due to Cherry's honeymoon, there were no Pan's People performances on 20-02-75 and 27-02-75.

06-03-75 – **Pick Up The Pieces [The Average White Band]**

13-03-75 – **Philadelphia Freedom [The Elton John Band]**

20-03-75 – **What Am I Gonna Do With You [Barry White]**

27-03-75 – **Play Me Like You Play Your Guitar [Duane Eddy and The Rebelettes]**

03-04-75 – **Girls [The Moments and The Whatnauts]**

10-04-75 – **Swing Your Daddy [Jim Gilstrap]**

10-04-75 – **The Funky Gibbon [The Goodies]** *(Pan's People dance while The Goodies perform in the studio)*

17-04-75 – **Get Down Tonight [KC and The Sunshine Band]**

24-04-75 – **Sorry Doesn't Always Make It Right [Diana Ross]**

01-05-75 – **The Night [Frankie Valli and The Four Seasons]**

08-05-75 – **I Wanna Dance Wit Choo [Disco Tex and The Sex-O-Lettes]**

15-05-75 – **Once Bitten Twice Shy [Ian Hunter]**

22-05-75 – **Sing Baby Sing [The Stylistics]**

29-05-75 – **Swing Low Sweet Chariot [Eric Clapton]**

05-06-75 – **I'll Do For You Anything You Want Me To [Barry White]**

12-06-75 – **Listen To What The Man Said [Wings]**

19-06-75 – **Disco Stomp [Hamilton Bohannon]**

26-06-75 – **The Hustle [Van McCoy and The Soul City Symphony]**

03-07-75 – **Misty [Ray Stevens]**

10-07-75 – **Have You Seen Her [The Chi-Lites]**

17-07-75 – **Barbados [Typically Tropical]**

24-07-75 – **Foot Stompin' Music [Hamilton Bohannon]**

24-07-75 – **Barbados [Typically Tropical]** *(Pan's People dance while Typically Tropical perform in the studio, though Pan's People's segments are actually repeated from 17-07-*

75)

31-07-75 – **It's Been So Long [George McCrae]**

07-08-75 – **Best Thing That Ever Happened To Me [Gladys Knight and The Pips]**

14-08-75 – **Fame [David Bowie]**

21-08-75 – **That's The Way (I Like It) [KC and The Sunshine Band]**

28-08-75 – **One Of These Nights [The Eagles]**

04-09-75 – **Summertime City [Mike Batt]** *(Pan's People dance while Mike Batt performs in the studio)*

11-09-75 – **There Goes My First Love [The Drifters]**

18-09-75 – **Feel Like Makin' Love [Bad Company]** *(This was the last TOTP performance to feature Babs Lord, who left to marry actor Robert Powell. She was replaced by two new members, Mary Corpe and Lee Ward)*

18-09-75 – **Summertime City [Mike Batt]** *(Pan's People dance while Mike Batt performs in the studio. This is a repeat of the 04-09-75 performance)*

25-09-75 – **I Only Have Eyes For You [Art Garfunkel]** *(A sextet again for the first time since April 1972, the line-up is now Cherry Gillespie, Dee Dee Wilde, Mary Corpe, Lee Ward, Ruth Pearson and Sue Menhenick. A routine for 'Solitaire' [The Carpenters] was rehearsed for this date, but wasn't used as the record went down in the charts)*

02-10-75 – **Who Loves You [The Four Seasons]**

09-10-75 – **No Woman No Cry [Bob Marley and The Wailers]**

16-10-75 – **Island Girl [Elton John]**

23-10-75 – **Hold Back The Night [The Trammps]**

30-10-75 – **Rock On Brother [The Chequers]** *(This is Dee Dee Wilde's last TOTP performance)*

06-11-75 – **Imagine [John Lennon]** *(A quintet again, the line-up is now Cherry Gillespie, Mary Corpe, Lee Ward, Ruth Pearson and Sue Menhenick)*

Look Wot They Dun!

13-11-75 – **This Old Heart Of Mine [Rod Stewart]**

20-11-75 – **Lyin' Eyes [The Eagles]**

27-11-75 – **Imagine [John Lennon]** *(This is a repeat of the 06-11-75 performance. A routine for 'Rocky' [Austin Roberts] was rehearsed for this date, but wasn't used as the record went down in the charts)*

04-12-75 – **First Impressions [The Impressions]**

11-12-75 – **Let's Twist Again [Chubby Checker]**

18-12-75 – (Are You Ready) Do The Bus Stop [The Fatback Band]

23-12-75 – **Barbados [Typically Tropical]**

23-12-75 – **Space Oddity [David Bowie]**

25-12-75 – **I Only Have Eyes For You [Art Garfunkel]**

25-12-75 – **I Can't Give You Anything (But My Love) [The Stylistics]**

01-01-76 – **In Dulci Jubilo [Mike Oldfield]**

08-01-76 – **Itchycoo Park [The Small Faces]**

15-01-76 – Let The Music Play [Barry White]

22-01-76 – **Midnight Rider [Paul Davidson]**

29-01-76 – Baby Face [The Wing and A Prayer Fife and Drum Corps]

05-02-76 – **December 1963 (Oh, What A Night) [The Four Seasons]** *(Mary is missing from this dance)*

12-02-76 – **Rodrigo's Guitar Concerto De Aranjuez [Manuel and The Music Of The Mountains]** *('Blue Peter' presenter Lesley Judd joined Pan's People for this one-off performance, making the line-up Cherry Gillespie, Mary Corpe, Lee Ward, Lesley Judd, Ruth Pearson and Sue Menhenick)*

19-02-76 – **Squeeze Box [The Who]**

26-02-76 – **Funky Weekend [The Stylistics]**

04-03-76 – **Let's Do The Latin Hustle [Eddie Drennon and B.B.S. Unlimited]**

11-03-76 – Wake Up Everybody [Harold Melvin and The Blue Notes]

18-03-76 – Take It To The Limit [The Eagles]

25-03-76 – **Yesterday [The Beatles]**

01-04-76 – **Jungle Rock [Hank Mizell]** *(This was Lee Ward's final performance with Pan's People. The remaining members would continue as a 4-piece)*

08-04-76 – **Paperback Writer [The Beatles]** *(The line-up is now Cherry Gillespie, Mary Corpe, Ruth Pearson and Sue Menhenick)*

08-04-76 – **There's A Kind Of Hush [The Carpenters]**

15-04-76 – **Theme From 'Mahogany' [Diana Ross]**

15-04-76 – **Disco Connection [Isaac Hayes]** *(Mary is missing from this dance, leaving just the trio of Cherry, Ruth and Sue)*

22-04-76 – **You Sexy Sugar Plum (But I Like It) [Rodger Collins]**

22-04-76 – **Jungle Rock [Hank Mizell]** *(This is a repeat of the 01-04-76 performance)*

29-04-76 – **More, More, More [Andrea True Connection]**

29-04-76 – **Silver Star [The Four Seasons]**

Although largely remembered today for their 'Top Of The Pops' appearances, Pan's People appeared on many other TV shows. During the late '60s, these were often for European TV shows rather than the UK, including 'Vibrato', 'Hits A Go Go', 'Beat Club', 'Beat! Beat! Beat!' and 'Moef Ga Ga'. Their many UK TV appearances include 'The Dickie Valentine Show', 'Bobbie Gentry', 'Happening For Lulu', 'The Golden Shot', 'The Frankie Howerd Show', 'The Price Of Fame', 'Cilla!', 'The John Denver Show', 'The Two Ronnies', 'The Jack Jones Show', 'Clunk-Click', 'Crackerjack', 'Jim'll Fix It', 'The Morecambe and Wise Christmas Show' and 'Blue Peter'. However, probably their most notable non-TOTP appearance was for their own episode of BBC's 'In Concert'. Taped on New Year's Eve 1973, and broadcast on 17th April 1974, the many dances include the infamously daring routine featuring Louise and Dee Dee in *extremely* daring costumes!

Pan's People rehearsing on 04-10-73, (L to R): Louise, Babs, Dee Dee, Cherry and Ruth.

Following the demise of Pan's People, both Cherry and Sue became members of the short-lived 1976 TOTP dance troupe 'Ruby Flipper', with Sue going on to join 'Legs and Co.' from 1976 until their demise in 1981. Mary popped up occasionally as part of the 1982 dancers 'Zoo'. Sadly, of the original 1968 – 1972 quintet, only Babs and Dee Dee survive. Flick died after a long illness in 2011, as did Louise in 2012, Andi in 2015 and Ruth in 2017. Babs is still married to actor Robert Powell, and Dee Dee is still dancing. As she recently told the author, 'Dancing is my life, and keeps me healthy and very happy, so to everyone out there who hasn't done it before give it a go! For my premise is: It's Never Too Late To Dance!'

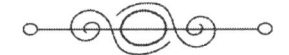

Peter Checksfield

If you enjoyed this book, you might want to post an honest review on Amazon…. and you may also want to read 'CHANNELLING THE BEAT! (The Ultimate Guide to UK '60s Pop on TV)'! Here's what others have said about the book:

'This really is one of the best guides ever to pop music TV'

(Keith Badman, 'Record Collector')

'Well done Peter, you've reminded us just how famous we all were!'

Mike Pender (The Searchers)

'A must-have for anyone with an interest in music's greatest decade'

(Jim Stewart, 'The Beat')

'It is my pleasure to be a part of this book, so have a great read and enjoy!' Brian Poole (Brian Poole and The Tremeloes)

'Of help to any writer about the pop culture of the sixties'

(Roger Stormo, 'The Daily Beatle')

'A concise and extremely well-researched tome'

Steve Ellis (Love Affair)

'A vital addition to any swinging sixties connoisseur's library'

(Alan Clayson, 'Ugly Things')

'This is my favourite book… a brilliant look at who and why. I can't put it down!'

Peter Noone (Herman's Hermits)

'A must buy for anyone with more than a passing interest in UK TV/pop music'

(Rob Bradford, 'Thunderbolt')

'A fantastic reference archive… a 'must have' book for any music lovers'

Tony Crane MBE (The Merseybeats)

'This is a valuable labour of love"

(Kieron Tyler, 'Mojo')

Look Wot They Dun!

BIBLIOGRAPHY & WEBSITES

1974 – Diary of a Rock 'N' Roll Star – Ian Hunter (Panther)

1974 – The David Bowie Story – George Tremlett (Future Publications)

1974 – The David Essex Story – George Tremlett (Future Publications)

1974 – The Gary Glitter Story – George Tremlett (Futura Publications)

1975 – Bay City Rollers – Michael Wale (Everest Publishing)

1975 – Slade – George Tremlett (Future Publications)

1975 – Slade in Flame – John Pidgeon (Panther)

1975 – The Marc Bolan Story – George Tremlett (Future Publications)

1976 – Alvin Stardust – George Tremlett (Future Publications)

1976 – Rod Stewart and the changing Faces – John Pidgeon (Panther)

1976 – Suzi Quatro – Margaret Mander (Future Publications)

1976 – The Bryan Ferry Story – Rex Balfour (M. Dempsey)

1976 – The Rod Stewart Story – George Tremlett (Future Publications)

1980 – The Electric Light Orchestra Story – Bev Bevan (Mushroom Publishing Ltd)

1982 – Bryan Ferry and Roxy Music – Dafydd Rees, Barry Lazell (Proteus)

1984 – The Rolling Stones: The First Twenty Years – David Dalton (Random House)

1989 – David Bowie: Moonage Daydream – Dave Thompson (Plexus Publishing Ltd)

1990 – Stone Alone – Billy Wyman, Ray Coleman (Viking)

1991 – Leader: The Autobiography of Gary Glitter – Gary Glitter, Lloyd Bradley (Ebury Press)

1992 – Marc Bolan: Wilderness of the Mind Paperback – John Willans, Caron Thomas (Xanadu Publications Ltd)

1992 – The Show Must Go On: The Life of Freddie Mercury – Rick Sky (Harper Collins)

1993 – The Guinness Who's Who of Seventies Music – Colin Larkin (Guinness World Records Ltd)

1993 – Twentieth Century Boy: The Marc Bolan Story – Mark Paytress (Sidgwick & Jackson)

1994 – Rod Stewart: The Biography – Ray Coleman (Pavilion Books)

Look Wot They Dun!

1995 – Elton John: 25 Years in the Charts – John Tobler (Hamlyn)

1995 – Record Collector – 2-part 'Bolan on TV' feature – Cliff McLenehan (Diamond Publishing)

1995 – The Sensational Alex Harvey – John Neil Munro (Firefly Books Ltd)

1995 – X-Ray: The Unauthorized Autobiography – Ray Davies (Penguin)

1996 – Beat Merchants: Origins, History, Impact and Rock Legacy of the 1960s British Pop Groups – Alan Clayson (Blandford Press)

1997 – All the Way to Memphis - The Story of Mott The Hoople Paperback – Philip Cato (ST Publishing)

1997 – Kink: An Autobiography – Dave Davies (Hachette Books)

1998 – A Little Bit Funny: The Elton John Story – Patrick Humphries (Aurum Press)

1998 – Wham Bam Thank You Glam: Tribute to the Seventies – Jeremy Novick (Aurum Press)

1999 – Avro's Top Pop – Richard Groothuizen (Tirion)

1999 – Rod Stewart: Every Picture Tells A Story – Lloyd Bradley (Aurum Press)

2000 – Bye Bye Baby: My Tragic Love Affair with The Bay City Rollers – Caroline Sullivan (Bloomsbury Publishing PLC)

2000 – Glam Rock (20th Century Rock & Roll) – Dave Thompson (Collector's Guide Publishing)

2000 – Jeff's Book: A Chronology of Jeff Beck's Career 1965-1980 – Christopher Hjort, Doug Hinman (Rock 'n' Roll Research Press)

2000 – The Worst Band in the World: The Definitive Biography of 10cc – Liam Newton (Minerva Press)

2001 – Freddie Mercury: An intimate memoir by the man who knew him best – Peter Freestone, David Evans (Omnibus Press)

2001 – Groove Tube: Sixties Television and the Youth Rebellion – Aniko Bodroghkozy (Duke University Press)

2001 – The Beatles After The Break-Up 1970 - 2000– Keith Badman (Omnibus Press)

2002 – A Charmed Life: The Autobiography of David Essex – David Essex (Orion)

2002 – Sir Elton: The Definitive Biography of Elton John – Philip Norman (Pan Books)

2002 – Top of the Pops: 1964-2002 – Jeff Simpson (BBC Worldwide)

2003 – Last Orders Please: Rod Stewart, the Faces and the Britain we forgot – Jim Melly

(Ebury Press)

2003 – Shang-a-Lang: Life as an International Pop Idol – Les McKeown, Lynne Elliott (Mainstream Publishing)

2004 – Midge Ure: If I Was... The Autobiography – Midge Ure (Virgin Books)

2004 – Rod Stewart: The New Biography – Tim Ewbank, Stafford Hildred (Piatkus)

2004 – SAHB Story: The Tale of the Sensational Alex Harvey Band – Martin Kielty (Neil Wilson Publishing)

2004 – The Kinks – All Day and All of The Night: Day By Day Concerts, Recordings and Broadcasts, 1964-1997 – Doug Hinman (Backbeat Books)

2004 – The Thrill of it All: The Story of Bryan Ferry and Roxy Music – David Buckley (Andre Deutsch Ltd)

2005 – 1000 UK Number One Hits – Jon Kutner, Spencer Leigh (Omnibus Press)

2005 – Strange Fascination: Bowie - The Definitive Story - David Buckley (Virgin Books)

2006 – Bolan: The Rise And Fall of a 20th Century Superstar – Mark Paytress (Omnibus Press)

2006 – Chris Spedding: Reluctant Guitar Hero – Kimberly Bright (i-universe)

2006 – Cum on, Feel the Noize: The Story of Slade – Alan Parker, Steve Grantley (Carlton Books Ltd)

2006 – Performing Glam Rock: Gender and Theatricality in Popular Musi – Philip Auslander (University of Michigan Press)

2006 – Shang-A-Lang: The Curse of the Bay City Rollers – Les McKeown, Lynne Elliott (Mainstream Publishing)

2006 – Truth... Rod Stewart, Ron Wood and the Jeff Beck Group – Dave Thompson (Cherry Red Books)

2006 – TV's Grooviest Variety Shows of the '60s and '70s – Telly Davidson (Cumberland House Publishing)

2007 – All the Young Dudes: Mott the Hoople and Ian Hunter – Campbell Devine (Cherry Red Books)

2007 – Born to Boogie: The Songwriting of Marc Bolan – Carl Ewens (Aureus Publishing)

2007 – Ronnie: The Autobiography – Ronnie Wood (Macmillan)

2007 – Tony Visconti: The Autobiography: Bowie, Bolan and the Brooklyn Boy – Tony Visconti (Harper)

2007 – Top of the Pops: Mishaps, Miming and Music – Ian Gittins (BBC Books)

Look Wot They Dun!

2008 – Brian May: The Definitive Biography – Laura Jackson (Piatkus)

2008 – Marc Bolan: Born to Boogie Paperback – Chris Welch, Simon Napier-Bell (Plexus)

2008 – Ronnie – Ronnie Wood (Pan)

2008 – Unzipped – Suzi Quatro (Hodder Paperbacks)

2009 – Glam Rock 25 Outrageous Songs From Rock 'N' Roll's Revolutionary Era – VARIOUS (Hal Leonard)

2009 – Sparks: Number One Songs in Heaven – Dave Thompson (Cherry Red Books)

2009 – The Elton John Story – Mark Bego (JR Books Ltd)

2009 – The Man Who Sang Blockbuster – Brian Thomas Manly (Somehitwonders)

2009 – Your Pretty Face Is Going to Hell: The Dangerous Glitter of David Bowie, Iggy Pop, and Lou Reed – Dave Thompson (Backbeat Books)

2010 – Children of the Revolution – Dave Thompson (Cherry Red Books)

2010 – Children of the Revolution – Dave Thompson (Cherry Red Books)

2010 – Elton John: The Biography – David Buckley (Andre Deutsch Ltd)

2010 – Life – Keith Richards (W&N)

2010 – Up and Down with the Rolling Stones – Tony Sanchez (John Blake Publishing Ltd)

2010 – Who's Crazee Now? My Autobiography – Noddy Holder, Lisa Verrico (Ebury Press)

2011 – Freddie Mercury: The Definitive Biography – Lesley-Ann Jones (Hodder & Stoughton)

2011 – Had Me A Real Good Time: The Faces: Before, During & After – Andy Neill (Omnibus Press)

2011 – Music in Dreamland: Bill Nelson & Be Bop Deluxe – Paul Sutton Reeves (Helter Skelter Publishing)

2011 – Pop TV 1960-1975 – Richard Groothuizen (BR Music)

2011 – Queen Unseen: My Life with the Greatest Rock Band of the 20th Century – Peter Hince (John Blake Publishing Ltd)

2011 - The Beat of Different Drums: How I Left Behind Glam Rock and Went on a Journey of Many Lifetimes – John Richardson (Fitzrovia Press)

2012 – All the Madmen: Barrett, Bowie, Drake, the Floyd, The Kinks, The Who and the Journey to the Dark Side of English Rock – Clinton Heylin (Constable)

2012 – All the Madmen: Barrett, Bowie, Drake, the Floyd, The Kinks, The Who and the

Peter Checksfield

Journey to the Dark Side of English Rock – Clinton Heylin (Constable)

2012 – Cosmic Dancer: The Life And Music Of Marc Bolan – Paul Roland (Tomahawk Press)

2012 – Mick Jagger – Phillip Norman (Ecco Press)

2012 – Starman: David Bowie - The Definitive Biography – Paul Trynka (Sphere)

2012 – Talent is an asset: The Story of Sparks – Daryl Easlea (Omnibus Press)

2012 – The British Television Music & Light Entertainment Research Guide 1936-2012 - Simon Coward, Richard Down, Chris Perry (Kaleidoscope Publishing)

2012 – The Cost of Living in Dreams: The 10cc Story – Dave Thompson (CreateSpace Independent Publishing)

2012 – The Man Who Sold The World: David Bowie And The 1970s Paperback – Peter Doggett (Vintage)

2013 – Bay City Babylon: The Unbelievable but True Story of The Bay City Rollers – Wayne Coy (Hats Off Books)

2013 – David Bowie Is – Victoria Broackes, Geoffrey Marsh (V&A)

2013 – Glam Rock: Dandies in the Underworld – Alwyn W. Turner (V&A)

2013 – Look Wot I Dun: My Life in Slade Hardcover – Don Powell, Lise Lyng Falkenberg (Omnibus Press)

2013 – Mick Jagger – Philip Norman (Harper)

2013 – Over The Moon: My Autobiography – David Essex (Virgin Books)

2013 – Pan's People: Our Story – Babs Lord, Ruth Pearson, Cherry Gillespie, Dee Dee Wilde, Simon Barnard (Signum Books)

2013 – Ride a White Swan: The Lives and Death of Marc Bolan – Lesley-Ann Jones (Hodder Paperbacks)

2013 – Rod: The Autobiography – Rod Stewart (Arrow)

2013 – Somebody to Love: The Life, Death and Legacy of Freddie Mercury – Matt Richards, Mark Langthorne (Blink Publishing)

2013 – The Boys of Summer: A Rock 'n' Roll Nightmare with Showaddywaddy – Dave Bartram, Amanda Holden (Fantom Films Limited)

2013 – Tin Pan Alley: The Rise of Elton John – Keith Hayward (Soundcheck Books)

2013 – Top of the Pops: 50th Anniversary – Patrick Humphries, Steve Blacknell (McNidder & Grace)

Look Wot They Dun!

2014 – Roy Wood: The Move, Wizzard and beyond – John Van der Kiste (CreateSpace Independent Publishing)

2014 – The Lost Roller: The Autobiography of Nobby Clark (Strategic Book Publishing)

2015 – All Mapped Out: The UK Tour of a Lifetime – Dave Bartram, Amanda Holden (Fantom Films Limited)

2015 – Aren't You Glad That It's Not Christmas Everyday? Memoirs of a Wizzard Drummer – Charlie Grima (Mirage Publications)

2015 – Elton John: From Tin Pan Alley to the Yellow Brick Road – Dr Keith Hayward (Wymer Publishing)

2015 – Jeff Lynne: The Electric Light Orchestra - Before and After – John Van der Kiste (Fonthill Media)

2015 – On Some Faraway Beach: The Life and Times of Brian Eno – David Sheppard (Orion)

2015 – The World According To Noddy: Life Lessons Learned In and Out of Rock & Roll – Noddy Holder (Constable)

2016 – David Bowie: Changes – Chris Welch (Carlton Books Ltd)

2016 – David Bowie: The Golden Years – Roger Griffin (Omnibus Press)

2016 – Hero: David Bowie – Lesley-Ann Jones (Hodder & Stoughton)

2016 – Shock and Awe: Glam Rock and Its Legacy, from the Seventies to the Twenty-First Century – Simon Reynolds (Faber & Faber)

2016 – The Complete David Bowie (Revised and Updated 2016 Edition) – Nicholas Pegg (Titan Books)

2017 – Bowie: The Illustrated Story – Pat Gilbert (Voyageur Press)

2017 – Captain Fantastic: Elton John's Stellar Trip Through the '70 – Tom Doyle (Polygon)

2017 – Chris Glen: The Bass Business – Chris Glen (lulu.com)

2017 – David Bowie: The Man Who Fell to Earth – Paul Duncan (Taschen)

2017 – Marc Bolan - Beautiful Dreamer – John Bramley (Music Press Books)

2017 – Mick Ronson: The Spider with the Platinum Hair - Weird & Gilly (Music Press Books)

2017 – So Here It Is: How the Boy From Wolverhampton Rocked the World With Slade – Dave Hill (Unbound)

2017 – Spider from Mars: My Life with Bowie – Woody Woodmansey (Pan)

2017 – The Glam Rock Files – Diana Wilde (Independently published)

2017 – The Sweet Book – Brad Jones (Self-Published)

2018 – Captain Fantastic: The Definitive Biography of Elton John in the '70s Paperback – David DeCouto (Independently published)

2018 – David Bowie: A Life – Dylan Jones (Windmill Books)

2018 – Glam Rock: Music in Sound and Vision – Simon Philo (Rowman & Littlefield)

2018 – I Ran With the Gang: My Life In And Out Of The Bay City Rollers – Alan Longmuir, Martin Knight (Luath Press Ltd)

2018 – Let The Good Times Roll: My Life in Small Faces, Faces and The Who – Kenney Jones (Blink Publishing)

www.10cc.world

www.45cat.com

www.allsparks.com

www.ayshea.me.uk

www.beat-magazine.co.uk

www.billnelson.com

www.blackfootsue.com

www.brianmay.com

www.bryanferry.com

www.chicorytip.co.uk

www.chrisspedding.com

www.cozypowell.com

www.davidbowie.com

www.davidessex.com

Look Wot They Dun!

www.davidpaton.com

www.deedeewilde.co.uk

www.eltonjohn.com

www.hardprog.pagesperso-orange.fr

www.heavymetalkids.co.uk

www.helloband.co.uk

www.imdb.com

www.ina.fr

www.jefflynneselo.com

www.jefflynnesongs.com

www.leosayer.com

www.lesmckeown.com

www.lieutenantpigeon.co.uk

www.mickronson.co.uk

www.middleoftheroad-popgroup.com

www.missingepisodes.proboards.com

www.mottthehoople.com

www.mudrock.org.uk

www.nzentgraf.de

www.one-for-the-dads.979225.n3.nabble.com

www.paper-lace.net

www.queenlive.ca

www.queenonline.com

Peter Checksfield

www.queenpedia.com

www.recordcollectormag.com

www.rodstewart.com

www.rollingstones.com

www.roxymusic.co.uk

www.roywood.co.uk

www.rubettes.com

www.sailor-music.com

www.showaddywaddy.net

www.sites.google.com/site/vintagerocktv

www.slade.uk.com

www.sladeinengland.co.uk

www.spencemusic.co.uk/bilbomusic

www.steveharley.com

www.suziquatro.com

www.theglitterband.co.uk

www.thekinks.info

www.thestrangebrew.co.uk

www.thesweet.com

www.thesweetband.com

www.tv.com

www.tvpopdiaries.co.uk

Look Wot They Dun!

ABOUT THE AUTHOR

An acknowledged expert in his field, Peter Checksfield is the author of the acclaimed 'CHANNELLING THE BEAT! (The Ultimate Guide to UK '60s Pop on TV)'. He has also contributed to 'Record Collector', 'Now Dig This', 'Fire-Ball Mail', and various websites. His interests include collecting rare music TV footage, walking, cycling and local history. He lives near the coast in Kent, UK, with his partner Heather. 'LOOK WOT THEY DUN!' is his second book.

www.peterchecksfield.com

peterchecksfieldauthor@gmail.com

Printed in Great Britain
by Amazon